The Magic
of Belgrade

D1584803

Momo Kapor

The Magic of Belgrade

Ilustrated by the Author

KNJIGA
KOMERC

BELGRADE IS BELGRADE

"Do you know that my son's coming back?" – an elderly lady, mother of one of my high-school mates, approaches me, excited and twittering, resembling a freshly painted yellow canary.

"Why?" I ask.

"He cannot stand it there any longer!" – says she. "He tells me that everything is OK, you know, as far as work is concerned, but, Mom, I can't stand it there any longer, Belgrade is Belgrade!"

I have spent years and years poring over hundreds of written pages, trying to solve the riddle of the spirit of Belgrade and to understand what it is that draws us back into its embrace, and here I am, knowing today less than I knew at the beginning.

Neither is the old lady, just out of her hairdresser's, quite clear about her son's reasons for this sudden return from the world out there, knowing that for many years he was quite content living in it. What is he going to do here, with no apartment, no job and no money?

Отвори мапу
Београд нађи
Па онда плови
На Бео̃злази

Сава

Дунав

How very strange is our love for Belgrade! It has its share of caprice, of vehemence, of noisy disputes which end with us packing up and promising never to come back; there is in it repulsion, as well as a fatal attraction; and, above all, as in teenage heartbreak, full of tenderness and tears, we constantly return to it.

While in Belgrade, we grumble about the smog which chokes us and about the streets packed with cars. We complain about our insupportable climate. We explain that there is nothing worth showing to foreigners, we write letters to editors pointing out that the city is unkempt, untrimmed, slovenly, dug up, that it lacks this or that... Then we fly to some other cities all over the world, better-looking and happier, we admire the sediments of centuries past – their palaces and boulevards, their treasures and sumptuous fountains. We select the best restaurants and praise the service and the cutlery, the quietness and the flower arrangements on the table, and then, on the spur of the moment, we order lettuce, and – look! – Belgrade is sneering at us from the edge of the plate: it is not the taste of our lettuce! It looks nicer at first glance, the leaves are bigger, cleaner and greener, but we have the feeling of being cheated and of chewing plastic. We drink liters of mineral water, but our thirst is still unquenched. And there were times when a glass of water from the kitchen tap would suffice.

We remember our cafés under the linden trees, our neighborhoods and the old man who, having had one too many, would sink into slumber by his sidewalk scales for exact weighing, showered with small change. What are our old flames doing now, do kids still play ball in the schoolyard, do girls run on rollers in that small park, does the ex-minister from No. 6 still talk to himself while taking a walk, do housewives still haul wicker baskets full of red peppers from Zeleni Venac market to pickle them for winter, do Gypsies still play in our yards, do kids still run after the jets of water from the street-cleaning cars – what are they doing without me over there?

And the longer we stay abroad, the more attractive Belgrade is to us: we count the days till our return and listen to our hearts beating fiercely while we cross the bridge over the river, above the sluggish barges and the anglers – we are going back to our old love, which has not even noticed that we were away.

Are we the flora that cannot be transplanted? Once we pull ourselves out of our old neighborhoods of Čubura, Palilula, Dorćol, Zvezdara, Neimar or Bulbulder, do our roots remain deep down below the asphalt?

My buddies are coming back from the long years of living abroad, already gray-haired but excited like children. They bring along their wives, elegant strangers, to whom they used to explain, during countless nights over there, that Belgrade is beautiful, the only place in the world where one can really live, and the wives keep silent now and look around – they don't seeing anything special.

How to make them see? How to translate the spirit of Belgrade into foreign languages?

It is hard. They endure for some time, wait for their husbands, together with their mothers-in-law, to come home for lunch, but it takes awhile; finally they appear, obviously tipsy and beaming, the way they never were over there, they cross their hearts that they had only two drinks while it is clear that there were many more. By then the wives are fed up and they go back to where they came from, claiming their children need them... And the husbands, as if they were on holiday! They sit with their peers all day long in a near-by bar, mull over politics, read obituaries in the papers, tell old jokes about the eternal Mujo and Haso, play preference – in a word, they are taking a rest from the West.

THE SPIRIT OF BELGRADE

Belgrade does not like to have its picture taken.

It does not feel like posing for pictures. It squirms. It does not photograph well and always looks like some other place.

It is not Paris, which likes to cuddle with painters.

Nor London, which ingratiates itself with photographers.

Nor Rome, bedecked with souvenirs.

Nor Vienna, perfect for engraving on an ashtray.

Nor Moscow, which looks nice when put into a glass globe with snowflakes.

Nor Berlin – the bear, which can be turned into a key ring.

Nor Budapest, which likes to lie lazily at the bottom of bowls of hot fish stew.

Nor Istanbul, with its gold teeth.

Nor Athens, a stone paperweight for old manuscripts...

There are few things in it that I have not already seen elsewhere... Maybe only three: its rivers, its sky and its people. Out of these three primeval elements, the unique spirit of Belgrade is born.

THE SKY

The clouds swirl above the confluence of the Sava and Danube rivers, combining mists with eastern and western winds – a dramatic sky, like a huge theater of some celestial battle. At any time of the day, the spiritual state of the citizens of Belgrade is portrayed in this sky.

The people who grew up on the rocky hill beneath this exciting panorama cannot but be of broad gesture, fierce character and changeable mood. These people, who, despite everything, stay in their city, that crossroad of winds, even as history tears it down and turns it into ashes, covering with earth and layers of leaves the traces of settlements and past civilizations, are capable of rebuilding their city anew, time and again, in an easy-going and unpretentious way – a city of human proportions, comfortable as a well-known café we used to frequent since we were kids. A city that will not frighten the accidental traveler by its enormity, but will forever bind him to its heart with a hundred invisible threads.

THE PALM

Aerial photos of Belgrade make it possible to read its past, present and future, as if from the palm of someone's hand.

The palm of Belgrade is callous, scarred, with the grip of a friendly handshake, the strength of a dangerous fist, the softness of a caress.

Its fingers are roads leading to the great wide world – ancient roads, imperial roads, rural paths, dirt roads, highways, expressways, roads crossing the sky, leaving behind long white streams.

The character line: the contours of ravaged Kalemegdan fortress.

The life line: long and often intersected by battle scars.

And here is the line of the heart: the shores of Ada Huja, Ratno Ostrvo, Ada Ciganlija and Mala Ada islands...

The line of exceptional fortune: the course of its rivers.

THE HEART

Where is the heart of Belgrade?

It is everywhere and nowhere.

It hides in the refined nonchalance of a shoe-shine boy who says "You name the price", in the philosophically balanced relaxation of its old men who have lived through so many wars, in a morning joke, told in a trolley car, which will improve the mood of gloomy passengers on their way to work, in the friendliness of the waiter who feels free to sit at his guest's table in the café "Under the Linden Tree" and have a glass of beer with him, in the hustle and bustle of streets where you rarely feel like a stranger regardless of where you come from, in the beauty of the graffiti on walls that nobody cares to whitewash, which depict a touching fresco of destinies, loves, swear words, insults, humorous remarks, results of football matches, names – all written on the mortar still bearing the warnings: CHECKED OUT – NO MINES! (in Russian), ALL TO THE POLLS!, WE'D RATHER GIVE OUR LIVES THAN GIVE UP TRIESTE! Above all that hovers a plaque of the long-gone SAVA insurance company, which was not able to insure anything, least of all itself, and the faded traces of old street name signs.

The spirit of Belgrade hides in the unique chaos of its green markets, but first of all in the supple walk of Belgrade women. Watching them on the city streets – for me it is like seeing a fantastic modern ballet, accompanied only by the clicking of their heels! Pale, abruptly grown city girls, raised on the asphalt, nourished by the yearning glances of passers-by, independent, impertinent and polite at the same time, with the inborn elegance of resourceful dress-makers and their cunningly hidden poverty – they are the most beautiful and the most attractive show which Belgrade offers to the newcomer's gaze, until the moment they disappear, as if at someone's secret command, and the streets remain inconsolably desolate and empty. And finally, the spirit of Belgrade is also in the feeling that you are at home, that no misfortunes can befall you, as you are among your own people, that at any moment you can borrow a few coins, a little bit of love, a roof over your head and some absolutely necessary complicity for pre-dawn pranks. This spirit gives birth to new vertical lines, to new city sections while old ones disappear, it spans the rivers and clears away the rusty tangles of railway tracks overgrown with grass, so as to have a better view of its rivers and the sky. It plays games with architecture and city planning laws.

If photographed from the air, regardless of the photographer's skill, the city will never attract a roaming collector of beauty.

To put it simply, it does not photograph well! But it will do something completely different: it will arouse an almost physical pain of longing in those who spent at least a couple of days in its streets, in the same way as an old snapshot of a long-lost love can inflict mortal pain.

The layout of its streets becomes something akin to a topographical chart of our hearts. The city will bewitch us with its charm, never disclosing the secret code of that strange love that we ourselves are not able to explain. We will forever remain its willing prisoners, having chosen Belgrade among many magnificent cities of the world to spend in it the one and only life given to us.

BELGRADERS

Belgraders differ from other Europeans in that their great-grandparents did not leave them houses to live in, and that their grandfathers did not leave them libraries full of books to read. Houses were torn down countless times, libraries went up in flames or were sold, and some people did not even have grandfathers – they were born by their grandmothers! Few people were in a position to leave anything to their decedents, save their scorn for wealth and the old notion that it is temporary and transient, the only eternal thing being the innate and broad gesture of hospitality and cordiality of Belgraders, who share their scant belongings with refugees and newcomers, as if they were next of kin.

PENSIONERS

They see before their eyes the mist lifting over the confluence of the two rivers, and farther out the Panonian plain – an enormous space luring them to abandon their worn-out, rickety bodies and to soar high above: a vanished sea which makes them realize the inconsequence of human existence. High up, on the Kalemegdan plateau, above the fortifications made of rocks and un-baked bricks, with mysterious corridors under-neath leading to underground passages and dun-geons, these honorable old men, who have served their turn, feel like the last defenders of a long-gone Belgrade, prisoners of the great riddle of the life that was, the life long ago erased from the present-day streets.

"Hey, man, see those buildings over there, there used to be marshes there with reeds this high, man! We used to drink water in the middle of the Sava, it was so clean!"

"How puny a human life span!", they brood before this vast space, which, by opening its mouth wide just once, can easily swallow up a

19

whole town, together with all its fortifications, palaces, ambitions, successes and vanities, and turn it into a miniature vedette on a faded hill.

A funny, long forgotten and quite superfluous hierarchy still reigns on the benches of Kalemegdan Park. There, ex-heads of departments first greet their ex-ministers, ex-counselors first greet their heads of departments, craftsmen first greet their former masters from 1937, retired captains first greet retired colonels, and the folks from back home first greet their former members of parliament...

NIGHT

We reach Belgrade lured by the promises given to ourselves, we arrive regardless of what's in store for us: we cross the huge, murky river, we arrive on foot, by train or truck, on the roofs of freight cars or in dusty buses, we come to our great adventure, knowing full well that Belgrade will accept us, like some good-natured relative opening his doors wide and telling us to feel at home, adding that "with a little bit of tolerance, there is room for everyone". And so we arrive, knowing that sooner or later these streets will accept us, like all those before us who also came looking for protection, happiness, a roof over their heads, jobs, a daily crust and a name. We arrive as nameless newcomers, carrying bundles full of dialects from back home, we wander and struggle, and then, one day, we start giving birth to born-and-bred Belgraders, who will soon sneer at our accent – long-legged, long-necked girls with an affected drawl and tall young boys, future basketball players of the Crvena Zvezda (Red Star) team. In this way we beget roots for ourselves in this windy city which has, at last, become our own!

BEZ VEZE[1]

Every spring I feel hunger seeping into my knees, that old hunger from 1957, followed by mild vertigo and an unfathomable yearning for scallions and for lettuce with a few remaining dew drops on its leaves. It is actually a fear resulting from vitamin C deficiency (felt mostly by tramps), a fear kept warm by hot asphalt, cooked with polished barley and noodles in the students' cafeteria, and drowned like meatballs in tomato sauce on some empty Sunday in April, when the cafeteria was sticky with misery and the streets were empty. It is the fear of an exile who walks on suburban streets and watches happy families having dinner under the cherry tree. He looks at children and dogs in the grass, trimmed bushes, creaking verandas and white napkins. The radio is broadcasting *Time for Sport and Recreation.* Smoke and

---

[1] *Bez veze* – a universal negative comment, whose exact meaning, depending on the context, can range from "nothing special" to "no good whatsoever", from "unimportant" to "what a letdown", from "boring" to "stupid"... The drawn-out first syllable of the second word is typical of Belgrade speech.

dust. The body is heavy, and sweat drenches old trousers and makes them stick at the knees. Free of their winter coats, Belgrade girls cut with their breasts the air full of excitement. Their bodies and the taut arches of their legs resemble the wooden sculptures of girls adorning the bows of pirate ships. These girls, who bloomed overnight, who shower twice a day and eat the first ripe strawberries with cream, these pussy-cats – the pampered daughters of diplomats and IBM representatives for the South-Eastern Balkans, these goldfish in the spring, when your knees buckle and your skin burns and makes you wish to get out of it and leave it in the first garbage can, and take off to the agreeable climate of your ancestors, naked and innocent like a new-born child or a baby snake just wriggled out of its last year' skin – those March beauties make my strolls even more miserable, as their beauty hurts.

I notice, with the passage of time, that the girls are becoming more beautiful, more slender and softer. They resemble, more and more, the dream girl who reached us, in the mid-1950s, by way of the pages of *Paris Match* magazine stolen from the French library (Brigitte Bardot running across the grass). Hungry for pretty faces, we cut out the photos and stuck them on the walls of our solitary rooms, hoping they would save us from misery and our hairy landladies. (Those were our only icons, those faded photographs on the wall. We nailed them onto the barrack walls, covered our soldiers' chests with them, and pasted them on the inside of closet doors in which our memories and our old sneakers rotted away.) Here they are, these girls who sprang up overnight, with their humid Babmi-like snouts, overtaking us aged strollers; but we no longer exist for them, we are nothing but empty air through which they pass, passers-by, the wall of the crowd, a mass, people queuing for trolley-buses, a background of smog, the gray-ness of pavements and façades; we are just name-less strollers that they pass through, and if they say 'pardon me' it is an absent-minded excuse not directed at anyone, while they hurry to meet some lucky boy of their own age.

We no longer exist, we are the leftovers of a different joke, whose point made us laugh like mad so many years ago. But our dream has turned into reality! We rub shoulders with unattainable copies of Brigitte Bardot, Geraldine Chaplin, Jean Seberg... Oh, God, the same pert little nose, the same freckles and the supple walk on the pave-ment! Lord, those doe-like eyes, those blue lakes which send us back the reflection of our age and our tiredness, that crazy and joyful March beauty on Terazije, the impertinence and the dimples on their cheeks – naughty tufts of hair pushed back from the forehead of a photograph come alive, which, a long time ago, adorned the cover of our soldiers' chests.

Now they are within reach, they are here, in restaurants, cafés, pubs and bistros, in supermarkets, in matinee movie halls, sometimes they even sit at our tables with a Coupe Jacques, and we try to talk to them, to translate into their language, as simply as possible, the years of waiting for them to appear here, under this sky, where women for ages carried their children on their backs and ran into the hills, waited in lines for bread and milk, cleared away the ruins of their homes by passing old bricks to one another, dug up corn and went back to their musty kitchens. Actually, we try to tell them how many things needed to happen in order for them to be born, so young and pretty. How much longing before those poor walls came alive and before the photos opened up and let their models come down into our streets, how much distress and misery. We try to tell them all that, and they look at us, with their lips around the straw, pouting and meowing affectedly:

"Bez veeeeeeeze..."

And look, at that very moment we go back to our soldiers' chests and to the 1960s, at the very same moment we tell ourselves that we are sitting again in some drafty loft in March and talking to the photo of Brigitte Bardot from the *Match* – so, it is still a dream, and the creatures at our table, they are only photographs, tasteless, odorless, weightless: surely some wealthy relative sent us those uncalled-for dolls, all bought in the same

27

mechanical toyshop, manufactured on the same assembly line, the only difference being that, when pushed, they do not squeak out "Mummy" but *"Bez veeeeze!"*.

We have been duped once again – they are not real McCoys!

Bez veze!

SPRINGTIME

In springtime, we are certainly the most beautiful people in the world!

In wintertime, many countries and many cities beat us in elegance, but once mink coats are taken off in London, once make-up starts melting under the crazy Roman sun in April, once people get out of the houses and cars which speak volumes about their owners, once those fantastic hats are taken off in Paris – our five minutes have arrived! In the sun, the mother of the poor, a pair of jeans and a T-shirt are enough for us to beat with our naked bodies the decadent English paleness, the Roman tradition and the Parisian beauty full of artificiality, nourished for a long time on frozen meat and vegetables. It does not matter any longer where you live, what car you drive, what your possessions are – the spring grabs everything that is beautiful by its hair by and pulls it out onto the street! The street turns into a huge arena of love, where looks full of hints and promises collide with each other: everything is on offer to famished eyes and impatient skin.

Young bodies vibrate beneath the denim covering the long legs which devour the pavements, the canvas is stretched over taut thighs....

How wonderful it is to be alive! What beauty is missed by those who hastened to die!

"To sleep with your own wife, that's pure incest!" a recently divorced man of fifty tells me, turning to look at the beauty disappearing into the night.

BEAUTIFUL WOMEN

At the time when I still passionately strolled along Knez Mihailova Street, in the perennially same murderous circle, there were only about ten beauties in Belgrade, and we all knew and admitted that they were real lookers! They passed by, as if they were our own private princesses, mysterious as if stepping down from some movie known only to them, magical and untouchable – wrapped in a whisper of admiration. They were aware of being the most beautiful girls in town, and that made them even more beautiful.

The years passed in a jiffy, and then, one day, startled from my sleep, I noticed that all girls on the old corso were beautiful and long-legged, and that there were many blond girls – a rarity in my time. All the girls were beautiful! You couldn't tell which one was more beautiful. I also noticed that these girls addressed the princesses of my youth as "grandmas"! They were walking unnoticed, preoccupied, hurried, each carrying her own drama in her bag. These days the girls of my youth seldom dance. They have wrinkles around their eyes and they really smoke too much.

But, lo and behold! When we accidentally meet in the street, we become kids once again: they are the beauties and we are only modest strollers. By the minute, they become more and more beautiful in our eyes. Elderly housewives turn into coquettish girls. "Ladies' turn" from the

old dancing halls is here again, and once more it is not us who are chosen for a dance, but always somebody else, who has more luck!

And, lo and behold: they are aware of it! They are aware that today they are beautiful only to us, and that they'll remain beautiful to us even when they turn eighty, because we are the guardians of their beauty, entrusted to us for safekeeping a long time ago. In these happy hours, there is no place for those young kids.

"Why are you staring like that?" a young girl asks me. "Surely that lady must have been beautiful?"

"If only you knew..." I tell her and go to have a drink.

BELGRADE GIRLS

As opposed to the past, present-day Belgrade girls are never alone: they are constantly in company – always in a nomadic tribe with its own language, style, way of life and rules of the game. They grew up together with boys, shared school desks with them from the first grade, wore the same type of blue jeans and T-shirts – played basketball on the same team. The mist of that wonderful secret of the sexes has been dispelled a long time ago: the Third High School for Boys, the Seventh High School for Girls... The glimpses in passing, the mystery of that first touch at a New Year's Eve party, when "ladies turn" still existed and the English waltz was danced at midnight.

The Belgrade girl has changed indeed. She is no longer that slightly plump little woman, who used to disarm us by her helplessness – with her large dark eyes shaded by sensuality. Today, Belgrade girls are marked by their slenderness, their long legs, narrow hips and broad shoulders, their nonchalant sportive step, while the last thing that you notice are their eyes, their look and what is behind it. The present-day Belgrade girl is liberated, independent, aware of the cruel advantage of her age. She is not embarrassed when her peers use four-letter words in her company. She has been taught in school that sex is a precondition of procreation, she knows every detail of fertilization involving male and female cells, and the macho-dominated city is no threat to her: she is capable of standing up to it and of controlling its streets.

The streets are her corridors: the public park is a replacement for her vanished backyard, and the street corner where she meets with her pals is her drawing room! Her everyday vocabulary is practical, reduced to about one hundred words. Everything that could sound like sentimental rubbish is eliminated.

When she feels like hearing some romantic terms of endearment, she goes to see a movie for her helping of celluloid dreams, spiced by violence. But the semi-darkness of the movie house will not corrupt her prudence. The threatening avalanche of sentimentalities will be prevented on time by some bold comment, followed by spectators' bursts of laughter – and the magic is broken.

Their clothes and make-up mount a fantastic painting with no rules whatsoever, in which remote echoes and reflections of international fashion are discernible. There is no trace of concern that they might look ostentatious, they are completely indifferent to what others might think. Their gaudy elegance is not a sign of a luxurious life, but of a deeply hidden desire to make an impression in passing, a certain amazing tendency to disguise, a yearning for beautiful things. All that they possess is on them! In this they resemble somewhat the Turkish cavalry – all their property is invested into their armor. Although far from the world fashion capitals, they are more elegant than boutique owners because they possess the freshness of the generation using cosmetics, while still preserving the fragrance of a young skin.

Every last drop of their mothers' desire for revenge on the male gender is channeled into them through English, piano and ballet lessons, basketball training and, not infrequently, the mastery of karate! The mothers prepare their daughters for a life happier than their own, knowing full well that every kind of life has its price. Those rosy girls are actually their mothers' secret weapons against their own unhappy past, full of misery and poverty, when beautiful things were scarce.

I wonder while looking at them: will they be willing to make a sacrifice in the name of love, as their mothers were? How will they grow old and what will they look like then? Will they be like our mothers, or will they be different women, parting with heavy hearts with the beauty of their prime?

But, nevertheless, if you scratch their confidence, disrupt their habits or puncture their chewing gum bubble, beneath the urban glamour you will discover the same gentle and vulnerable little girl like her mother and grandmother used to be.

IN THE FAMILY WAY

Belgrade turned green overnight, its leafy tree crowns hiding its shortcomings: façades shedding their pre-war ornaments, toothless neon signs with missing letters. The streets turned into mysterious green tunnels, promising exciting and unexpected encounters and small miracles. Fill up your pockets with sunflower seeds and take a stroll – you'll find out that anything is possible in the month of May!

All of a sudden, the pavements are brimming with an incredible number of young women in the family way. They lick their ice-cream, sluggish and somewhat absent-minded, and try to calm down their skinny husbands scared to death before the prospect of becoming fathers so soon. They are beautiful, even so drowsy and clumsy in their wide, waistless dresses; they have strange cravings, like eating grapes in May, and they feel a little bit dizzy. Girls of their age look at them with envy, while they proudly push forward their swollen tummies, as monuments to a generation which will conquer the world.

"Look, it's moving!" says a freckled one to her young husband, putting his palm on her taut stomach.

"It is, no shit! Here, it's moving again..."

Their mothers, future grandmothers, are, as one would expect – desperate! Their fathers keep silent and smoke. They do not want to meddle.

"I have nothing against it" says a future grandmother, 38 years old, " but we wanted our child to finish her studies first and to enjoy life a little before burying herself..."

"Look who's talking! As if you had finished your studies first!" calls out her mother, soon to be great-grandmother. "Oh, come on!"

"It was different then."

But the times never change. The future Belgraders always arrive unplanned, always at the most inconvenient of times. They could not care less that they will live in rented rooms, they could not care less that their parents are jobless and still studying, that their fathers haven't done their army service yet! They arrive, and later all things fall into place by themselves. In what way? Nobody can tell, but everything works out fine.

Belgrade in May is drowsily beautiful, as if it also were in the family way.

THE COUNTRYSIDE

"Well? Which do you prefer, the town or the countryside?" my elderly aunt would ask me every time I went to stay with her for a couple of days, skinny and pallid, in need of some fresh air.

Naturally, I would reply that it was much nicer in the countryside, while already yearning for the town. Nevertheless, my aunt's question is still open, and although I spent countless years looking for an answer, I am back at the beginning.

If it is truly nicer in the countryside, why the hell do thousands of country people settle in towns every day? And if it is nicer in the town, why, then, do thousands of city dwellers run head over heels to the country every Friday afternoon?

We promise ourselves that the day will come when we'll leave everything behind and go to live in our great-grandfather's house, with both feet firmly on the ground. We are fed up with the impure air we breathe, with neighbors above and on both sides of our apartment, we have enough of seeing animals only in cages and on TV, and seeing milk only in cardboard packages, we are also fed up with living by installments; and then, after only three days in the country, the silence begins to drives us crazy – the flies from the stable get on our nerves, there is no place to buy newspapers at ten at night or cigarettes at midnight, we cannot go to sleep with the hens, nor wake up with the cocks. And so we are in a constant collision with our own dream of the countryside. Our kind and generous hosts cannot go to bed, as we are not sleepy yet, and cannot perform their morning chores as we are still asleep. Closed in on all sides by various walls (fence, barn, stable, hen house, gate, a neighbor's house), it dawns on us that in Belgrade there is much more of what we call "nature". As woods go, the one in Košutnjak Park is much denser than this one in the countryside, fenced in and sparse. As for rivers, ours are much deeper and wider than this brook, only just finding its way among the rocks. As for food – it is true that it abounds in the country, but it is monotonous, as it comes from the vegetable patch behind the house, and is not comparable to any green market in town; besides, country people cannot prepare those fresh and good ingredients the way they deserve to be prepared. As for TV, we did not have to travel some 200 km away from our favorite armchair in order to watch the same programs.

Since we so abruptly changed our living rhythms of urban neurasthenics, the general languor and serenity of the countryside get on our nerves. It is with a sigh of relief that we go back to the hectic throng of our native asphalt. This is our life! The country – it is our daydream which we dream every time we feel we are not going to make it on the asphalt. Only with both the town and the country in our hearts do we feel complete!

It is beyond doubt that it is nicer in the country, but the town is my great love, and, as with every great love, there are frequent quarrels in our relationship. When it comes to that, I leave the town to be unfaithful to it with the countryside, but after a while I return repentantly, to share my destiny with it.

When I feel like seeing the grass, I walk over to the tiny park in the block, with several square feet of something supposed to be grass. It is enclosed in a fence to prevent it from running away home to the country for the weekend.

IN THE STREET

What a strange people we are!

There are few places in the world where people comment so much on other people's appearance. You dress up to the nines and with your nose up in the air go out for an evening stroll, without any forebodings, but, look, you meet an acquaintance! He does not even say "Good evening", let alone ask how you are: he makes an appraisal of you on the spot. If, by chance, you've put on some weight, he spreads his arms in sympathy, makes a "tsk, tsk" sound and shouts as loudly as he can: "Wow, man, you put on weight! Do you have any idea what you look like?"

Not realizing that he has pushed you into the deepest despair, he bounces off and forgets you right away. You go the nearest street weighing scales and, starting from the following morning, you stop eating completely, you lose weight daily and only long to meet him again. And, here, the day has come! You go out for a walk, slender as a spruce, and – there he is, coming your way! This time he does not spread his arms nor make the "tsk" sound, but looks at you suspiciously, as if you were contagious, and deadly serious shakes his head: "What's the matter with you? You've lost a lot of weight. You should see your doctor..."

It is obvious that he suspects you of having the worst of diseases. Your knees start to buckle. You go back home and begin to stuff yourself with food, until the next time you meet, when he'll tell you again that you are overweight.

In any case, no one ever tells you that you look just right! You're never told that you look great. Why do they do it? Is it because they love us and care for our well-being, or they want to hurt us because they are mean and envious? Or, simply, because they have nothing better to do but to mind other people's business and to prattle meaninglessly?

Who will ever satisfy everyone?

Yet, when we are in a faraway country, among unfamiliar and polite people, we miss this intrusive, occasionally unbearable concern of our compatriots. We walk, lost in the crowd, and wish for someone familiar to stop us, spread his arms and tell us, with the inevitable "tsk" sound, that we are awfully overweight! Surely, we would feel less lonely then...

BELGRADE IS BELGRADE,
AFTER ALL

Belgrade is best explained by these five words which we say out loud as soon as we enter its airport, on our return from abroad. They include love, warmth, admiration and a sense of security; also, happiness that we live in such an appropriate place as Belgrade. For, if you did not achieve anything particular in your lifetime, it is sufficient that you have managed to live in Belgrade – the unfulfilled dream of many people from the interior.

The very fact that it is much easier to get to Sydney or San Francisco than to get a cab to take you from the Main Railway Station to Terazije Square, as no taxi driver will let you into his car for such a short ride, is the best proof of its exceptionality.

That is the reason why, every time I come back to Belgrade, I raise my head high and tell the taxi-driver: "No, no, Belgrade is Belgrade, after all", and he, as a rule, agrees with me.

For, when the whole country is out of electricity, Belgrade heroically shines with its toothless neon signs! And when at eleven p.m. all other towns in the country close their cafés and hotels for the night, you can rest assured that there will be at least one café in Belgrade open until as late as eleven fifteen! It is a metropolis, after all!

Actually, many places in the interior are deserted nowadays because of Belgrade, as all the people have moved here! Together with their love for city life, they brought along their hatred of nature, from which they escaped willingly. To start with, these newcomers banned horses from Belgrade, so as not to be reminded of their villages and stables. One can see horse riders and horses in the middle of Fifth Avenue in New York, and no one is bothered by it, in spite of indescribable traffic snarls. To put it simply, the Americans conquered the continent on horseback, and that is why they love and revere horses. Were it not for those unfortunate five or six ponies at the Zoo, Belgrade kids would see horses only on TV! There is another thing: those who escaped to Belgrade from their villages hate trees from the bottom of their hearts (they remind them of the woods), and therefore they cut them down wherever they can, meaning everywhere. Asphalt is their dream! The more asphalt the better!

Belgrade is the most ideal place in the world to run away from for a weekend in the country. Those who remain behind are the true Belgraders. They have no one in the country. Belgrade is the only city in the world where the waiters are more graceful than their guests. Belgrade is the only city in the world where everybody will eye you with distrust when you enter a café. Like, "What's he doing here?" You swallow it somehow, then sit down and start eyeing the newcomers with the same expression: "What's he doing here?"

Belgrade has the famous No.2 tram line, which goes in circles all day long, the same as our lives.

Belgrade needs much less time to create a whole new street than to name it. That's why many new streets in our capital are named "Nova" – The New One, and most house numbers are "no number"!

Only in Belgrade you remain young for a long time, as store owners address you as "son", or "kid", even if you are over forty.

Even elderly single children find their siblings in Belgrade, as people call each other "brother".

And, finally, Belgrade is the best place in the world where to catch a bus for Zemun.

Because, Belgrade is Belgrade, after all!

THE FLEA MARKET

At the very outer margin of Belgrade, where dusty gardens stretch forth into the Panonian plain, a big flea market, called *Buvljak* or *Rondoš*, is expanding and sprouting week after week. This is where I spend my Sunday mornings. Over it, regardless of the weather, there is always a pearly gray cloud, bringing showers usually around noon.

The flea market is the saddest place on earth. It does not have the centuries-old pedigree of London's Portobello Road, where Carol Reed filmed his *A Kid for Two Farthings*, nor the refined cunning and the decorative sense of Paris's Clignancourt, where on Sunday mornings well-to-do antique dealers disguise themselves as vagrants to cheat naive and gullible foreigners and dump false candlesticks on them. It is not the flee market at Porta Portese in Rome, which excited me more than the cellars of the Vatican, nor is it Delancey Street in southern Manhattan, surrounded by red-brick buildings with fire escapes – a Mecca for the poor! All the outcasts of this happy Babylon are to be found there, pushing, crawling and swarming.

The flea market is a partly asphalted barren patch of ground, where there suddenly appear, as if dropped from the sky, a creaking merry-go-round, a shooting gallery, rows of counters and a huge mass of people. This is by no means a dilettante's playground. Here the poorest purchase clothes and footwear, try on winter coats of unknown deceased persons, buy spare parts for their jalopies, or furniture left uncovered in the rain for days on end, or bird cages. Here people eat and drink – corn cobs are cooked and sausages grilled – sell badges, stamps, old coins, reading spectacles with no lenses, telephones without receivers, transistor radios, knives, icons, scissors and all kinds of tools... To some, the flea market is a village fair which they left behind upon moving to the city, recreated from poverty and peasant misery! To others, it is the final stop of a dangerous chain of smuggling, whose path leads across the border to Romanian villages and Hungarian pusztas, Italian depots and Thessalonica warehouses.

The flea market is a morning cocktail party for those never invited to one. It is the business premises of the unemployed, the last resource of the resourceless, a polygon for young thieves, a springboard for future millionaires, the promised land for collectors of trivia, a homeland for those who strayed from their birthplaces, a tonic against loneliness for the lonely, and hope for the hopeless...

There are people who are annoyed by flea markets. They are annoyed by this chaos of misery, contraband, slyness, recalcitrance, laughter, drunkenness and petty trading risks. It is my impression that these people are annoyed by life itself! Their image of the world is that of a well ordered military barracks, where everything and everybody have their preordained place. For these people the flea markets are meeting places of thugs, thieves, drunkards, whores, individualists and, generally speaking, a breed from the margins of life. They believe that this gang of wretched characters and ruffians, out of pure spite, oppose all well designed plans for healthy and honorable life and a smiling future. But, the flea markets are tougher than dogmas. They are more tenacious and indestructible than life itself. If you kick out a flea market from the corner of a regular green market, it will appear, like a weed, on a completely different patch of ground, even bigger and more chaotic. That is what happened to the postwar flea market at Cvetkova Mehana, which, after having wandered through the city, crossed the river and went into the plain, finally settling down in New Belgrade.

You go there when there is absolutely no other place to go, when you are forced to take out the last possessions from your home and put them on a stand, beaten but peaceful somehow, knowing that you cannot go any lower and that no worse predicament can befall you.

THE ČUBURA YARD

When away from home, somewhere in the wide world, I often think of a yard in Belgrade, in the neighborhood called Čubura, in Šumatovačka Street.

It is located behind a narrow iron gate and a small, ordinary-looking house. I am not going to disclose the house number, not only since I don't want its dwellers to become aware of the charm of this enchanting space, but mostly to prevent people devoid of inner content to rush to it, the kind of people who overnight conquer every site in the city, once they are told about its meaning and its value.

To put it in a nutshell, it is a yard with an old linden tree in the middle, with clothes lines spreading out in all directions from its lower branches. A wooden swing hangs from one of the branches.

Under the linden tree there stands an old worm-eaten table, washed by many a rain and sagged by the weight of past snows. There are two benches as well – it is, therefore, a kind of a classical square; it is where neighbors meet to share a freshly baked cheese pie (in mild autumn days), to have a couple of beers (in summertime) or to discuss some local drama: for example, the case of the postman's daughter, who is expecting but isn't sure who the father is.

This yard is a town in itself and it can stand even the longest city planners' siege, as there is a regular supply of drinking water (the tap in the middle of the yard), plenty of food (already preserved for winter) and plenty of booze – jars of sour cherry brandy fermenting in every window. During this hypothetical siege, the yard dwellers could send out messages even without a phone, as deep down in the yard there is a pigeon coop with some fifty carrier and tumbler pigeons.

I find this to be the most appropriate space for living. First of all, in this yard one is never alone, unless one explicitly wants to be. Although every dweller has his own little house and roof above his head, he is not deprived of the blessings of common living. In about ten little houses on both sides of the yard, one has at one's disposal a complete little town with its strangest inhabitants.

In one of these little houses (as if on an asteroid from Saint Exupéry's *Little Prince*) lives the legendary Drunkard. In another, the Quarrelsome Man, followed by the Defeated One, the temporary Lovers, and the lonely Bully. This yard is also inhabited by the Grumbler, the Miser, the Florist, the Ex-Man, the Pigeon Breeder, the Jasper, the Clerk, the Whore, the Widow, the Other Grave Digger, the Artist, the Cook, the Car Mechanic, the Shoemaker...

These little houses, whose walls are covered by creeping vine bearing sour Čubura grapes, usually consist of two tiny rooms: the kitchen, acting also as the living room, and the bedroom, acting as the guest room and the storage place for old stuff. The richest yard dwellers also have a little shed where they keep firewood and coal, bicycles and the baby carriage. The kitchen is entered directly from the yard, so that in wintertime one is struck by the smell of fresh snow, and in springtime by the scent of the linden tree.

Two wooden privies are situated at the very end of the yard, while bathrooms are in Mišarska Street, or in summertime, in the Sava river. In springtime they all bathe in a tin tub or in a huge oak barrel, always brimming with rainwater and floating pigeon feathers. What a delightful chance to take a peek at the lavish and mature bosoms of the Divorcee, while she takes her bath in a rosy silk slip!

If you look up, you'll see a piece of blue sky surrounded by tall apartment houses, where neighbors do not know each other. The dwellers of these tall houses look down from their windows upon the yard dwellers and feel sorry for them for their lack of comfort. But the yard people, sitting under the linden tree, say, as a rule, that they would not exchange their yard for anything in the world, not even for a one-and-a-half room apartment in a high-rise, the dream of every normal citizen of Belgrade.

Actually, the best thing is that no one from the outside can perceive that behind the green squeaking iron gate, there exists another, totally different and self-sufficient world. But once you pass through that gate (the house number must remain a secret), which is never locked, you feel a desire to stay there forever.

KEVA[2]

Even those not related to her call her – *Keva*!
Keva, pass me that. *Keva*, iron this! Leave it,
Keva will do it later!

For those not knowing what I'm talking about,
suffice it to say that *Kevas* are elderly and somewhat fat women of short stature (a dying species,
unfortunately) who pass their time of day mostly
in their kitchens, and who, like some demigods,
carry on their shoulders not only the entire household, but also the family, life and the world...

From time immemorial, they are always
dressed in the same way, in simple house dresses
made of cheap darkish calico or fustian, of a
shapeless cut: not because they have nothing else
to put on, but because they couldn't care less
about their appearance. The pockets of their robes
are full of multicolored pills, for the liver, stomach, headache, and those pink ones, for high blood
pressure... Their legs are thickset and varicose,

<hr>

[2] *Keva* – a slang expression for "mother"; very approximately like "Ma".

and on their feet they have worn-out slippers of plaid felt, which lost their shape and color a long time ago.

Only very rarely are they given presents. Everybody knows – *Keva* does not need anything. Only that we are all alive and well! And if we occasionally bring her a hundred grams of coffee beans, she prepares coffee for us right away.

Those fortunate ones to have a *Keva* in their homes will have the privilege of eating the most exotic dishes, forgotten a long time ago and unknown to many. *Keva*s are the last creatures in Belgrade who can make pasta squares with sautéed cabbage, potato dumplings with noodles or *'papazjanija'* – a stew made of various ingredients found in the kitchen, not to mention plum-stuffed dumplings or "crescents from the well", given this strange name who knows when, because the dough had to be kept in the well for a while in order to rise.

It is also a fact that *Kevas* are wary of ready-made filo pastry and that they prefer to "roll" dough on their kitchen tables, even for soup noodles. In spite of all scientific proof, they still thicken all cooked dishes with a roux made of flour and ground paprika. They are maestros in making *ajvar* – the so-called "Serbian caviar", as a French traveler fittingly called it, for which they roast peppers on ancient tin stoves in the yard. Until recently they used the same stoves for baking

plum jam, and in war times for making soap out of suet and lye, which, once firm, they would cut into squares with wire. They never throw away jars, covering paper and elastic bands, because they will be needed for storing *ajvar*. They will be happy to present you with a jar of quince preserve, but on the condition that you return the jar.

Amusingly, *Keva* hardly ever eats with her household members at the kitchen table, but yet she has problems with weight. The explanation is probably that she, spending all her life in the kitchen, by the stove, inhales nourishing vapors and nibbles on or tastes the food before she is satisfied with its taste.

When their grandchildren get sick, *Kevas* immediately throw the antibiotics prescribed by the physician into the trash. They bring the fever down with grape brandy, corn flour and wine vinegar; they treat mumps by putting bacon behind children's ears, they also use 'animal fat washed in nine waters' as a cure, and they keep a collection of various teas in their cupboards: the marshmallow, chamomile, sage, mint, thyme tea. The very magic of these names has a healing effect.

Kevas are the last persons on earth who still mend torn clothes which no tailor would accept. For this purpose they keep a collection of *ibrišim* threads of all colors.

They are the most tolerant beings in the world. Abdullah, the Albanian who helped with the household chores, often sat at the table with us, but was invariably served food prepared especially for him, as *Keva* knew that his religion forbade him to eat our food. During the Ramadan fast, she did not even eat in front of him, so as not to hurt his feelings.

The only calendar she respected was – the church calendar. Her only outing was the annual visit to the cemetery – for All Souls Day. Even then, while we all ate to the memory of the departed, she would incessantly serve the buried.

Even if you are over fifty, *Keva* will never fall asleep before you come back home. On the kitchen stove, regardless of the fact that you already had your dinner, your favorite childhood dish will be kept warm for you – spinach with ground meat patties. How could you resist that?

Kevas, those priestesses and guardians of long gone times, when people lived quietly, honorably and comfortably, unfortunately did not pass on their little secrets to anyone.

Only when they are gone, leaving behind the ancient *Pata's Cookbook* and a shoe box stuffed with snapshots from our childhood and youth, do we realize that the dishes we eat today are totally devoid of taste...

THE HOMELESS

Belgraders are usually born homeless.

That is because in Belgrade people can never leave any inheritance to their descendants. The only thing that Belgraders can inherit from their fathers is a tendency to put on weight, high blood pressure, a liking for white wine with water or the habit of taking a nap after lunch.

Each new generation starts from scratch!

It is much easier for the newcomers from nearby villages. In order to become Belgraders, they sell their livestock, their fertile fields, their grandfathers' woods... Since they are closely knit together tribally and familially, like at the village mass harvest, they join forces to build their houses of concrete on the outskirts of the city, moving slowly on to downtown. Their best men bring in the cement, their neighbors are in charge of bricks and tiles, their brothers raise the roof beams, their sisters-in-law prepare food, and they all jointly mix the mortar over the weekend. They put their garages in the basement, so they can easily be turned into inns or single rooms, which one day they will let to native Belgraders. Being in a genetic state of war with the city, their houses resemble bunkers.

Not knowing what's in the store for them, Belgraders, free of any worries, ride their bicycles along the river banks and play tennis.

They feel somewhat aristocratic. They grow up in their parent's small flats. Once they decide to start their own families, they will have to leave that sweet, extended childhood residence and become subtenants in their own native city! Namely, they'll have to make up their minds whether they want to keep their marriage or the parental roof above their heads.

And so they become the world champions in walking on tiptoe and closing doors quietly. For years, they take baths in other people's bathrooms, always with a sense of guilt...

When they hear that a house with a garden in the West costs less than a two-and-a-half rooms apartment in Julino Brdo, many of them will emigrate to faraway countries, to make careers, get rich and stay there forever...

In New York City, for example, those who stand on their dignity flee as far away from Manhattan as possible, while in Belgrade they strive to live in "strict" downtown. (By the way, why is downtown here always "strict"?)

And so the years go by... Although their mothers were sickly all their lives, it was their healthy fathers who died first, leaving those poor widows to mind the remnants of old-fashioned furniture, the china tableware for twelve (never eaten from) and the tenancy rights to the apartment.

Everybody wonders why our man from Caracas, a famous oilman, a true dollar millionaire, who owns a palace there, tennis courts, a stud farm and three swimming pools, when in Belgrade does not stay at the Hyatt hotel, where he belongs, but in the one-room apartment in Krunska Street, with his mother, who does not want to move to Latin America for the life of her. She cannot desert her dead ones. Every Sunday she goes to the cemetery to weed and water their graves....

But the man is aware that there is no hotel in the world where he could eat his *Keva*'s spinach with a sunny-side-up egg, nor would anyone wait for him at home past midnight, to warm up the leftovers of yesterday's stew for him.

But one day she passes away. After the funeral, our successful businessman is informed that the apartment will be returned to the Town Council of Vračar, to whom it belongs. He does not understand it! He wants to keep it at any price! Did he not deserve to keep these 40 square meters in his home town? No way. He is not listed as the titular of the tenancy rights to the apartment. All right, he'll buy it out... It is not for sale!

He wants to buy the whole block of buildings in Krunska Street, just for that tiny apartment in which he grew up on thin and watery *ajnpren* soup, within the familiar smell of the roux, lavender and resin from the fir wood, used for kindling the stove called "the horse carriage". He must not lose the turning of the seasons on the familiar tree tops in Krunska Street, beneath which he used to kick a rag ball, had his first French kiss ("like in the movies"), cried when that girlfriend left him for a Crvena Zvezda basketball player, while her name is still engraved in the entrance hall, which hasn't been white-washed since the 1950s,. What is he to do with all those relics from the past which survived his mother: walnut-wood wardrobes where he used to hide as a child, kitchen stools and the "Turkish corner"?

To take them out by the first of the following month, he is told. But, where? How to move out his childhood and youth? What would his English wife say if he tried to bring into her Victorian castle a sagging divan with its collapsed springs, the one on which he slept best, on which he recovered from all childhood diseases and on which he made love for the first time when his parents went to a spa in 1954.

And finally, after a long and useless battle with lawyers and city administrators, our successful but defeated man leaves his household furniture out in the rain and goes back to where he came from, never to return.

He also breaks all business connections with Serbia – because of a simple one-room flat, the only thing in his life he cared about, and which he could not keep…

GRILL COOKS

They used to come to Belgrade from somewhere in the south well before the war, poor, with neatly mended country-style clothes, with their irreplaceable southern accent; they toiled through apprenticeship, to become journeymen, to whom their bosses, afraid that their own children would ruin them, bequeathed their shops; they worked hard and in silence day and night, saved and gained, and then, like a bolt from the sky, were dispossessed of it all!

Naive as they were, they believed at first it was only a war of national liberation, until, some years later, all their shops were taken from them: green-grocer's and pastry shops, grilled-meat eateries, oriental bakeries and shops for filling siphon-bottles with club soda. Only then did they find out it was the Revolution, which they had not heard anything about before.

At first they were given jobs as clerks in their own shops (to maintain continuity), while the least able and the laziest of their former apprentices became their bosses. They worked until they could not stand negligence any longer, and then disappeared quietly from the *čaršija*, or downtown, where they had made names for themselves in the past.

That same *čaršija*, which they once held in high esteem, where a word of honor was more valuable than any written contract (you could cheat only once), turned into a pejorative word for the new authorities, consisting mostly of peasants from near-by villages. "It is the *čaršija* talking!", or "The *čaršija* is a political underground..." Serbian literature is brimming with stories about peasants afraid of going downtown to the *čaršija*, which is only its commercial center.

Already at the threshold of old age, but born as individualists, they embarked, without being aware of it, on a real secret war with the omnipotent System. If for no other reason but to escape from uselessly whiling away hours in their kitchens, they went out into the streets to sell cooked corn cobs in autumn. Some of them traded a little bit in trivia, dragging all day long their big, greasy briefcases full of bottles of perfume or lottery tickets. "Look, my dear ones, my whole store is packed in this briefcase..." (Uncle Maksa, 1950). If they happened to get a job as checkroom attendants in restaurants, they would be easily recognized, selling a couple of packs of imported cigarettes or lighters on the side. They also worked as illegal coffee cooks in offices and institutions, soon to become indispensable, as the coffee they prepared was the least expensive and the tastiest (a little secret: they never washed their coffee pots). They moved into the closed-down sports clubs on Ada Ciganlija, onto deserted barges, into empty barracks on the remote outskirts and started modestly, almost from scratch, their underground catering guerrilla with a baking pan of cheese pie and a crate of beer a day. Having learned from personal experience that in this country a businessman must not, for the life of him, expand his private business or become too visible, they would manage, at best, to have about ten tables in some rented garden, from which, one day, a pipe from the legendary, makeshift grill would start emitting its irresistibly appetising smoke and soon all Belgrade would hear about it!

Finding out that it had been tricked, the irate System would bear down on them with all its might – the hoards of inspectors, policemen, sanitary assessors and City Hall functionaries. Our grill masters would then collect their miserable little cooking utensils, a couple of burned-out skillets, the grill for barbecuing meat, an assortment of mismatched plates, salt shakers, cutlery and the best carving knife, and would move to another garden, another rowing club, and all Belgrade would follow them and their magical skill that nobody could take away from them.

We usually addressed them as Uncle Mile (or, when wanting to ingratiate ourselves – uncle Mi-

lence), as if they were our family – Uncle Trajče, Uncle Janićije, Uncle Kole, Grandpa Drlja or Uncle Giga, while they invariably, regardless of our age, called us – kids! "Come on, kids, time to go home! Closing time! Hey, you drank way too much, don't blame later your Uncle Mile for that!"

They were mostly somewhat plump old men of short stature and strong hands, gray-haired and with an occasional golden tooth, of surprisingly vivid gestures and small eyes as if floating in oil, dressed in shabby, worn-out clothes from the pre-war times. Like reliable war comrades, their wives, who all looked alike, stood by them at all times, adoring their husbands: Aunt Dana, Aunt Mileva, Aunt Živana, Aunt Zora – the anonymous winners of the long-lasting and exhausting war against the unjust State. Swallowing the pungent grill smoke for years, they put their children through school and made of them engineers, physicians, diplomats, professors, doctors and high-ranking officials (slightly ashamed of their parents' modest calling).

Fertilized by their sweat, toil and bones, present-day entrepreneurship is in full bloom and no one finds it strange. What a pity they did not live to see it!

Let us, therefore, mention them in our prayers...

HONG KONG ON REVOLUTION BOULEVARD

As a humble chronicler of Belgrade, I have to note that in 1990 a splendid Chinese restaurant was opened on Revolution Boulevard.

Revolution Boulevard used to be called King Alexander's Street (as of recently it's called that again).

Belgrade old-timers like to call their streets by their pre-war names. There is a little coquetry in it. If a person knows the previous street names, he shows, in a way, that he is not a newcomer to Belgrade. If you happen to remember that Borisa Kidriča Street used to be called Beogradska Street, and even earlier Hartvigova Street, you are an aristocrat, sort of.

The changes of street names offer us an insight into a long history of ideological violence. Krunska Street (Crown Street) earned its name because it led to the old Royal Palace. From the liberation until the historical "NO!"[3] it bore the euphoric name Moscow Street, and only when those

---

[3] Tito's break with Stalin in 1948.

who named it so were dispatched to Goli Otok camp did the Proletarian Brigades march through it. As if Proletarian Brigades could not have passed through some recently built boroughs, but, spitefully, just past the Royal Palace!

One day, I was telling a pretentious Belgrade lady that I bought something in March 27th Street, and she corrected me, as it seemed that I was not sophisticated enough:

"You mean in Kraljice Marije (Queen Mary) Street? "

"No," I say, "I mean in the former Ratarska (Plowman's) Street!"

By the way, the present day National Front Street used to be called, before World War II, Queen Natalija Street, but even earlier, before World War I, it was called Abadžijska Street (*abadžija* – a tailor who made peasant clothing)!

Farmers and peasant tailors are older than any dynasty.

But, to return to the Chinese restaurant that we did not get into yet.

The former Revolution Boulevard, once more renamed Aleksandrova Street, is given to naming its stores by exotic names... In addition to the legendary "Madera" restaurant, the "Costa Rica" boutique and the "Bombay" pastry shop, the Boulevard today also boasts of the "Hong Kong" restaurant!

As if some mysterious Asian lantern cast its glow on this suburban borough below Đeram mar-

72

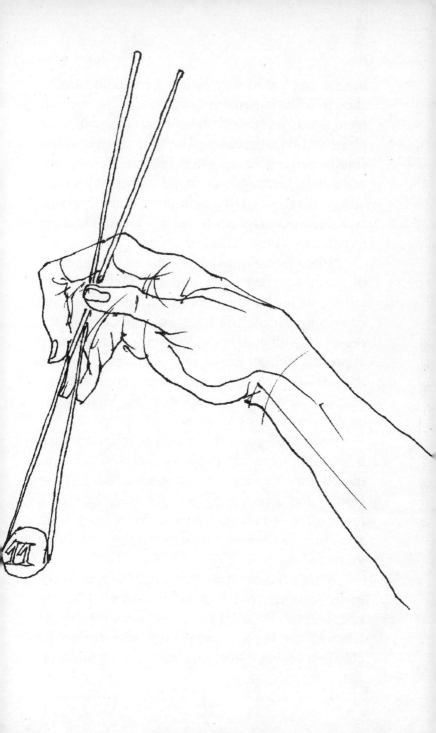

ket, having lost its way among the candle makers, shoe makers, bag makers, watch makers, second-hand goods traders and tinsmiths, who still make pipes and weathervanes. The faraway world has finally arrived here, where people know each other from birth and where old waiters with varicose veins see their guests through, from their first boyish drinking binges to the last glass of brandy, in memory of the deceased...

"Hong Kong" moved – where else but into the old tavern called Stari Vujadin (Old Man Vujadin), where the neighborhood people used to drop in for decades for a glass of cold beer and ten *ćevapčići* with onions. And so, one day, a marquee appeared with an impossible mixture of owners: the state-owned enterprise Stari Đeram and the Mandarin Pin Hua Hu replaced Old Vujadin (he could now eat his *pljeskavice* with chopsticks).

Instead of yesterday's oral menu, on which bean soup, tripe and pig knuckles in sauce simmered for decades, grilled meat absorbed the smoke and aspics trembled, we were offered a menu of 179 fantastic dishes, from shark's-fin soup to a bamboo shoots salad! Enough to drive you nuts!

What's the big deal, you might say: in every metropolis there are at least a dozen Chinese restaurants! That's true. There are even whole Chinatowns. I used to eat in them often (being the cheapest eating places), from Bangkok and Singapore, all the way to New York and Los Angeles... Before going to Chinatown in San Francisco I would stuff my pockets with warm rolls from an Italian bakery, as it is a known fact that the Chinese do not consume bread, but only rice.

The moment the Chinese waiter turns his back, I take a piece of the roll from my pocket and dip into the sauce. I cannot control myself! Namely, I come from barren regions of the country, where you eat bread with spaghetti, even with bread pudding!

And so, as soon as it opened its doors, everybody who is somebody in Belgrade dashed to "Hong Kong" to demonstrate their liking and appreciation for this exotic food. Diplomats with their wives, foreign correspondents, businessmen, experts in Asian languages and many other big shots, all booked tables two days in advance.

A dozen Chinese men and women, apparently mute, who ran away from their own Revolution, stranded (how ironic!) high up on our Revolution Boulevard, move among the tables, mysterious like shadows.

Two local guys, the local drunkards who spent all their life sitting in Starac Vujadin, cannot believe their own eyes. Until recently, they used to see only pink elephants, and now, for the first time, they see – the Chinese!

They stare at the dragons and larks on the walls and watch the guests eat with chopsticks...

They are baffled by every single item on the menu. Instead of the perennial sardines and hard-boiled eggs, they find "Northern and Southern Dish", "Buddhist Food", "Gong-Kao Chicken", "Eight Treasuries", "The Happy Family Meal", "Hiang-Ling Dish"...

"Hey, you Chinese guy, bring another bottle of Belgrade beer!"

"I have no money to sober up! Do you know how much it would cost me to get drunk properly again? That's why I only top up... It's cheaper!"

Another character is fresh out of medical treatment. First he made a tour of Belgrade. He says he couldn't believe how much the city has grown! When did they banish the cars from Knez Mihailova Street? What is that tall, dark building nearby the London intersection called? Since when are *pljeskavice* (grilled meat patties) called "McDonald's"?

He dropped by into his old neighborhood to see his buddies at Starac Vujadin – but they were gone!

"What jasmine tea! Give me another Belgrade beer!"

"Well, how are you and your wife getting along?" asks a friend of his.

"Like pigeons!", he answers. "Every now and then one of us flies through the window!"

By the way, do you know how the Chinese eat when they are on a diet?

They use one chopstick only...

P.S. Four months later, Hong Kong folded. Starac Vujadin won! On their last night before closing down, I saw, for the first time in my life, ten Chinese people drunk with despair.

ROAST LAMB

As if persistently fleeing from its nature and its essence, Belgrade in the last decade resembled a stunned upstart ashamed of its origins. Instead of reviving the old professions and crafts of its fathers and grandfathers, it plunged into opening fake Italian pizzerias, English pubs and supposedly European cafés. Judging by the number of video shops, one can conclude that we have, apparently, become a city of lonely TV addicts.

Belgrade women have fallen in love with a French word – boutique. How many of them there are in town – nobody can tell!

In earlier times, women used to have their own dressmakers. I remember those boutique forerunners, who used to make dresses for the ladies from the neighborhood in their kitchens, never foreseeing that their smart successors with two years of elementary school would one day run fashion shows for the diplomatic corps. Between their lips they held straight pins and safety pins, and around their necks there dangled a yellow-cloth measuring tape, like a ribbon of the Medal of the First Order with Double Back Pain.

Mrs. Petrović's calico, the fabric for comrade Petrović's suit, cuts, designs, various yarns tangled up into a ball, and the taste of the marking chalk... Instead of these poor martyrs, who, toiling at their secondhand Singer sewing machines put their children through school, we got hundreds of pretentious boutiques, whose owners claim adamantly that they are not dressmakers, but fashion designers!

Even an ordinary butcher's shop changed its name into "the meat boutique".

The offspring of Belgrade bakers seem to shun the warm, soft Balkan loafs with thick and crunchy crust and generous heels that everybody fights for at the dinner table. After a short stay in Paris, they decide to make croissants (with a rolling "r") and baguettes that go stale in less than two hours.

The first sex-shops also appeared in the country of Serbia, where, praise the Lord, "those things" are still done without artificial devices!

And so, running away from ourselves and towards some imaginary Europe, we were completely deprived of roast lamb, except for that served by the gram in the better restaurants.

I heard from some elderly Belgraders that before the war lamb from the spit was sold at every other street corner, and that all day long you could hear the blunt sound of the butcher's knife hitting the chopping block, while the vendors in their piercing voice with a southern accent called out to their customers:

"Come ooooon, peeeeople! Hooooot, roasted! For mamma to eat and for daughter to only watch, as mamma will eat it all!"

And when the police, having been given orders from higher places, forbade the vendors to lure their customers by crying out loudly, the owner of a low-price eatery, cutting the lamb loin with his carving knife, while the fragments of bones and meat flew left and right, yelled at the top of his voice:

"Woe is me, if only I could shout!"

Looking for years for the lost flavors of his homeland, the author of this brief essay on the spit tried all kinds of lamb, starting from the Australian ones (tasteless, just as the continent itself), the New Zealand ones, which is too soft, to the splendid fatty Arab mutton, stuffed with rice and raisins and various magic spices, all the way to the Greek lamb, roasted for Easter together with braided intestines, so-called "bear's foot", on Mount Pelion – the homeland of the centaurs.

But, after this long research, I can say with a clear conscience that the lambs from our regions are the best, particularly those feeding on the grass salty from sea winds, along the Dinara mountain range. In that meat you feel the fragrance of miraculous herbs and the mythical flavor of our rebellious ancestors.

Lamb from the spit is more than a dish – for us it is a national ritual; you do not turn a lamb on the spit every day. It is one of the few dishes that lose their flavor if roasted at home, in the oven. As the old people would say, lamb meat must pass through the serving hatch. Who has ever seen "lamb for two persons" on a menu?

The turning of the spit is a feast; a reward for the winner or solace in distress; it is booty or the sign of exceptional hospitality; but, above all, it is a chance to be together with the people we love while waiting for the last pouring of beer over the lamb (to make its skin crispy) and the final act – taking it off the spit and fighting for the best pieces, with the author of this essay only rarely managing to get hold of the kidneys or the tail!

Praising excessively the taste of the local lamb to an influential American businesswoman, the director of a firm from the interior told her, while she was helping herself, that the lamb, roasted in her honor, was so young that it had been "taken from its mother this morning, while it sucked her, and slaughtered at noon". The lady, shaken to the roots, fainted on the spot and the expected lucrative business deal fell through!

COFFEE

Coffee is the most important secondary thing in our lives. It seems we can do without everything but coffee! And even if there isn't anything else in our pantry, we'll treat our guests with the last remains of coffee from the coffee mill.

The manner of making and drinking coffee is a watershed between mentalities and civilizations. While the North and the West drink short espresso coffee, casually and almost in passing, leaning on the counter, the East has to sit down first, relax and peacefully recapitulate the day during this bitter-sweet repose from life.

In encyclopedias you can read that coffee (*coffea*) until the 15th century grew exclusively in eastern Africa, namely in Ethiopia. Then it was brought over to Saudi Arabia. The Turks adopted the custom of drinking coffee from the Arabs, and passed it along to us. That's why we call it "Turkish coffee"! A point of interest, once they made us dependent on coffee, they themselves turned to drinking tea. Be that as it may, when, some years ago, on the island of Rhodes, I ordered "Turkish coffee", the waiter almost threw me out of the inn:

"Sir", he said furiously "here we drink only Greek coffee. If you want Turkish, Asia Minor is right over there, just keep swimming..."

I can say that I have tried almost all kinds of coffees in the world, from the insipid one which people drink in the States from big cups for café-au-lait, to Latin-American "café negro", Italian espresso and cappuccino, via French filtered coffee, all the way to the overly sweet Greek coffee, served in thimble-size cups, and the Australian coffee, tasting like chowder with traces of caffeine... But never and nowhere have I come across that unique flavor and aroma of coffee prepared by the famous café owner Vejsil-effendi from Sarajevo, up there near Vratnička Kapija. He would roast it in the roasting pan, then crush it with a wooden pestle in the stone mortar and finally serve it with reverence, without any haste, as if we had all the time in the world, while the twilight was slowly landing on the roofs of the town in the valley.

A story has it that an elderly, apolitical effendi, in the difficult times of political upheavals and intrigues, ordered his usual coffee in his favorite coffee-house, and the waiter asked him whether he wanted Serbian or Turkish coffee. Deciding against coffee, the effendi said: "Bring me tea!"

"Russian or Chinese?" asked the waiter, and the effendi waved him off and said resignedly: "Bring me a glass of water."

In our country there are more kinds of coffee and more ways to drink it than in any other place in the world.

To start with, there are two basic kinds: *maksuzija* (prepared with love and welcoming, therefore *maksuz!*), and *sikteruša*, served when the host indicates discretely that the time of the visit is over.

In Bosnia they also have a poor people's coffee called *doljevuša*, when you pour water over coffee dregs, in order to prolong the pleasure.

The epoch of ubiquitous meetings and conferences bred a new automatic, absent-minded way of drinking coffee, tasteless and odorless, prepared by ill-humored coffee girls in government offices and institutions, and flavoured by their dissatisfaction with their low wages and lowly positions.

Here, it is with a cup of coffee that love is born, plots are hatched, hangovers cured, plans made, meetings held, disputes solved, widows consoled, and there is no chance that gossiping about others (the most outstanding national characteristic) would be possible without coffee-drinking sessions...

Coffee is our past, but also our future, since we are probably the only people in the world who predict fateful events by looking at the bottom of an empty coffee cup, first turned upside down on its saucer to "drain"!

In the black-and-white landscape of coffee dregs, we see our future travels, tears and joy, a person in uniform and a blond lady from afar, but also someone conspiring against us, which will come to nothing, as we see clearly that we are in for a gain!

Well, then, thanks for the coffee and we apologize if we offended you – we didn't mean to!

HORSES

In September of 1990, I saw a horse-drawn carriage at Ušće!

It rose, like a nostalgic specter, from the September mist in which Ušće wraps itself in the fall, so as not to catch cold. I thought it was a dream... It was the first horse-drawn carriage in Belgrade after more than thirty years!

Horses were banned from the city as early as 1956. Not all, though. Only the four-legged ones.

It was in the days when power was held by centaurs: half peasants – half people from the lower middle class. Neither here nor there. Naturally, they hated everything that reminded them of their village. They wanted to forget their origin as soon as possible, and therefore mercilessly felled the trees lining the streets and poured asphalt over grass.

Their architecture was the reflection of themselves – they built Marx and Engels Square, a cold rampart of cemented ideology, without a single blade of grass...

Just in case, they banned even goats in their native hills, secretly afraid that, if they happened to fall from power, they would have to look after them again.

Until that time we, naturally, used to live with horses. We moved from one place to another in freight carts pulled by tame, enormous horses from Styria. We jumped onto moving fiacres. The stables in Dorćol, Čubura and Dušanovac smelled of hay and manure. In winter we would warm our frozen hands on the warm horse's breath in front of Tabor, an inn at Kalenić market. The peasants used to bring us wood for winter on horses' backs; in summer they would bring us blocks of ice in bags, for ice-boxes... If we were anemic, we were fed horse meat.

Rumor has it that a milkman, going down the streets of Senjak with his horse, spotted a fully armed policeman standing in front of a luxurious villa, never guarded before.

"What are you doing here, my fellow countryman?" – he asked.

"I'm protecting the King of Arabia!"

"Shame on you!" spat the milkman. "You're protecting the King of Arabia, but you were not able to protect your own!"

The earliest horse races held in Belgrade, in 1842, were organized by foreign diplomats in honor of the Turkish representative Shekib-effendi. In 1863, Prince Mihailo himself chose the site for the race track, behind Tašmajdan Park.

Today, the Prince rides a bronze horse, and Belgrade kids call the near-by café "Under the Tail".

On the eve of World War I, on June 28, 1914, the Hippodrome was opened at Careva Ćuprija, where Belgrade beauties still show off their hats and middle-aged lovers.

An old chronicler of Belgrade, Milan Stoimirović, wrote that there lived in Belgrade a certain Hungarian, by the name of Kakashi, a former Austro-Hungarian officer who joined the Serbian army and, although a descendant of the noble Caroly family, fought bravely on the Danubian front, until severely wounded. Then he retired and devoted himself completely to horses. If he would happen to see someone striking this noble animal, he would immediately lunge at him with a cane! This is what he said once, in his broken Serbian:

"The Serbs brave, everybody knows that. A Serb go straight for the gun and the bayonet, for knife and cannon, he rush to the machine-gun and tank; he never stop before bombs or poisonous gas, do not fear zeppelin, even less submarine, but tell me please, why is it that this brave people feel such a deep antipathy toward the stick? The moment he see a stick, a Serb stop in his tracks..."

Although this legendary horse-breeder died in Belgrade at a ripe old age, he never learned Serbian properly. Rumor has it that he used to say, till his dying day: "He laughs best who laughs from behind!"

The last Guide through pre-war Belgrade cites five stations for fiacres and twelve for freight carts. The fiacres used to stand even by the

Prince's Monument, just as they still stand in front of the Plaza hotel in New York. Sometimes I feed them corn kernels, just for the fun of it. The policemen ride their horses daily along Fifth Avenue. The freckled English girls gallop through Hyde Park in London. Horseshoes echo through the old cobblestoned Roman streets of Trastevere... Other big cities are not ashamed of their horses as we are, although our whole history is linked to them!

In the best known Serbian painting, almost an icon, patriarch Arsenije Čarnojević rides on, surrounded by his horsemen. Even in front of the National Assembly building, "black horses are at play". Nevertheless, not counting those who appear occasionally at the Hippodrome, there are today in Belgrade only a couple of poor ponies at the Zoo. Our children can see horses only on TV. When they go to the countryside, they ask their grandfather whether the horse bites, and they offer it chewing gum. Isn't it high time to bring back, at least symbolically, several horses into their childhood? If New York, London, Paris, Vienna or Rome can do it, why can't we?

Maybe that enchanted fiacre, turned up suddenly at Ušće from the past, is the beginning of the return of horses?

What are we waiting for? What are we afraid of? In groceries, you can get goat cheese again. It seems that the time of the centaurs is over...

VAJFERT

For ten years at least I used to sit at the table of the legendary Mr. Miša Radan, in the small bar called Lasta, right by St. Mark's Church. I suppose that that old pal of mine chose this modest place for his headquarters for at least three reasons. He resided in the neighborhood and worked at a near-by bank, the waiters were more than polite, and while one sipped his drink there was no remorse, since one had the feeling of passing though one's own hometown while watching the buses leave for the airport right from Lasta.

And so we were sitting at Lasta, watching the employees from near-by offices, stores and companies dash in to have a quick one. These were the so-called office drunkards, who used to make regular rounds of about ten bars, along a precisely set route.

It is funny that we, the painters, and our colleagues by trade, the house painters, are believed to be prone to drinking, but it is less known that the highest number of illegal drunkards is recruited from the corps of ordinary office employees. Also, the highest number of vodka drinkers is among them, not out of particular love for things Russian, but because vodka neither stinks nor smells, and it is almost impossible to detect how many drinks one has had. That's where the famous sentence comes from – "No, on my word, I did not touch it – here, smell my breath!"

One day, word by word, at our table in Lasta the turn came of the story of the late Milovan Džudža from Čačak (God have mercy on his soul), who worked for forty four years as a night watchman at the National Bank in Belgrade.

The governor was a very famous Belgrade tycoon, Đorđe Vajfert, who also owned the brewery bearing his name, a strict but fair man of the old school, who had bought the ground for the bank in Kralja Petra Street from the Tzintzar family Kumanudi.

And, as many citizens of our city are at present divided into those who are fans of Crvena Zvezda and those who are fans of Partizan, or into those who read *Večernje Novosti* and those who read *Politika*, in those bygone days Belgrade was divide into those who drank Vajfert's beer and those who preferred Bajloni's.

Be that as it may, there was only one thing old man Vajfert could not tolerate – his employees drinking during office hours! If he would happen to catch a tipsy employee, that one would be fired on the spot. If this rule of Vajfert's were still observed in this day and age, Belgrade would soon be bereft of most of its male employees!

But, let's go back to the late Milovan Džudža, the night watchman who faithfully guarded the bank on New Year's Eve. He, poor soul, asked for a crate of beer to be brought to his box – to join in the celebration. But, as misfortune would have it, at the very moment the crate was being brought inside, the omnipotent Đorđe Vajfert made his appearance.

"What is this, for God's sake, Mister Milovan?"

In those days even the watchmen were "misters"!

"Beer, Mr. Governor..." replied Milovan, scared out of his wits.

"What do you mean "beer" in the National bank, Mr. Milovan?"

"Well, Vajfert's beer, naturally, Mister Governor! Not a chance that we would drink Bajloni's beer!"

And so, my friend finished the story at the table in Lasta, thanks to his wits Milovan Džudža made a splendid career as a night watchman, and remained on the job until the day he died...

Anyway, who is an alcoholic?

Only he who drinks more than his physician!

PARASOL-UMBRELLA

"He sells umbrellas!" is what old Belgraders still say for a person who, in tumultuous times, minds his own business and does not take sides.

While searching for the origin of this expression, there landed, right into my story, with his gardening umbrella wide open, Ćir Moša Avram, nicknamed Maca ("Pussycat"), a Serb of the Mosaic faith, owner of the First Serbian Umbrella Factory, looking like a Chagall rabbi in the Vitebsk sky...

Under his wide black umbrellas files of priests walked with dignity, to baptize or to bury, self-confident high-ranking official used them as walking sticks, brides went to the altar turning the handles of their parasols made of white lace; in the shade of Ćir Moša's umbrellas and canopies, people drank Bajloni's and Vajfert's beer in gardens strewn with crunching gravel; peasants liked to buy those heavy dark-blue umbrellas with massive handles, good for striking cattle or an insolent child.

"Umbrellas protect you from humidity and cold", reads the advertisement of the First Serbian Umbrella Factory – *they protect not only your clothes but also your reputation, as nobody looks well if drenched with rain; finally, every Serb and family man should carry an umbrella, lest he should look like a ragamuffin! One can go out without underwear, as nobody can see it, but not without an umbrella, as everybody sees it!"*

Devoted to the manufacture of his umbrellas, the masterpiece of which was a marvelous "parasol-umbrella", white until dry, serving as a parasol, and turning black when opened in the rain, Moša Avram, nicknamed Maca, watched in amazement the rebellions, coups, assassination attempts and political battles that shook Serbia in the early 19th century, refraining from meddling into affairs beyond his understanding or influence. Simply, he wanted to work quietly in his trade and to be of use, but apparently he was not allowed to, as in those days, just like now, the eternal maxim "he who is not with us is against us!" was in force.

I ask myself whether Ćir Moša, that fanatic Serb of the Mosaic faith, was a less good Serb because he did not want to belong to any party, belonging as he did, above all, to the great world fraternity of umbrella makers?

Anyway, do you happen to know who was the president of France in the summer when Van Gogh painted his *Sunflowers* in Arles?

What was the name of the political party which in 1302 banished the divine Dante Alighieri from Florence for life, as a result of which he died as an exile in Ravenna in 1321?

And so Ćir Moša went on manufacturing his umbrellas diligently, taking a well-deserved rest at noon in front of the Grand hotel and drinking much too sweet coffee, but his calm would be disturbed by a head-waiter, who incessantly bothered him with questions about politics, rallies and assassination attempts...

One day, the chronicler says, Moša blew up and snapped at the waiter: "I am Moša Avram, from the First Serbian Umbrella Factory. I have nothing to do with plots. I sell umbrellas!"

A whole century later, I still believe that Ćir Moša was right and that his umbrellas were more useful for Serbia than all those long forgotten scandals, proclamations, intrigues, strategies and political pamphlets. But the funniest thing is that in this day and age considerably more people discuss politics than make umbrellas. How shall we protect ourselves from the storms of hail-bearing and gloomy political clouds?

BRE![4]

In the spring of 1989, my old friend, Princess Jelisaveta Karađorđević, spent some time in Belgrade.

She came to pay a visit to her hometown. They kindly showed her Beli Dvor (White Palace). She made a tour of the parks where she used to play as a child. She visited the chapel where she prayed for the souls of her ancestors.

On the wide brim of her black straw hat, the peonies she plucked in Kosovo Field were gradually wilting.

Unlike the upstarts who turned rich overnight, and who criticize everything when they return to Belgrade from the wide world, the Princess fell in love with this city. She told me that she came to love the people, the tree-lined streets, our cuisine and our way of life...

When I first met her, in the fall of 1977 in New York, I divulged to her a secret – that as a boy I used to kiss every frog I caught.

---

[4] A colloquial interjection of unclear origin, expressing emphasis or wonder.

"Why did you kiss frogs?"

"Just in case," I said. "You never know when a frog could turn into a princess..."

In the meantime the Princess learned to speak Serbian quite decently and to write in the Cyrillic alphabet.

As all refined people, she spoke in a well-measured and quiet manner. We, naturally, speak from the top of our voices and in unison. That's why the Princess learned to say: "Don't holler!"

We were sitting in a boat restaurant on the Sava river, watching the strollers on the quay. All Belgrade girls looked like princesses from some enchanted, secret kingdoms of New Belgrade...

I remembered how, a long time ago, at Gino's on Lexington Avenue, I taught the Princess to say – *bre*. She did not know then what the word meant – if it is a word at all and not a particle!

For the first time, that distant year, I realized how much that three-letter Turcism is present in our everyday parlance, how multilayered it is, crammed with all possible meanings and nuances... It seems to me that we are not able to produce a sentence without having at least one *bre* in it, just like Bosnians who use their *bolan,* or Dalmatians their famous *eeee!* – with its thousands of meanings and intonations.

Said with admiration: He is a great guy, *bre*!
Said with scorn: Oh, go on, *bre!*

Said provocatively: What's all this fuss about, *bre!*

Said gently: Oh, *bre!*

Said lovingly: Come closer, *bre!*

Said haughtily: Look who's talking, *bre!*

Said philosophically: Come on, *bre!*

Said with astonishment: How come, *bre!*

Said imperatively: Play on, *bre!*

Said epically: "*Bre,* stop lying, you swarthy Moor!"

"*Bre,* I kept my mouth shut, *bre*, I shouted, *bre*, I threatened – all in vain, everything kept going wrong!"

How to translate this minute but so important word *bre* into any foreign language?

Because it includes spite, defiance, gentleness and casualness, there is something rebellious and unruly in it, something rowdy and overbearing... It serves to express agreement and admiration, but also disagreement and regret, wonder, invitation and warning, surprise, encouragement, stimulus and fostering, but also imploring.

We all fit into that little *bre*, with all our flaws and virtues – it seems to be our very quintessence... And if we would, one day, disappear from the face of the Earth, we would most certainly rise again, out of these three letters.

And, then, the time came for Princess Jelisaveta to go back to the wide world...

I told her that she never looked more beautiful, not for the sake of compliment.

"Don't holler!", she answered, going down Makedonska Street.

"Oh, go on, *bre!*" I told her, but she did not hear me.

HATS

When we leaf through albums with the pictures of old Belgrade, the first thing we note, on its streets, squares, café tables under the linden trees in full bloom, is a multitude of ladies' and gentlemen's hats – that essential part of the pre-war Belgrade costume. It seems that those people, long gone, found it rude to leave their houses with their heads uncovered.

Tall black top hats, clerks' respectable bowler hats, Borsalino hats worn by respectable tradesmen, the wide-brimmed romantic hats on hotheaded poets and bohemians; Panama hats made of straw for strolling in the shady paths of Topčider in summertime... Who could name them all! Good urban customs prescribed that a young man, upon finishing high school, should get his first hat and a black walking stick with a metal handle – two attributes needed to join the world of grown-up and mature people.

As for ladies' hats, they always reflected the wild fantasies of their owners and the milliners who made them, casting a furtive glance towards Paris – the homeland of hats. On those old photos one can clearly see the movable gardens on the pretty heads of Belgrade ladies; black hats with a veil studded with dots, beneath which the eyes take on a mysterious, *sfumatto* shine full of intimating promises, as well as those, worn in springtime, whose excessively wide brims resemble birds with wings broken by strong emotions; not to mention the minute pill-box hats, which so charmingly became Daisy Duck and fatal Deanna Durbin...

Let us take a look at the present day Belgrade streets... not a single hat to speak of! As if they had been banned by law. Were it not for theater plays (where hats are always worn by negative characters), and horse races at Careva Ćuprija, where some ten or so hats make their appearance at the derby, we would almost forget that hats existed at all! Truth be told, Belgrade is the only European capital which banned hats, those mortal enemies of scarves, progressive berets, cloth caps and leather caps, on an ideological basis.

I watch with melancholy the photos of beautiful women with the light of some long gone day in May passing through the straw brims of their hats and painting their faces with freckles... The frivolous Belgrade hats from the 1930s could not possibly envision what, starting from 1918 in faraway Mother Russia, the cloth caps worn by

Lenin, Stalin and Trotsky had in store for them.

That old fear of post-war guardians of the strict socialist morals, which considered the hat to be a symbol of the defeated middle class, was passed down the line from mothers and grand-mothers all the way to their grand-daughters, who prefer to go out in the street with their hair either pink-colored or shaved off than with hats on their heads. It seems that the strict morals, manufactured in the laboratories of the engineers of human souls, found it easier to make a peace pact with the ragged hippie style than with the hat, which still haunts it in its dreams, reminding it of all things it had crushed and turned into dust and ashes. As in the song, "all that was hidden at the bottom of our hearts, in the ashes down below, was fanned into flames by our comrade Tito, comrade Tito, comrade, Tito," and so on, and so forth.

Be it as it may, in those two or three remaining, impoverished shops which used to manufacture and sell hats in the pre-war era, today you can find only the white wedding ones, while gentlemen's hat shops are replaced by workshops manufacturing cloth caps, sailors' caps, *šajkača* (a Serbian peasant cap) and fur hats. It's interesting that gentlemen were not as annoyed by the disappearance of hats as ladies, who now look at them with envy only if they travel to some more fortunate country, where gods and hat-makers are not on bad terms with each other.

Belgrade is a city of absurdities: it found it easier to re-establish the multiparty system than to bring back the nice custom for ladies to wear hats!

In any case, it turned out that the old saying "The boot protects your head, not the hat" was not correct.

Namely, the boot unwaveringly stamped out the hats, as well as many a head of those who, naively, wanted to wear them in those times.

In the meantime, the caps' cloth lining grew threadbare and the caps themselves worn-out...

They've had it!

BELGRADE IN HALF AN HOUR

Whenever someone accuses Belgrade of an alleged intolerance to other nations, religions and languages, I feel like taking their hand and propelling them out onto a certain street, quite ordinary at first glance, where they will learn a lot about tolerance.

It is Sedmog Jula (7th of July) Street, which before the war used to be called Kralja Petra Street (King Peter's Street), a name reinstated in recent times.

In a way, Kralja Petra Street connects two civilizations: from its top you can see our tame and domestic Sava, while at the spot where it ends you feel the breath of the cosmopolitan Danube. Two rivers and a street, as if thrown defiantly across the city's backbone, like a taut arch between two civilizations...

First we come across the Serbian Orthodox Cathedral, built in 1845 by Prince Miloš, who had commissioned the craftsmen from Pančevo to construct it in the Baroque style for a fee of 31,000 silver forints. The Patriarchate and the School of

Theology round up the portrait of the Serbian Zagorsk – the center of Orthodoxy in these parts.

Right across the street is an old-fashioned tavern, which, at one time, was named by its impious owner "At the Cathedral", but the church fathers rebelled and demanded that the blasphemous name be changed. Since that time it is called "?", the strangest name on Earth, as its owner was at a loss how to rename it. At The Question Mark you can find equally strange guests, the last of the Belgrade bohemians, aspiring artists and students of the nearby School of Applied Arts. The specialty of the house: "Šumadija tea" (mulled brandy), mulled wine, sauerkraut, meat aspic and hand-holding with young artists idling their time away.

At the very crossroad of the fashionable Knez Mihailova and Kralja Petra streets, there used to stand the legendary Pelivan Inn, (today called Snežana, or Snow White), with comfortable divans, wide pillows, free tobacco from skin bags and chibouks lit on the eternally burning braziers. Old chroniclers wrote with nostalgia that at Pelivan's one could always get a delicious suety pilaf with mutton, as well as tripe, cooked mutton, cheese pies or *burek* and dry *takuša,* all served in copper bowls or plates.

The end of the Oriental era was heralded by the opening of one of the first European-style restaurants in Belgrade, called Dva Jelena (The Two Deer). There the first balls were held, attended by new arrivals from Europe.

But, you would be wrong to believe that "those wild Turkish times" have gone from this strange street for good. Going downhill, you come across the old Bajrakli Mosque, leaning onto Kralja Petra Street. This Islamic place of worship, with its harmonious arches, is the place where all Belgraders of the Mohammedan faith come to pray. It is a small Islamic center of a kind, successfully presided over by mufti Hamdija Jusufspahić, let Allah reward him with good health and a long life!

A couple of hundred of meters further on, there is the Jewish Community Center, with its artistic and cultural societies and lecture halls, where the long Hebrew tradition of the Dorćol Jews, who presented Belgrade with their precious, noble and sensuous tones in poetry and painting, is painstakingly kept and preserved.

Across the street is the Royal hotel, until recently called Toplice, patronized mostly by our Russian brothers and other travelers from East European countries. In front of the hotel, as well as in its hall and in the near-by bars one could buy, at half price, original vodka, caviar in small jars and wooden *babushka* dolls, holding a second *babushka* inside, then a third one, all the way to the tiniest *babushka*, which held...

The luxurious Benetton boutique is located in the immediate vicinity of the oriental pastry-shop, managed by a diligent man from Gora, while the

Italian pizzeria "Košava" is only five steps away from the elite pre-war Aero Club and the memorial home of the painter Petar Dobrović.

Is there a stranger and a more tolerant street on Earth!

At its very end it flows into Dorćol (in Turkish Dort-jol means the crossroad of four roads or four alleys), a vanished Jewish quarter, where Serbs, Macedonians, Tzintzars, Greeks, Armenians, Bulgarian gardeners and Romanians lived happily next to one another – a true little Babylon situated in Belgrade!

Taking all this into account, I see this modest street as a true lesson in tolerance and friendship, a lesson often impossible to grasp in many better-to-do main streets in enlightened Europe.

THE GATE

Once upon the time there lived on the Belgrade hill of Topčider, in the quiet and shady Kačanski Street, a native Belgrader by the name of Obrad Simić.

He was a sturdy man with a shaved head and a long white beard, resembling that worn by Nikola Pašić in the past. He lived quietly in the house designed before the war by Aleksandar Deroko, architect, painter and travel writer; he owned a parrot called Ara who could talk, and a boat-house on the Sava, where he used to swim from early spring to late fall.

The above-mentioned Mr. Obrad was an excellent connoisseur of the English language, and he translated the comic *Bringing Up Father* for many decades and with a great passion, transforming the Anglo-Saxon spirit into the spirit of Belgrade, full of Vinaver-style juicy idiomatic pranks.

In present day Belgrade everybody translates from English, and there is nothing out of the ordinary in it, but before World War II you could count on the fingers of one hand the true Anglophiles and connoisseurs of English, which became fashionable with us only in the last decades.

Speaking of languages, it should be known that Belgrade from time immemorial resembled a true Babylonian ant-hill. Apart from Serbian, Turkish had been spoken for centuries equally, and Ladino arrived together with the Sephardic Jews expelled from Spain, enriching Serbian with many strange words and sayings.

Also spoken were Greek and Tzintzar, said to be a corrupt mixture of Greek, our language and Romanian. If we are to add to this galimatias Roma, Armenian, along with the idioms and dialects of boatmen, merchants, craftsmen, carpetbaggers, mercenaries, musicians and chapel-masters from Carinthia, the idioms of adventurers, gigolos and tramps, of traveling magicians and illusionists, of consuls and spies, we will realize the enormity and richness of the idiomatic heritage left to its children by this exciting, windy town, through which even today foreign words fly like bullets.

Is there, for example, another nation on earth which can boast of as many different names for a "mean woman" as we have? Just take a look: viper, bitch, hag, harpy, shrew, harlot... to name only a few! Who could know their origin and their roots!

It is a well-known fact that in the noble circles of Belgrade between the two wars, French was the language of choice. Namely, Belgrade is the only place in the world which had its own branch of French surrealism, not to mention "French salad", "French cap" and a dish called "French potato".

During the war, though, one had to learn some German, for the purposes of black-marketeering and surviving.

From October of 1944, all the way through to the break-up with the Big Brother, Russian ruled mercilessly, so that the typical affected French rolling "r", rolled, out of fear, under the French double bed.

Russian was particularly popular with those who did not have patience to devote themselves to really learning a foreign language. By pronouncing Serbian words in a soft manner, they imagined that they spoke Russian perfectly!

At that time, Obrad Simić's beard reached almost to his waist, as he had vowed not to shave it off before the downfall of the communist regime, and he gave them one month at the outside!

Those who, like Mr. Simić, spoke English, resembled members of some small, ostracized sect, in which he, by virtue of his corpulent body, independent spirit and rather extravagant behavior, stood out like a white crow, particularly because, to make matters worse, he was employed at the American embassy!

This is not easy to understand from the present-day point of view, when Belgrade is flooded

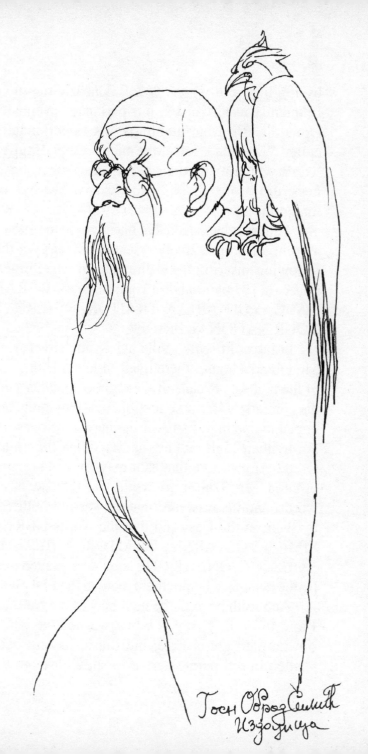

Госн Ображениик
Изгобница

by English, and when "O.K." is nearly the most frequently used word in our parlance. Even McDonald's Big Mac hamburger is affectionately called "Mekica", let alone many other English words which made their home here: super, business, drugstore, disco, jeans, derby, bye-bye or marketing...

Well, so it happened that one night in the 1950s, a group of progressively-oriented citizens put the following inscription on the gate of Mr. Simić's house, in red paint and in capital letters: OBRAD SIMIĆ, YOU ARE A TRAITOR, WHERE IS YOUR NATIONAL PRIDE?

In the confiscated villa across the street from Mr. Obrad's house, there lived Milovan Đilas, one of the highest officials of the regime, together with his comrade-wife. It is possible that they grew annoyed by having to answer the inevitable question put by their high-ranking guests, about the traitor Obrad. Anyway, be that as it may, the then regime ordered Mr. Traitor to white-wash those nasty words, and he answered that he was not bothered by them in the least and that the words OBRAD SIMIĆ, YOU ARE A TRAITOR, WHERE IS YOUR NATIONAL PRIDE should be painted over by the persons who put them there in the first place.

And truth be told, the members of the National Front from the borough white-washed the letters on the pale green gate, but these, having been written in red paint, started to show through the whitish coat, particularly on rainy days, because it is a well-known fact that the color itself is always more durable than the superficially colored excuses.

Many tumultuous years passed by and the high-ranking official, the one-time master of life and death, who considered everyone who spoke English to be a traitor to the proletariat and who, while in power, ordered that high-school children be taught only Russian, plunged into studying English at an advanced age, and into meeting with American diplomats and journalists, to tell them how he had grown disappointed with his wartime comrades, until at some historical assembly he was demoted and proclaimed to be the traitor of the people!

The white-washed sentence OBRAD SIMIĆ, YOU TRAITOR, WHERE IS YOUR NATIONAL PRIDE was turning more and more visible, the same as the fact that English was turning into a universal language. The villa across the street was not frequented any longer by high-ranking guests. One day the ideologist was walking all by himself on his neglected lawn, when Mr. Traitor called out to him:

"Hello, neighbor," he said, "I have a present for you, this gate which I don't need any longer and now it refers to you..."

Or, as my late grandma used to say, no morning sun shines the whole day!

BELGRADE TRUSTS NO-ONE

Knowing my city and its inhabitants inside out, I have been pretty sure, until yesterday, that there is nothing that Belgraders can surprise me with. And then, yesterday at noon, in the spacious café of the Moscow hotel, at the orchestra stand, I saw a cello tied up to a double bass with a chain!

Like two prisoners, bound to each other, these two tall instruments endure their sorrowful destiny next to the piano sneering toothlessly at them with its black-and-white keys.

What have they done to deserve such severe punishment? Perhaps in Belgrade's last animation orchestra they faultily played some potpourri or overture by Franz Lehar, whose music actually never found its way to the hearts of our music lovers, or perhaps the poor cello tried to play Bach's suites for solo cello, not suited to this repertoire? Who can tell? I've seen all kinds of things in my lifetime, but a string instrument tied by a chain thick enough for an elephant's leg, that surely I haven't seen anywhere!

I know, of course, that Belgraders bind their bicycles, motorbikes and even doormats with chains...

Belgrade urbanites are also wary of public phones and machines. Nobody is slapped as often and as much as those poor, miraculously surviving phones in phone booths, turning blue from so many beatings. Even if they spit out the token, they are nevertheless slapped again, in the hope that they'll spit out some more. As if the telephones were the slot machines!

Our people believe that all machines are given to stealing. Every morning in my supermarket I witness a scene in which furious housewives slap the wretched coffee mill, suspecting it of having stolen several coffee beans from them. The coffee mill suffers in silence.

Belgrade is actually the only city in Europe in which even the parking meters made of steel had to succumb to countless shellackings and perfidious kicks.

They were not able to digest any more cleats, hair pins and old coins, so that now they just stand desperately on pavements, looking like Martians lost in space.

All this holds only for Belgrade. It is, of course, somewhat better in the interior! There are no coffee mills or parking meters out there...

THE MOSCOW HOTEL CAFÉ

There is, during Belgrade's summer nights, a period (between seven and nine p.m.) when it is impossible to stay indoors. Through your open windows you listen to the sounds of an agitated city, the murmur of its warm pavements, the clicking of heels, the laughter of the young, the cat-calls and whistles - and your ears are caressed by that special, affected Belgrade accent, suggestive, full of summer promises and some dormant defiance, which seems to be resisting the tenderness of a mild summer night.

I find Belgrade the most attractive in these very hours, while the night is still young. The hope that something exceptional is going to happen gives that particular twilight glow to the eyes, and makes the bodies move in the rhythm of an exciting urban ballet, the choreography of which is an invitation to love.

At this hour it is best to sit in the wicker chairs in front of Hotel Moscow and watch the jostling crowd – a huge urban whirlpool swallowing up both faces and fates...

And amidst that endless, undulating fabric of life, flowing from Terazije to Slavija Square, once upon a time, when I was still young, the last Viennese-type café orchestra played its music, like a handful of shipwreck victims on an elevated raft, washed from all sides by indifferent waves.

There was a time when no fine restaurant could be without such an orchestra. But gradually, one by one, these music families would leave the old hotel buildings emulating Vienna's unsurpassable Sacher hotel, taking with them little marble tables, velvet-upholstered chairs and warm pastry under the glass bell, as well as the refined guests who still knew how to sit there in a proper way, like "trees dying upright". Those were the last musicians who knew the overtures from *Countess Maritza, The Student Prince, Orpheus in the Underworld, The Light Cavalry, The Chocolate Soldier, Night at the Persian Square*, or the potpourri from *La Belle Hélène*...

In those bouquets of withered melodies the petticoats rustled, kisses abounded in shady arbors, hands and palms perspired in secret, forbidden touches; there was also dizziness induced by the wine, glossy floors and polished shoes, reflecting the lights of crystal chandeliers. This kind of "Grand Hotel" is on its irreversible way out, just like some old lady in her worn-out fur, whose once high pension is nowadays only peanuts, insufficient to live on. These hotels die before our eyes, deserted like empty sea shells on the beach, whose lives are wasted and pleasures sucked out to the end.

Together with the old lady's corpse, undertakers take out her shabby furniture, and the ornate Secession buildings turn into snack-bars and supermarkets, while bed-linen with embroidered hems is replaced by the hospital-like impersonality of sheets covering new love nests.

How long will it take us to grasp the beauty and charm of the extinct Middle-European café – that drowsy oasis of a vanished civilization of "Singer" sewing machines, the Orient-Express train, faded watercolors, horse-drawn carriages, waltzes, corsets, blooming gardens on wide-brimmed hats, veils, "tin Omega watches", mistresses, testaments, adulteries and sweet sins?

The express train called "Nostalgia" roars across the Europe of yester-year.

This is what I think about while I listen to the last Belgrade animation orchestra playing *La Vie Parisienne,* and a lady member of the orchestra weaving the Ariadne's threads of her flute solo around the drowsy summer evening. Good Lord, how beautiful and how sad!

I sit in front of the Moscow hotel café and watch the tumultuous sea of blue jeans. The narrow hips, naked backs of these young sportswomen, strong muscles under T-shirts with emblems of overseas universities, braless breasts, the glow of white teeth and naughty hair tufts – the throng of svelte bodies, flat stomachs, tanned legs – the milky sensuality of their skin, grinding its teeth in the thunder of the night chaos, drumming on the hot asphalt, growling and hissing, swallowing the octanes, electricity, coins for parking meters, energy, youth, sweat and sperm...

And amidst this chaos, like a leitmotif which has lost its accompaniment, a moldy theme by Jacques Offenbach wanders aimlessly through some unfamiliar epochs, looking for an audience among the deaf, not knowing that a completely different syncopated rhythm pulses and roars in their blood vessels and nerves.

CABBAGE

Come November, cabbage heads roll in the streets of Belgrade.

Beautiful women go down to Bajloni Market, their high heels clicking down Cetinjska Street, and they touch the cabbage heads with their polished nails – they select only the hard ones, of medium size, good for making sauerkraut. A man can achieve much in his life, forget his native roots and turn into a sophisticated intellectual, but it is only a matter of time when you'll come across him dragging a sack of cabbage heads on his shoulders. Cabbage is a must! Indispensable for *sarma* with spare ribs, for the sautéed sauerkraut called *podvarak*, for pasta squares with sautéed cabbage, for brine... Along with beans and potatoes, cabbage is the third basic dish in our national cuisine. Not to mention the sauerkraut salad, sprinkled with red hot ground paprika from Horgoš! How it is possible to live without this salad?

Just take a look at this esteemed philosopher, who with great love and care puts the cabbage heads into a barrel scalded with boiling water, pouring salt over them and carefully arranging chilly peppers and horseradish roots. He sets aside his important work or his university lectures, and, like a ghost, goes down to his cellar, a candle in his hand, twice a week, to stir the brine. Why all this effort and toil? Is there no sauerkraut to be bought in groceries? There is, of course, but we as a people have a deep mistrust of the "public sector" cabbage. In our own barrel, each and everyone of us will find the country home his father came from, if not even we ourselves. And it is of no use that new, modern high-rises with bold lines are being erected; the smell of sauerkraut will find its way into the elevators and reach even the most tightly closed living room.

It is common knowledge that a heavy stone we select to press the cabbage heads with should be firm, and certainly not white, as it crumbles. The bigger the stone, the better for the cabbage. All right, but how to find a fitting stone in Belgrade? It's a piece of cake for those who own some modern sculpture, something like one of Jean Arp's, but the rest must find a way to solve this problem the best they can. Once, at midnight, I saw a certain respected man below Kalemegdan fortress staggering like Sisyphus under the weight of a stolen stone.

Luckily, not all Belgraders pickle their own cabbage – otherwise Kalemegdan would quickly be robbed of all its stones and rocks.

WINTER FEASTS

Belgrade awakes from its deep winter sleep, crawls listlessly though the dark tunnel of February and exits into the precocious spring which titillates its nostrils and senses...

Its cats meow their enticing cantilena in our backyards, in moonlight.

"The sexual activity of cats is the strongest in February, after the winter hibernation", reads a textbook on cats, "and it has therefore been considered to be the cat month from time immemorial!"

In the meantime, somebody stole our *košava*! We almost suffocated with smog.

"The *košava* used to blow for seven days in a row, beating fiercely on creaking gates" – wrote an old chronicler of Belgrade – "to fell roof tiles and to whistle through the telephone cables, playing some devilish symphony. The *košava* was the most efficient street sweeper in Belgrade. It carried away both the sand and the dust, and it squeezed snow into all, even the tiniest, invisible holes. Caps and hats would disappear in the whirlwind, as if lifted and carried away by some invisible force..."

To make matters worse, a certain custom officer opened by accident a case full of London fog, and for a whole week we were not able to see a thing!

But as for eating – we ate aplenty!

An old song says: "And I'll find your little mouth even in the dark", which we changed into "my little mouth".

Each winter the citizens of Belgrade put on at least five kilos, the reason being that Belgrade is a mercurial city, given to celebrating all kinds of things!

It started with feasts on public holidays. Three days of *sarma*, cold roast suckling pig, spritzer made of rosé and club soda and of staring at the TV, would end with a grandiose hangover and Alka Seltzer.

Our patron saints' days followed – St. Archangel Michael, St. George, Saints Cosmas and Damian...

For St. Nicholas – the guardian of seafarers – we would eat carp cooked in wine, as St. Nicholas fell in the period of fasting!

In order to help our Croat and Slovene Catholic brothers overcome loneliness, we would celebrate with them their Christmas Eve and their Christmas the following day, with roast turkey and *mlinci* pasta.

Thanks God that Bairam is a summer holiday – we wouldn't be able to digest the okra!

We hardly had time to recover, but – look! – here comes the New Year! It would be wise not to describe the genocide of suckling pigs and the streams of bubbly!

We made a solemn oath that, come January 1st, we would turn a new leaf and not touch a single drop of booze! Also, that we would go on diet. But, lo and behold, here comes the Orthodox New Year. How can one refrain from eating and drinking if the Dragačevo trumpeters are in the vicinity?

In the meantime, we celebrated Orthodox Christmas, and for St. John's Day we ruined ourselves utterly! At the first place of call we would help ourselves to smoked ham from Užice, at the second – to pigs' trotters and ears, at the third we would drink extra strong *prepečenica* plum brandy, at the seventh - beer...

Plastered!

If we add several weddings, birthdays, baby showers, graduation celebrations and house-warming parties to the list, we will get a clear picture of what Belgrade had to live through this past winter. Even the largest cities in the world would not be able to digest all that.

Belgrade awaits its future with apprehension. March 8th – International Women's Day – is already smiling at it, while two Easters and a May Day are approaching from afar.

Those who live will tell the tale!

THE GOOD OLD TIMES

Ever since I can remember, I have lived in the worst of times.

Never in good times. Everything was always more expensive than the year before, the taxes higher and the wine worse than ever. In the past, summers were real summers and winters real winters...People were more honest, the air cleaner, and the meat we eat today can't be compared to the meat of....

Today we remember with melancholy the days of abundance of ten years ago. Those were the days!

Ten years ago we used to say that we couldn't take it any more and that things were much better five years ago.

Thirty five years ago we used to say that everything would be much better in forty years' time.

Twelve years ago – that the end of the world was upon us...

While other, smarter nations, lived in the present, we were turned towards our bright future.

125

When it fell through, we turned to our bright past. I was never overly interested in the past, and I have no time for the future. Am I a flippant character if I want to live a little right now? I mean, right away. Is it so much to ask? If not now – when?

In the meantime I began to feel more and more claustrophobic in my own country. The list of cities I am able to visit is getting shorter by the day.

I choose a voluntary exile. I ramble through foreign parts. But I don't find that things are better over there. They say that they are also living through the worst of times. Everybody longs for something that he misses...

Those from Durmitor snivel because every winter they are snowed in and cut off from the rest of the world.

Once I celebrated New Year in Singapore, with an outside temperature of 35 degrees. In the largest park in Singapore I saw an enormous machine for making artificial snow and the children paying for the pleasure of watching it fall!

In Caracas, apples are the most expensive and the rarest of fruits. For what you pay for a kilo of apples, you can buy ten kilos of pineapple, mango and coconut.

In the garden of my friend Puriša, in Čačak, the apples die a natural death. They fall off the branches, and rot in the grass, as there is no one to pick them. The whole of Čačak used to pass by the window of a local supermarket and watch with yearning and admiration a single, withered pineapple (how did it ever get there?), but there were no buyers, as it was too expensive.

Once I went to the Berlin Wall. It was night and my friends lifted me up on their arms to see what it was like on the other side. It was dark on the other side. East Berlin longed for a chance to have a hamburger at the McDonald's in West Berlin, at least once before passing away.

Sophisticated Berliners from the West side took me through Checkpoint Charlie all the way to East Berlin, to have blini with caviar at a Russian restaurant and to listen to Hungarian gypsies play at Mátyás Pince.

The Easterners were fed up with both Russians and Hungarians.

The Westerners – with McDonald's!

I saw colored girls in New Orleans ironing their naturally curled hair to make it straight and color it blond, to achieve the ideal of platinum Nordic beauties.

At the same time, Swedish girls were paying dearly to have their hairdressers curl their hair for the Afro-look!

"Not smoked salmon again!" cried the children of Icelandic fishermen over dinner, while a Swiss banker paid a small fortune at the Walliserkanne restaurant in Zurich for the same meal.

In New York, the Russian Moskovskaja vodka was more expensive that the most expensive whisky, which, on the other hand, was the unrealized dream of many Russians.

In Scotland, every farmer drinks whisky, and in Champagne every grower drinks the best French champagne, which in Glasgow is a treat only at weddings or New Year's celebrations...

In Fresno, California, an old and rich immigrant on his deathbed yearns to have a taste of cornmeal mush from Zlatibor, from which he fled half a century ago, vowing never to return!

I go back home... They ask me whether I learned something on my travels.

I did. I realized that even these awful years would one day be looked upon as the good, old times.

You only have to live to see it.

FROM WELL-INFORMED SOURCES

The party I like most is the cocktail party.

It unites all. It is, in all honesty, the only party which is capable of bringing together the leaders of the most diverse and quarreling parties. They chatter contentedly under the watchful eyes of diplomats and foreign correspondents. Every glass-clicking or back-tapping is assumed to be of historical significance...

Foreign correspondents in Belgrade are mostly our people, who differ from other Belgraders in that they speak a foreign language. There are, among them, ladies from good homes, who learned languages in their childhood, and who are in the habit of conveniently dropping a foreign word here and there. Foreign newspapers find it more profitable to employ our people as their correspondents, as they would have to pay their own much more. Our people are satisfied with what they get. Besides, there is also a matter of comprehending all that is going on on this soil. Even we, the locals, hardly understand anything!

When at press conferences foreign correspondents put nasty questions to our ministers, one could swear upon the Bible that they are not one of us. They enquire about the situation in their own country, as if they arrived here only yesterday. Interestingly, true strangers usually ask questions in Serbian, while our people do it – in English! Who knows how many times, when hearing them speak Serbian, I praised them for having mastered our language so well! Sometimes I wonder how they converse with their mothers? In English, probably.

At cocktail parties, foreign correspondents look upon us with a certain superior concern, like when during the break between classes the best students meet the worst ones, expelled from school. Had I not repeated the seventh grade in high school, just on account of foreign languages, perhaps I would also have become a foreign correspondent from Belgrade, starting my reports with: "As we learn from well-informed sources..." Maybe I would also behave as that theater critic who praises highly a play in which the actors are his neighbors and men from his home town. But, as it is, I barely made it to a local correspondent. Therefore, the only chance I get to cast a surreptitious glance at foreign correspondents is at cocktail parties.

DISSIDENTS

It is self-explanatory that the cocktail party was named after the cocktails served at it. Cocktails themselves never took root in Belgrade, where only hard drinks are consumed. But the cocktail parties did!

Our best known and only cocktail is still that lethal potion called *beton* ("concrete") – a mixture of beer and brandy. In lieu of the cherry in a Manhattan, this one is spiced with the inevitable cigarette ashes dropping into the glass and giving it a special flavor.

In earlier times, dissidents were also invited to cocktail parties, for decorative reasons. But they ran out of luck. Communism seemed to have vanished into the ground! Overnight, dissidents were left both without a profession and important topics; to put it simply, there wasn't anything they could protest about any longer... Their books became insignificant the moment one million people, gathered in front of the Parliament building, cried in unison: "Thieves, get out!" Is there anything else to be said, as awful, as short and as true?

Readers were already becoming bored with books about the persecution of dissidents. Much more in demand were love stories about two people in love and a third one making trouble for them.

Many a dissident turned into a respected politician overnight, writing speeches instead of books. They are not invited to cocktail parties any longer. Now they are the ones who invite!

A person who spends his morning hours addressing masses from flag-ornamented platforms can hardly be able to devote his evening hours to nuances, self-irony and self-doubt, the ingredients of good literature. That man has forever ruined his emotional mechanism. Once the madness of power is over, what will they live on?

By God, it's been a long time since a book was banned in Belgrade! With a little bit of luck, perhaps those horrible days of bans and blacklists will come back! Once they come to power, perhaps the former dissidents will start banning books and movies, thus giving birth to a new class of dissidents!

Зуко Џумхур

ON EUROPE

My first encounter with Europe took place at the small frontier station in Villa Opicina. Europe was there, on carts loaded with bananas, tangerines and chocolates, as well as with bottles of Coca-Cola, which until then we could see only in the movies.

Having dived out of an overly long dark tunnel of misery into this affluence, I could hardly believe my own eyes. When director Puriša Đorđević saw these same oranges and chocolates in 1947 in Trieste, where he was directing a movie, the commissars told him that Europe was actually starving, but that it had sent all its goods to Trieste to show us that capitalism was better than communism.

Somewhat earlier Europe made its debut here in the form of a magic ball-point pen, with a beautiful girl painted on it: if you turned the pen upside down, the lady's bathing suit, made of ink, would drop down! Europe, actually, was situated in Knez Mihailova Street, in the Air France window, where we used to stand for hours and stare into the movable photos of famous travelers and to watch enviously the wonder of aviation – the model of a Caravelle!

I believe I spent half of my life trying to decipher the secret of our eternal love for Europe. I traveled its length and breadth, I lived in it, and every penny I earned in it – I left there! After my greatest successes I would go home with just enough money for the cab fare from the airport, and on one occasion I did not have even that much, so that the cab driver had to wait for me in front of my house while I fetched the money.

After the unassuming America, Europe seemed to me like a worn-out, dilapidated amusement park, painted over with cheap paint God knows how many times, where a man, regardless of how hard he tried to hit the target with a ball or an air-gun, would never ever gain anything.

Rambling through the verdant Serbia one year in spring, I happened to come across St. Roman's monastery, quite off the beaten track. I put my palm onto the fresco depicting the warrior angel, painted on the rough wall still warm from the summer heat. While touching the baked ocher, gold coating and ultramarine from the 13th century, I remembered, smiling to myself, the essential difference between Europe and us.

When in a Roman church, for example, you wish to see a certain painting, you have to put some euro coins into the machine. Only then, for three minutes, the painting will be illuminated. Those who have no coins, see no art, let alone touch it with their palms.

You get only as much Caravaggio as you pay for.

And in St. Roman's monastery, the mother superior asks you inside and offers you coffee and plum preserve, enquiring whether you have eaten yet.

The thinnest cutlets I ever ate were in the homes of our people who turned into the biggest Europeans in Europe. I am talking of a particular kind of our Europeans (God forbid if they all were like that!) who, when visiting the old country, bring Europe to their mothers living in villages, but on their return they take with them smoked ham, cheese and period furniture.

They invite us to visit them there... But how, when we are penniless? We are old-fashioned people, we never go visiting without taking flowers, or at least a bottle of brandy, for our hosts. It is much easier for Europe to come to us. It always comes empty-handed. Europeans seem to despise these conventions so typical of the Balkans. They are above them!

The richer they are – the bigger misers they become.

It's all trifles to them – we try to absolve them in our own eyes. They don't even notice that something has to be paid for, such as a taxi, lunch

136

or flowers, and to push some cash into the musicians' instruments – it is simply not their custom! Only we, the penniless, pay attention to such things.

At that, we keep forgetting that our guests from Europe are wealthy just because to them each euro is precious.

"I am just watching you squandering your money..." says one. "As far as I can see, you'll never be Europe!"

INAT

Come spring, it seems that all my acquaintances from abroad swarm into Belgrade at the same time. For days I do nothing but show them around town and take them from one meeting to another. I have lunch twice a day, dinner three times a day, not to mention all those drinks taken on the run! Also, being the host, I have to explain to them things I myself don't understand...

"What kind of people are Belgraders, actually?" asks Bill, a Slavist from Ohio. "What is their most prominent trait?"

"Out of all Serbs," I tell him, "Belgraders are the ones who above all love to be loved!"

"Who doesn't like to be loved?"

"No one, certainly, but it seems that Belgraders have a pathological need to be loved..."

"How do you explain it?" asks the ever-curious Bill.

"It is probably because," I say by way of explanation, "since their childhood they are being told that their city is the most beautiful in the world, that it is the only one rising above two big

138

European rivers, and that throughout history all kinds of invaders have fought over it. This is where you live best, eat the most savory food, breathe the best air, sleep better than anywhere else. Belgraders are the most courageous, the most honest, the most charming and the most talented people; they are lady killers, revelers, handsome guys...

"Well," says Bill, "is it really so?"

"In all honesty – it is!" I say, blushing, because I have fallen into my own trap.

"What is the problem, then?"

"The problem is", I say, "that Belgrade has finally noticed that not everyone in Europe loves it."

"What did you do then?"

"We turned to convincing those who did not love us that they actually did, only they were not aware of it! The people actually adore us, it is only the governments that hate us!"

"But didn't they elect their governments?"

"They probably did..." I say, and try to draw his attention to the most beautiful pair of legs I have seen that spring in Knez Mihailova Street. Look, what a bird! But, in vain.

"So, what's going on now?"

"Now we resort to *inat.*"

"Inat?" Bill takes out his pocket dictionary. "What is it – *inat*?"

"Your dictionary will be of no help!" I tell him. It says in the dictionary that *inat* is deliberate, provocative behavior against someone's will; defiance, quarrel, wrangling. *Inadžija,* according to the dictionary, is an aggressive, quarrelsome, defiant person, sarcastic, teasing and unruly... But it is not true in the least! *Inat* lies at the core of our being, it is deeper and more comprehensive than any definition. Look at this town of ours! Forty times it has been raised from dust and ashes, out of *inat,* at the very same location where it had been destroyed before. Anyone with common sense would have given up on such a jinxed place long ago! Our best-known national hero ploughs the imperial road out of *inat*! When they quarrel with state authorities over the price of milk, our farmers, out of *inat,* give it away for free at the markets. Out of *inat* we join a political party, which we were attacking only yesterday, as soon as it starts to lose power. Out of *inat* we get married, out of *inat* we get divorced. Out of *inat* we cut down the tree with musicians on it..."

"What are the musicians doing up there?"

"What do you mean – what are they doing? We put them up on the branches to sing for us like birds at our weddings."

Well, since despite all my endeavors, Bill apparently did not grasp any of my explanations about unrequited love and *inat*, I told him the following story, as a parting gift:

A foreigner who many years before the war had been studying our mentality and our customs,

140

returned to Serbia after a long time and asked a certain farmer whether he still eagerly wanted for his neighbor's cow to drop dead.

"No," answered the farmer. "Now I want my cow to drop dead!"

"Why your cow, for God's sake?", asked the flabbergasted ethnologist.

"Well, to see then who is Mrs. Mileva going to buy her milk from!

A POET IN JAIL

Is there a more idiotic question than: "Did I wake you up?"

Good Lord! Did he wake me up at nine a.m.!

"If you had any qualms about calling me this early, why did you call then?" - I mumble through my pillow.

Regardless of how long he has lived in the city, our compatriot has a genetic fear of sleeping late in the morning – an ancient, deeply ingrained peasant habit that one must get up before dawn. At that, it does not count whether you worked throughout the night or not! Morning is morning!

I also find it rather annoying when my readers stop me in the street, asking for an autograph and saying: "What's the next order of business?"

I usually reply that it is to put my flat in order, which is absolutely true.

To put it in a nut-shell, it is much nicer to be in the dog-house! You keep company with the members of your family and your closest friends, or sit all day long under the linden trees and shuffle through history.

"Listen to this case", says one of the collocutors. "You certainly remember that classic of ours who had his book of poetry, written before the war, printed during the German occupation, and for that our authorities put him behind bars?"

When the newly appointed Serbian Minister of the Interior made a tour of the prison, he was told that the great Serbian poet was confined in it. The Minister asked to be taken to his cell.

"Are you the famous Poet?" asked the Minister.

"I am."

"Since when are you in prison?"

"Since the Liberation!", replies the Poet.

The following night two soldiers appeared in his cell, with automatic rifles across their breasts, to take him away.

"Who is the poet here?" cried the first soldier.

"I am!" said the Poet proudly, with his knees buckling.

"Come along!", ordered the second soldier.

The same cell also housed an actor, a black-marketeer, an opera singer, a thief and an ex-minister.

The poet kissed them all good-bye and distributed the remains of his bread among them, since he wouldn't need it any longer. While being led by the soldiers through a long underground corridor, he was mentally composing his last sentence which one day would be quoted in textbooks.

He was taken into the office of a young Inspector, whose eyes were fixed on an open notebook. It should be pointed out that the Inspector, who was attending night school, was about to take an exam for the fourth grade of elementary school. The master of life and death!

"Are you the Poet?" he asked.

"Yes, I am!" replied the Poet, proudly lifting his head and still composing his last message.

"Tell me, whether *"is it"* is written together or separately?"

"Separately..." admitted the Poet.

"Thank you!" said the Inspector. "Take him back to his cell..."

THE GARDEN PARTY

When invited to a garden party, I put on my only dark suit as if it were some kind of punishment. I call it "table red wine" and when I put it on the moths start flying in all directions. I take a cab to Dedinje, where the fortunate people live, those who still have something I have forgotten about a long time ago – a garden with trees and flowers.

The cab driver eyes me suspiciously: who am I to be going to such an elegant district? If I belong there, he'll hate me, and if I don't, he'll despise me...

We pull out of the gray, dirty, muggy and sweaty city and enter a different climate that my poor lungs are not accustomed to. God, how much grass, ozone and chlorophyll, how much flora! How many cotyledons per person! I inhale deeply the smoke of my cigarette, just to be in touch with something familiar.

Naturally, everybody goes to a garden party by car or by chauffer-driven limousine. My battered cab, with its peeling paint, shrinks in shame to the size of a child's go-cart, and returns, head over heels, back to the city.

When you go to a garden party, you should not get there either too early or too late. If you get there first, you will find yourself standing alone in the middle of the lawn, like a scarecrow, not knowing what to do with your hands. Therefore, you will grab a glass, meaning you'll not see the end of the party sober. If you arrive among the last guests, nobody will notice you, the food will be long gone and the ice melted.

However, if you get there at the proper time (which means half an hour later than the time indicated on the invitation), someone will escort you to the long table loaded with food and ask you to help yourself. It is my sincerest advice not to touch anything, otherwise you'll find yourself in a lot of trouble! After you take a plate, knife, fork and napkin, you make a tour of the table, taking a bit of this and a bit of that. How can you resist sampling the dishes you don't see every day, how to say 'no' to a pampered salmon, medium done roast beef, cold turkey white meat, asparagus and artichokes, squid risotto with mushroom sauce... By the end of the tour you'll realize that your plate is overloaded and that a waiter has thrust a glass of rosé upon you. There are no chairs or tables anywhere in sight, as at garden parties people are supposed to stand. Besides, your burning cigarette, which you put momentarily at the edge of the table with food, is threatening to set the batiste tablecloth on fire.

Naturally, there is no ashtray in sight (well-bred people don't smoke while eating), no bread (well-bred people don't eat bread), and worst of all, there is no salt (well-bred people do not use salt). How to put out the cigarette without being seen? The trimmed English grass looks at me with hostility, while I long with all my heart to convert to Hinduism and turn into a many-handed Shiva!

And while you stand there as a living monument to a provincial – a plate in one hand, a glass in the other, fork, knife and napkin under your arm – someone important you have been longing to meet approaches you and wants to shake your hand. Good Lord! You can't just put everything down on the grass. Those more experienced and cunning have already taken possession of various corners, low walls and staircases...

Then come the "garden party phrases", known for their amiable irrelevance which caries no weight:

"Oh, certainly we must meet soon! No, no, I'll get in touch with you..."

"Are you here in August? You are not? Great! Then see you in August!"

"Give me your phone number. What, you have no phone? Splendid, I'll give you a call soon..."

My black jacket is turning into a Finnish sauna – an instrument of torture. Streams of sweat flow down my back Someone asks me if I am all right.

"Never better!"

Unlike us Belgraders, Westerners do not perspire at all, as if they are from another planet! Even when the heat is at its worst, when we have long ago taken off our jackets and pocketed our ties, they don't loosen their collars or ties by even a millimeter.

I asked a stiffly-buttoned diplomat how that was possible. He looked at me calmly and said: "I don't want to be hot!"

And so the garden party comes to an end and the doormen start to call for long black limousines, which slide in and quickly swallow up the distinguished guests, while you, as there is no cab in sight, set out on foot, down the long, deserted street with no numbers, along shady gardens and villas hidden from passers-by, thinking to yourself: "Boy, these people sure know how to live!"

THE DIPLOMATIC DINNER

The ambassador received me in his pyjamas.

I found it somewhat strange, since I had arrived slightly but elegantly late, as you are supposed to do in the world of diplomacy.

"How are you?" asked the ambassador.

"We are fine, thank you," I said and added: "Two ice cubes...

The ambassador went on sitting in his pyjamas and watching TV. He did know what to think. Neither did I.

Let me add that the ambassador is of my age. My generation! And while he, at my age, is already ambassador, I am nothing. Here I am still considered to be 'a promising writer'.

I have noticed that ambassadors are prone to feeling nostalgic for their own countries. But it was not the case with this one. He feels completely at home in Belgrade. As soon as he opens a newspaper, he sees reports on strikes, protests, resignations, ethnic gatherings, inflation...

Actually, both of us, the ambassador and I, are doing time in Belgrade...

We could have landed some other, better country. But, here we are!

Interestingly, the ambassador to whose house I went for dinner and found him in his pyjamas, is not married.

It is an unwritten rule that our ambassadors must be married. That's probably so in order to have someone to keep an eye on them all the time. Ambassadors' wives are constantly tired, as at receptions they have to stand next to their husbands and shake hands with all kinds of characters.

But the ambassador I'm talking about was not married. I asked him once why that was and he answered me by way of a proverb from his small, distant and friendly country:

"You love your wife most on two occasions: first, when you carry her in, and last, when you carry her out!"

The ambassador admitted once that he hated diplomatic receptions, but that he had to throw an occasional party himself, the reason being that he was expected to return the hospitality of other ambassadors whose parties he attended. So, twice or three times a year he opens the doors of his residence, shakes hands with other ambassadors and repeats how happy he is to see them again. He also invites some ten or so locals, to mix with the ambassadors. They are usually our former ambassador in his country, a former consul with a wife sporting a gold tooth, a former correspondent

151

from those regions and the only person in Belgrade who speaks the ambassador's mother tongue, a painter, a writer, a beautiful single woman everyone is in love with, a priest from the Patriarchate, two local diplomats, a surgeon who took out the ambassador's appendix, a man that nobody knows anything about, a party crasher who dropped in to have a free drink, and finally, a character who looks like an ambassador but is, actually, only some ambassador's driver.

And so the two of us went on sitting, drinking, gossiping about Russians and Americans and exchanging topics of mutual interest for our two small and friendly countries.

Being single, the ambassador likes to roam through the streets of Belgrade unescorted. He tells me that the day before he came across a graffiti on a wall that he did not understand, and asks me to explain it to him. The graffiti reads like this:

BELGRADE GIRLS, DO NOT CHEAT ON US WITH GREEKS!

YOUR ARABS.

After an hour or so, I ask the ambassador, still sitting in his pyjamas, where the others were.

"What others?"

"Well, other dinner guests?"

"Dinner is tomorrow evening..." says the ambassador calmly.

IN THE WIDE WORLD

The West allows the Belgraders who behaved well over the year to spend a week in their hometowns for Catholic Christmas.

"Are you going to stay for Orthodox Christmas?" we ask, and they first make enquires as to the date of it and then say that, unfortunately, they can't stay, as they have to go back to work.

They arrive with their wives, who look like Christmas trees, clinking with gold. Their full-length, expensive fur coats trail on the ground, and our streets, if you'll excuse us, out of pure spite turn muddy, while Belgrade ill-humoredly wraps itself in a tattered coat of sleet and smog.

They get into the backyards of their homes in the boroughs of Voždovac, Senjak, Bulbulder and Čubura...

Stray dogs and layabouts from the banks of the Sava snarl at their pampered little dogs – almost insects, carried in their owners' arms like babies.

They find everything to be small, somehow; only the *sarma* rolls are bigger than anyplace else!

The mothers of the Belgraders who made it out there, in the world, sit in their kitchens and save electricity by not heating their rooms any longer. The guests will sleep once more in cold beds, just like they used to do, a long time ago, when they were kids...

The Western Belgraders turn on the boilers right away and their mother turn them off in passing.

The Western wives grumble and endure. But to think that they could have gone to Ibiza or the Caribbean!

Once in a while we pay them a visit, out there in the West, where the streams of milk and honey flow.

What's the use of having a twelve-room house, a tennis court, a lawn, a pool and a sauna, if they are not seen by someone from Belgrade, who will tell stories about them when he returns? They escort us through their houses, from cellar to attic, via boiler rooms, servants' quarters in the loft and children's wings.

"And the children", we ask, "where are they?"

"With their grandmother, in Belgrade," they answer. "They find it boring here..."

They show us their collection of vintage wines (while we drink only those bought in the supermarket) and go on displaying their riches, and we admire them with all our might. Serbs will be Serbs! What's the use of being rich if no one envies them for it.

We easily recognize those of our kind when they put salt on their food before tasting it, as well as by the famous sentence:

"Here we have no contacts whatsoever with our compatriots!"

Truth be told, in Belgrade you choose the company to your own liking. In the West, you have to keep company with those who are there.

Nevertheless, all over the world, the Irish stick to the Irish, the Italians to the Italians, the Greeks to the Greeks. Only my people brags about not keeping company with itself! But, who with, if not with those of our kind!

Or, as the saying goes: "He may be a son of a bitch but he is our son of a bitch."

"Keep away from our people! They are dangerous..." I have been advised by the Western Belgraders, and, lo and behold, only Westerners are present at their formal dinner parties; the table is sagging with food – roast suckling pig (an aunt brought it from Belgrade), cheese and spinach pies, French salad, an enormous cake...

Westerners praise these delicacies and the fact that the hosts speak without an accent, and enquire after the names of the dishes. And then they say: "Well, this coming Saturday we expect you for dinner at our place! Right, Frances?"

For these occasions (which are rare) our compatriots carefully prepare their clothes and their accents. They take me along, praising in half-

155

tones their hosts for being rich and influential. Once we get there – everybody is served a brandy and a canapé, with something like a pigeon turd on it! See what I mean?

One of our Western Belgraders blew his gasket and returned to Belgrade to stay. Here he fell in love with a girl who topped him by a head.

"But, I am a lot taller than you", she said.

"Never mind", he answered. "When I stand on my wallet, I surely top you..."

BELGRADE IS THE WORLD

Belgrade is not all in Belgrade.

A much bigger part of Belgrade is in the yearning for Belgrade, which makes it more beautiful than it actually is.

Belgrade is in Belgrade restaurants (cafés, taverns) all over the world, where "our people" get together... Skadarlija in Richwood, N.Y., The Balkans in Sydney, The Four Birches in Brussels, La Chosa in Caracas, Belgrade in Munich, King Peter in Washington...

Belgrade is in a cherry at the bottom of the Manhattan cocktail, sucked by a happily married, lonely lady from Belgrade, who in the Café Greco in Rome summarizes her life – was it really worth it: would she be happier had she stayed in Voždovac and married her Miki?

Belgrade was also present in the Old Serbia restaurant in Brussels, next to the Grand Place, when its owner, Dobrila, once "a black lady of Serbian poetry", enquired about the poet Branko Miljković, and we told her that he had turned into a monument in Kalemegdan. She was flabbergasted! What do we mean, a monument, when she mended socks for this monument and cooked beans for him when he was a nobody?

Belgrade is also in Hamilton, Canada, where an elderly cavalry officer of the Royal Yugoslav Army asked whether the south-easterly *košava* wind still blows for three, seven or twenty one days, not knowing that the *košava* stopped blowing a long time ago... Seems that it got bored with not being able to blow us off this hill, and now it whimpers and whines somewhere out there in the steppes of Russia...

Belgrade is also in the homes of those who were forced to leave, having taken along a tiny part of it, a dried Kalemegdan flower from the herbarium, a book, a recipe for making eggplant moussaka, nicknames of long-lost beauties, both boys and girls, the photo of the graduates of the Third High School for Boys (school year 1956-57), a drawling, affected Belgrade accent, which resists being spoilt even by English. The old Knez Mihailova Street, with its peeling façades and pavements full of potholes, does not reside in Knez Mihailova any longer! It is on the soles of elderly strollers, who were not able to transfer the rhythm of their former *'štrafta'* (corso) to any boulevard in the world.

Belgrade is on the photos of late mothers, fathers, grandfathers and grandmothers, who during their lifetime never ventured farther than Zemun, and now from their photos on the walls they gently watch a living room in New York, crawling with people chatting in seven languages.

Belgrade is also in the washbasin where we make just one head of cabbage into sauerkraut, to make *sarma* (pickled cabbage leaves stuffed with minced meat) and to boast about our food before Australians and Argentineans.

Belgrade is in the way that Belgraders receive their guests all over the world; Belgrade is on the icons of St. Nicholas and St. John, the most frequent patron saints in Belgrade – the icons which traveled to Canada and New Zealand; Belgrade is...

Belgrade is not in Belgrade.

Belgrade is in all those Belgraders who still cannot or dare not come back.

I am also not here any longer, but somewhere else, desperately trying to return to myself...

Belgrade is not in Belgrade, as Belgrade, actually, is not a city – it is a metaphor, a way of life, an angle of looking at things.

Belgrade is in the idea which fertilizes the place where its spirit is transposed. It is in a certain joke, in an accidental gesture, in the innate easygoing way of accepting both victories and defeats, it is there where the unit for measuring style is – charm.

Belgrade is in the names of little children in Switzerland, France, Sweden, Germany and the United States, whose mothers are Belgraders.

Belgrade is in our index finger when we dial 011.

Belgrade is in the expression *bez veze* regardless of the continent where it is uttered.

Belgrade is scattered on all four sides of the world.

I long to see the day when all these Belgraders will be reunited in one place.

OUR PEOPLE IN THE WIDE WORLD

When they go abroad, into the wide world, Belgraders immediately convert all prices into dinars! The operation greatly reduces our enjoyment of the marvels of the world. We feel the prick of consciousness for squandering money, while, on the other hand, we realize how poor we actually are.

The worst thing that can happen to us in the West is to be invited to dinner by a Belgrader who struck it rich. We buy overpriced flowers (and the bouquet nevertheless looks miserable) and take a cab to carry us to some fashionable, residential area kilometers away.

Namely, the rich people never reside downtown, like the rest of the normal world, but, just like here, on near-by green hills and valleys. When we add up the cost of the flowers (immediately taken away by the maid lest they should mar the interior) and the cab, we could have bought new clothes, top to toe, at some bargain sale! And dinner, if only it were something to write home about – but it was lettuce and transparent roast beef! Bread was not served. Five times I asked for it – they did not react.

After dinner we talked some.

The lady on my left asked me whether my books were translated into English or French.

Unfortunately no, madam!

Why is that?

Because I am a local writer. I write only in self-defense and exclusively for my street. What I write about is absolutely untranslatable!

And where do you live?

I tell her.

What kind of people are you?

I tell her that we are a small people who had its shining moments. Those moments when, on the stage of history, the leading tenor of the Opera suddenly loses his voice, and – there! – from the last row comes dashing forward an obscure extra, who pulls off the highest C – a formidably clear tone which makes the crystal chandelier burst. We had such arias in 1914, 1941, 1948...

But it can be worse if you are invited by a wealthy Belgrader to the most sumptuous restaurant in town, for the purpose of showing off, and right at the start he asks what wine and what vintage we would like to have. Feeling like poor relations from the interior ready to sink through the floor, we leave him to confer with the waiter.

It is on such occasions that I remember with nostalgia those Belgrade taverns full of smoke, and how we used to join tables and sit together. When someone among us ordered tripe, we all soaked bread in his sauce. Where else can you do that? Just imagine the reaction of our host, together with his reserved wife (who finds me suspect, anyway), to my soaking bread into his French oyster sauce! Surely they would faint, both of them!

At the end of the meal he asks for the bill, which will be deducted from his taxes at the end of the year. Once more he made money at our expense! Money makes money! We are upset because we are not in a position to return his kindness, as one should. But where could we take him, with our bucks? To a hamburger stand at the railroad station? Or treat him to hot dogs from the kiosk?

We thank him profusely for the dinner and say goodbye in front of our wretched hotel.

Naturally, they'll run us down behind our backs and we'll return the favor.

Nevertheless, our sleep is sounder. If nothing else, our children, unlike theirs, speak Serbian. Theirs – not a word! Their own grandma talks to them via an interpreter!

We sleep and dream of Belgrade...

CAFÉ NOSTALGIA

The prettiest Belgrade girls do not live in Belgrade.

Having been exceptionally beautiful and smart, they are now happily or unhappily married to foreigners, who were lucky enough to take them away from us.

To feel better in the wide world, the first thing they did was to change their husbands' names. So Timothy became Tića, Guiseppe – Đuza, Peter – Pera, George – Đoka, and Gaston – Gane.

The Belgrade girls measure all boulevards in the world by the length of Knez Mihailova Street, in which they learned to walk. Piccadilly Square is Slavija to them, Central Park in New York is Kalemegdan, and the Champs Élysées become Kneza Miloša Street.

The Belgrade girls living abroad spend a pretty penny on phone calls. Not a day passes without them dialing 011, and asking their mothers whether stuffed green peppers are covered with potato or tomato slices.

The prettiest Belgrade girls often cry on the line to 011.

La Closerie des Lilas

171, Bd du Montparnasse, 75006 PARIS · TEL. : 01 40 51 34 50

They taught their husbands to swear like troopers. They listen to them swearing and laugh. They miss swearwords.

When I visit them from time to time and we start yarning our stories, we usually do not notice that their husbands silently make small balls out of bread while we tell them who had the best figure on the Zvezda float in 1961!

"*Nema problema*!" says Gaston, nicknamed Gane, smiles at us and goes to his study.

"What do you call him?" I ask my beautiful hostess.

"I'm her Pussycat!", says Gaston who came back for his glass. "Meow! I'm Meow Maca..."

There is nothing sadder than dinners in two languages. Actually, there is! It's dinners in three languages.

The pretty offspring of these Belgrade girls are partially-Belgrade girls, who find it hard to communicate with their grandmothers. The partially-Belgrade girls look at their mothers in wonder when they root for Crvena Zvezda (Red Star) and not for Inter. Who else can they root for?

They live for those twenty or so days they spend in Belgrade each year. They arrive in their long, shining cars and show off their expensive dresses, jewelry and fur coats. The neighbors are speechless with amazement. Their first love has in the meantime lost his hair, but gained a belly and a job. They will sleep at their mother's, in their former childhood rooms, surrounded by teddy bears, doggies and old issues of *Politikin Zabavnik*. Their husbands will sleep on the living room sofa and wake up stiff, as the sofa is too short, but the Belgrade girls will not let them move to a suite at the Hyatt, regardless of how rich they are. Gaston will say: "*Nema problema*!"

What bothers our Belgrade girls most is that the wide world has not yet discovered the blessings of the neighborhood. Who to have your morning coffee with, while husbands are at work? On your left live some unfamiliar people, on your right some even more unfamiliar persons. Across the hall – no one.

The Belgrade girls yearn for Belgrade, but after only two days in their hometown they find nothing to their taste. For example, the house, starting from the cellar, via the elevator and all the way to the attic, stinks of sauerkraut. They can hardly wait to go back to Brussels, The Hague or Rome.

But, once they return, they are annoyed that there is no place where you could buy a single head of sauerkraut for *sarma*. They would pickle the cabbage themselves, but nowhere in the West can one buy a plastic barrel with a tap. As for the stone to press the cabbage with, they would find a way out: their husbands have stone sculptures by Henry Moore in their drawing rooms – but the barrel is the problem!

And so the time comes again when the prettiest Belgrade girls in the wide world turn gloomy, when they smoke too much and more and more often sip their drinks in the morning. Even their own daughters don't understand what's the matter with them.

They feel like going home, at least for three days. In their nostrils they feel the smell of roast chestnuts on the Boulevard.

"*Nema problema*" says Gaston, smiling over his pipe.

HIGH SCHOOL GRADUATION ANNIVERSARY

Every ten years, on the anniversary of our high school graduation, we turn into high school kids again, we are young and handsome once more, particularly if the lights in the banquet hall are discreetly dimmed.

To tell the sad truth, I don't even know who I graduated with, as I often failed to pass makeup exams in August, I was expelled from school twice and once I had to repeat the year, and in the light of these facts I celebrate the graduation anniversary with whoever invites me!

And so we get there, excited and dressed to the nines, in order to find out who has aged more: ourselves or the rest of the class.

Some of our school mates died and some, even after such a long time, are not allowed by their lawful wives to see their high school flames again.

The best and the most talented ones, not needed by their own country, moved away to far-away lands, living on their brains, which we here seem to have in superabundance. How sorry we felt for them when they left with their suitcases to look for employment elsewhere, and look at us now! Earning less than their baby-sitters.

But, of course, we pretend that we are having the best of lives. A life like ours is not to be had anywhere!

I was lucky to have been born in the cockiest nation of them all!

What other nation has the saying: *"Speak Serbian, so that the whole world can understand you!"*

Or: *"All that was invented by the Serb, and manufactured by the German..."* Not to mention the famous phrase: *"No-one has what a Serb has!"*

Every class has one gray, inconspicuous man who stubbornly claims that he shared a desk with you at school, but you can't remember him at all.

Also, one from a well-known, wealthy family, who was the first to own a wrist-watch, a fountain-pen and a motorcycle, while the rest of us longed for a ball-point pen – but he took to drinking and squandered all his property.

And another one, who, starting from nursery school and the first grade of elementary school, was a member of all committees – in the pioneer, high-school and youth organizations. While the rest of us were fooling around, he kept climbing, until he reached very high positions. So high that he did not even stoop to come to our graduation

170

anniversaries, having, seemingly, forgotten us all. Later on, when he fell from grace, he suddenly remembered that we existed. Now he attends our parties and sits with us, albeit a little bit depressed and disillusioned in the Idea, but here he is, nevertheless!

And another one, who was the first to sleep with a girl (and told us how it was), while we eyed him as if he were some strange bird, because at that time it was a rarity. Even propaganda, so to say!

And a fat one, with bowlegs, who could never jump over the "horse" in the gym (and that's why he would stay back in the classroom, to mind our belongings), and who later became a famous expert, nobody knows in what field, out there in the West.

Also, an ex-beauty (the handsomest boy in the whole school) that the *belle* in our class was in love with, but who looks like shit today. After he stopped playing water polo, he grew fat as a pig and lost his hair, maybe as a result of wearing the water polo cap.

And still another one, desperately in love with our class *belle* to this day and hour, although she has been married and divorced three times so far and now more often than not sips her vodka before noon.

And another one, who was always a war orphan, and on account of that was given stipends, winter coats from UNRRA, free summer and winter holidays. Only later was it found out that he had both parents, who were alive and well and rather well-off somewhere in the interior.

And a girl, who brought her jealous husband to our anniversary party, because he never lets her go by herself. She sat there rolling her eyes and apologizing to us when he moved his eyes off her.

And also one...

We say good-bye to one another, rather tipsy and with firm promises to meet again, in ten years time, at the same place.

If they make it that long, I think to myself.

As for me, I'm going to make it.

One, who was not able to come to our graduation anniversary party, asked his buddy how it had been, and this one told him that it had been great, that the girls were still beautiful and that we went with them to hotel rooms... Great!

At the thirtieth anniversary, the one who had enquired about the previous party was again not able to attend, and his buddy told him that it had been fantastic – lamb and suckling pig to your heart's content, and wine and beer in excess.

At the fortieth anniversary, the enquirer yet again did not make his appearance, and when he asked his buddy how it had been, he received the following answer: "Fabulous, I was seated at the end of the table, closest to the toilet!" Great, indeed!

TO LIVE IN BELGRADE

To live in Belgrade means to drink turbid water smelling of chlorine and to sleep in noise fit to wake the dead.

To live in Belgrade means that market prices are twice as high as elsewhere.

To pay for the air and water, also for garbage disposal, as well as for flowers that grow for free elsewhere.

To pay parking tickets and fines for jaywalking.

To pay for lawn mowers in the gardens of those who until recently mowed their grass themselves.

To live in Belgrade means to endure all insults without retaliating, in order to spare the feelings of those insulting us.

To live in Belgrade means to apologize all the time to those who do not live in it.

Belgraders are, let it be known, the least fortunate people in the country.

They have the two biggest rivers, but they must not bathe in them because of pollution.

They have the safest river fleet, because many years ago it has been pulled out into the docks, below Kalemegdan, and it does not sail its rivers any longer. Belgraders have underground tunnels but no subway!

But, still, of all towns in the country, only Belgrade has turned into a Wailing Wall, where complaints are placed by all those whom their own humane and progressive milieus do not even want to hear out.

To live in Belgrade means to observe, with philosophical calmness, how ex-singers from roadside inns, turned rich overnight, buy the villas of impoverished aristocratic families in Senjak.

Born and bred Belgraders still remember how, following the war, their houses were confiscated by the liberators, who despised private property above all. So they liberated the ex-owners from their houses and gardens.

Times they are a-changing: the same people who during the war used to execute their comrades, almost adolescents, if they picked a plum from someone's garden in passing, lived to be a hundred under somebody else's plum tree in the gardens of Dedinje.

Unlike them, the illiterate folk singers at least paid for their newly acquired palaces, which in any case is a historic step forward.

One thing is certain, though: you may or may not visit other places, but you must come to Belgrade at least once, if for no other reason than to get a visa from some foreign embassy, before pushing off forever from your homeland.

Also, you may think of Belgrade whatever you want, but many parents long to see their children studying in Belgrade.

Hypochondriacs from all over the country dream of being treated in Belgrade hospitals.

All actors wish dearly to play on Belgrade stages, and all snobs would like to be seen at some of its festivals.

All gourmets would like to eat Belgrade grilled meat, all thieves dream of Belgrade Railway Station, and all whores would like to operate in Belgrade hotels...

That is why Belgraders, of all Europeans, have the highest number of guests at their lunches and dinners!

Every now and then somebody raises his voice against Belgrade being the *prestonica*[5]. How can it be the *prestonica* when the king's been long gone?

I am not opposed to the idea of transferring the capital to some other town; although I hate to move from one street to another, I nevertheless feel like living in the provinces for a while.

Nevertheless, one day in the bright future all people will live in Belgrade!

Maybe even in Zemun?

"If this morning you woke up in Belgrade," Duško Radović said once, "you have done enough for one day!"

---

[5] *Prestonica* – capital. The word is derived from *presto* – throne, thence the pun.

THE WEEKEND

Let it be noted: in these miserable times, Belgraders have it toughest, as they, in addition to everything else, have to pretend every morning to be gentlemen and to wear white shirts and ties, which are a must at their places of work.

I don't mean to say that farmers don't have it tough, but a farmer, by and large, has all he needs in his own yard. For one thing, he does not pay rent since he has a roof over his head, unlike most Belgraders. Besides, a farmer has no other boss but God Almighty, who sends down fertile and lean years; he does not have to sit at boring meetings and to buy flowers for birthdays.

I don't mean to say that miners don't have it tough (they are constantly cited as examples), but hardly a miner is without some arable land and brothers over the hill which he mines. Five days a week, he digs the ore, and the other two – his own land.

It's not easy for the suburban farmers, either: they see the town before their eyes, but yet they are not urbanites. When hard times come by, they take revenge on the city folks. Who knows how many Persian carpets, crystal chandeliers, gold cutlery and silver candlesticks ended in the hands of suburban farmers during the war. They were exchanged for a sack of corn or a bucket of lard. Even today, when at an open market a farmer from the Belgrade suburban area pulls out his wallet stuffed with big notes, he can easily buy any old philosopher, together with his doctoral degree.

But what about a poor intellectual, Belgrade-born, and a subtenant to boot, without a single square meter of living space to his name?

His grandfather was a civil servant, his father a clerk. He did not inherit anything but a naive belief that civil service is the best. Of course it is, provided that the state is stable. He crammed foreign languages into his head, being told that "you are worth as many men as the number of languages you speak", and now he translates for his semi-illiterate bosses, who don't speak even their own language properly.

And old Belgrade ladies, in order to survive somehow, sell pieces of furniture which are family heirlooms and rent out their shabby, once elegant apartments for the filming of music videos featuring stars of "newly composed folk", formerly singers in the roadhouses along the Ibarska highway. Once the filming is done, these stars will contemptuously throw a handful of coins on the highly polished dining table which seats twelve.

Come May, true Belgraders become the loneliest human beings in Europe. On weekends the only people left in the city are those who have no relations in the country.

In brief, people without roots. All the rest, enticed by the call of their native villages, will dash out there to plough, dig, weed, plant, graft and trim, slaughter and scald. Once they put their feet on their own piece of land, they feel twice as strong as anyone from the asphalt.

In Belgrade parks even the grass is fenced in, to prevent it from running away to the country for the weekend!

Late on Sundays, all roads leading to Belgrade are clogged with columns of engorged cars, heavily laden with sacks of mother's "unsprayed" potatoes and onions, free-range chickens, bacon, eggs and sides of freshly slaughtered meat.

It is the metropolis coming back after two and a half days of breathing, eating, drinking and stowing supplies in order to survive somehow till the following Friday afternoon.

The penniless elegant urban intellectuals watch with contempt their neighbors who unload and drag up the stairs the supplies fetched from the country, and then, half-starved, take their children to the Kolarac Concert Hall to enjoy Bach's fugues and toccatas.

THE OEDIPALS

Judging by the amount of complaints lodged by Belgrade women, one can conclude that nowhere in the world are there as many Oedipals as in our white city[6]. If that is true, it is probably because nowhere on earth do self-supporting mothers go through such hell to bring up their boys, then later find it hard to accept when some awful harpy, who never lifted a finger, comes along and takes away their only son.

How to spot the Oedipal son?

At first, while he is courting you, my dears, he looks perfectly normal and you are surprised that some other fortunate girl hasn't already grabbed him. Soon, when you marry him, you'll see the reason why!

You'll never make stuffed zucchini better than his mamma.

If you prepare beans, there will always be something lacking in them, something special, maybe a bay leaf or a couple of carrots, I don't know?

---

[6] The name *Beograd* is made up of the words meaning "white city".

Unlike you, his mamma always ironed his shirts with a sharp edge along the sleeves.

And just when you finally get a day off, he'll have to take his mamma to see a specialist.

Whenever you drive her into a corner with your logic she'll naturally claim to be sick, but she'll outlive everyone by at least a quarter of a century!

God forgive me, it seems that she could hardly wait for her husband, a drunkard and a bully, to die, so she could finally be alone with her precious boy.

She will, most surely, hate your short skirt and will refuse to look at your holiday snaps, where you are seen topless.

She will know better than you how you should bring up your own child!

The poor Oedipal will be between two fires all the time.

Finally, the famous question will be posed: either her or me?

Who do you think he'll opt for?

And, then, one day, you too will get a daughter-in-law...

THE WEDDING

The bride and groom were indeed young and handsome and they decided against a big wedding – just the two of them and the two witnesses.

Being a part of the new generation, which likes to hang loose, they intended to give a slap in the face to petit-bourgeois rituals and to appear before the magistrate in worn-out jeans and sneakers.

They would arrive at the magistrate's office on two motorcycles (no wedding rings or flowers wrapped in cellophane) and, after stopping by for a couple of glasses of Coca-Cola in their favorite café, push off in an undisclosed direction.

No wedding gown, no tuxedo, no bow tie, no boring family in the wedding hall, no formal dinner at the hotel, no orchestra mutilating melodies neither urban nor rural, no tipsy relatives, no stupid jokes, along the lines of:

"Why should you be luckier than the rest of us!"

"You'll see what you are in for soon, once she turns a new leaf!"

"Hey, best man, throw us some coins for luck!"

"I won't meddle!" said his mother. "If she is good for you, she is good for me too, *I* am not going to live with her, but, let me tell you, there is no way to stop me from coming to my only son's wedding, come hell or high water!"

They had to yield, but it turned out that the bride's mother had been weeping for a week and that she had some heart trouble, so they had to invite her as well, with the bride's father in tow, who couldn't possibly survive being the only one left out. On hearing the big news, the grandparents almost suffered a stroke, so they were invited as well. As the bride did not have a grandfather, her grandmother (who had actually raised her) would be accompanied by her best man, who isn't allowed go anywhere without his second wife.

Can you imagine the scandal which would arise if their cousins from both sides of the family were not invited! They would not be on speaking terms with the newly-weds for the rest of their lives.

But her mother's younger sister, her aunt, (who will, naturally, come with her husband) cannot leave her two children alone, so they'll come, too, to carry the wedding gown veil.

"What wedding gown!" said the astonished bride. "I'm going to get married in my blue jeans!"

"Oh, no, you are not!" screamed her mother. "What will these children do – carry the legs of

your trousers? Next time you marry you can do as you please, but this time you'll do what I tell you!"

Then they had to invite their best men's best men, uncles and aunts with their wives and husbands, as well as all the in-laws in the family, so the idea of going to the wedding on two motorcycles fell through. They had to rent thirty taxis, splendidly decorated with carnations and white towels by their neighbor, whom they also had to invite, but he, actually, was no bother at all, as they had to invite the groom's bosses and colleagues from work (in order not to insult them), while some army buddies of his also announced their presence, and, in turn, the bride invited her classmates and her piano teacher, who brought along the piano tuner, who engaged an inexpensive six-piece band and, apart from that, a retired tenor from the Opera choir, to pull out the high C when necessary, and it is common knowledge that his friend, an old lady who used to sing in the choir, sings harmony, after which the bride and groom engaged two photographers to immortalize the event, and then they also invited...

And there they are, in a cheaply rented company cafeteria, with the tables arranged in the shape of a gigantic letter U. She – in her white wedding gown, he – in the tuxedo with the bow tie, resembling a waiter fired from his job.

They sit among two hundred and sixty seven tipsy guests, between the two families who eye each other with suspicion and mild dislike, and listen to the lyrics of a wedding song which goes something like this: "With her foot on the footboard, she is crying: No! / Winking at the best man to tell the driver: Go!"

Their dream about getting married in blue jeans is gradually being permeated by the stench of onions from a table weighed down with half-done and hairy suckling pig roast stuck among the toppled beer bottles.

CONVERSATIONS IN BELGRADE

This is the list of things that Belgrade wives should never say to their husbands:

Where are you going?

Where have you been?

You're drinking again!

It's your third one!

Look at yourself!

It is high time you took a shower!

You don't have to turn after every broad...

You made a fool out of yourself once again!

Where shall we go for the winter holidays?

Everybody has already made reservations for the New Year's Eve party.

Is this what I sacrificed my career for?

How many packs a day do you smoke?

Did you think nobody noticed how you stared at her all night long?

Am I feeble-minded, or what?

Look, I have nothing to wear...

Of course you cannot eat, you already had dinner at her place!

She could be this and that, but my mother always minded our children. And what about your parents?

How come I don't know her?

Can I go to that bachelor's party, too?

You ruined my life!

And here is what Belgrade husbands should never say to their wives:

Where are you off to?

Where have you been?

The spitting image of your mother!

What, lunch is not ready yet?

Stop tip-tapping with your high heels!

All you need is a dog!

A widower – no such luck!

Not now – we'll do it in the morning...

We are out of bread again!

My mother was right when she told me...

Don't use up all the hot water!

I'm fed up with your childhood piano!

You may have studied English, but you never graduated...

You've been to the hairdresser's again?

Do you always have to be late?

Is this what you call dinner?

Oh, the way my mother prepares this dish!

Didn't I give you some yesterday?

What do you need them for? You already have five pairs...

Well, do turn the leaf for once!

What are you fantasizing with that hairdo?

Where is that shirt of mine?

"How long has it been since we've made love?" How can I make love to an investigating judge?

Don't you have any female friends at all, like other women?

In case, God forbid, that one of us dies – I'll move to the coast...

This is not a marriage – this is a madhouse!

Damned if I'll tell you!

SUMMER VACATION

Slobodan! Slooobooodaaaan! Get out of the water! Not a second more! Look at yourself, you've turned all blue! Your teeth are chattering! Get out right away, do you hear me? You also tell him to get out! You're his father! Look, he is all blue!

You re not normal! You couldn't care less! You are driving me nuts!

This child could easily drown right in front of you and you wouldn't lift a finger! The same as when that traffic policeman insulted me to his heart's content! What did you do? You laughed so hard you could barely breathe, instead of taking my side, like a man!

Me, it was me who started that one! I only told you that you had been speeding and that you always drive too fast and that you think you are the smartest and that you overtook that cistern, and that if you went on like I would take the child and get out of the car in the middle of the highway, and then the cop gave you your license back saying that he was not going to fine you (am I not telling the truth?) as you had already been sufficiently punished by having to stand a wife like myself! Yes, that's what he said! And you – you did not lift a finger! What? What were you supposed to do? No, you were not supposed to fight with him, but at least you could have said something in my defense, instead of laughing like an idiot!

Well, really now... I wonder why you got married in the first place? Actually, you would be better off had you stayed single! You are not a marrying type at all. Come on, put away these newspapers and admit: wouldn't you be happier without the two of us, eh? Come on, be a man at least once and tell the truth!

Good Lord, who am I talking to?

What does he do every single blessed day? He either dozes or reads newspapers or drinks beer...

Some vacation!

I would have had a five times better time had I stayed in Belgrade. I would darken the room, make a draft and sleep to my heart's content.

Now, what? All year long I wait for these two miserable weeks at the coast, and we get to the beach at noon, when everybody in their right mind leaves to have lunch.

You made it possible? Who are you to make anything possible for anyone? And what is it that you made possible for me, tell me, I beg you?

To live in a chimney, six hundred and eighty steps above the expressway? Yes, exactly six hundred and eighty! I counted them the other day...

To bathe on this smelly public beach, stinking of coconut oil?

To pretend I don't see you gazing all the time at those topless tarts over there? You think I did not notice that you are staring at them? Why don't I take my top off? Because I am a fool, I nursed the baby and ruined my breasts, not like those whores who think only of themselves! That's why I don't take it off, if you want to know!

Other husbands take their wives to all those hamlets, macbeths, bethovens and chopins, and you take us out to *ćevapčići*! As if I couldn't have eaten *ćevapčići* in Belgrade, where they are much better anyway and they don't stink of olive oil?

What else did you make possible for me? To drag myself to the market and back and to make sandwiches for you two, to eat them at the beach in order not to spend money! But just see how much you spend on cigarettes and beer day in day out. Just make a calculation!

What did I do to deserve this kind of life! Look at other married couples! They stroll on the beach at night, hold their hands, talk... They have things to talk about. They don't stare at the newspapers and beer glasses!

God! He's fallen asleep! Well, this is the last straw...

Slooobodaaan! Sloobodaaan! Get out of the water right away!

OUT OF THE DUMPSTER

I see a dumpster on the pavement.

A young woman in a shabby fur coat that has seen better times leans over the edge of the dumpster and peers into it. She is looking at something. She is addressing someone.

I see a dark-skinned girl coming out of the container. She reminds me of one of Bellini's angels. She rises from the garbage like a little Venus from the shell and sea foam.

The girl tells her mother: "There isn't any..."

Is there a shorter and a crueler word in our language than the eternal "there isn't"? The word that has been with us far too long.

The mother says:

"Look some more..." and the child disappears into the garbage once more.

It's dusk. The dumpsters are burning as if Belgrade had been set on fire. Someone threw the embers from the heating stove into one, and the gray plumes of smoke hover over the city like street censers lit for the salvation of our souls.

I stand motionless, astounded by this sight.

A friend of mine, rather poor himself, never throws bread into the garbage. He puts what's left of his loaf of bread into a plastic bag and places it by the dumpster. The bag disappears magically, as soon as he goes back inside.

You have four eyes when you're hungry.

Having been hungry for centuries, we buy more bread than we actually need. And later we throw it away. Bread in the dumpster is not a good sight. It bodes ill. And ill never fails to come.

Our ancestors taught us to pick up a piece of bread fallen onto the ground, to breathe on it, to kiss it and make the sign of the cross over it. A good, but long forgotten custom, full of respect for bread. Forgotten just like an old word – endowment.

In the past, Belgrade merchants, later proclaimed to be heartless capitalists, used to leave their endowments to the city. And the new ones?

Today there are people much richer than those old Belgraders were, but no one gives anything away. They keep their purses tight and their mouths shut. Among them – our people who made it abroad. Oilmen, bankers, industrials... Not a single one to make a fountain, to build something, to donate a sculpture, to give a stipend, to ensure hot meals for the poor... Who are they going to leave all their riches to? But, it is a fact – one generation saves money and the following one squanders it. No one will take anything to one's grave.

All religions have been lost save the religion of acquisition.

Even if they had been robbing, stealing, exploiting and hording money stingily, the old merchants nevertheless left all their wealth to their fatherland, to save their souls somehow.

What can we leave? What are our endowments?

Perhaps we could start with something small, almost insignificant? The world is not bettered by grand gestures, but by small ones. Maybe, for starters, we should leave the remaining bread in a plastic bag by the dumpsters? Two stale hot dogs, a half-empty cup of buttermilk. Worn-out shoes. Endowments reflecting our times! They can all fit easily into a plastic bag.

I leave mine by the dumpster and, after having taken several steps away from it, I look back. It is gone!

This little endowment of ours used to be called *sevap*[7].

What is *sevap?*

It is when you do a good deed, but remain anonymous. Someone's gratitude would enhance your vanity.

The dumpsters are burning, sending plumes of smoke over the city.

Elderly gentlemen in their altered pre-war Crombie overcoats make tours of open markets

---

[7] *Sevap* (Turkish) – a good deed.

and pick up discarded cabbage leaves, a couple of potatoes that rolled away from the counter, a forgotten carrot, two leaves of lettuce...

They dig into the dumpsters and take out old newspapers and cigarette butts. They are called – garbage selectors! One of them wears a checkered cloth cap that once belonged to my friend Peđa. They are not obliged to be gentlemen any longer. They have been liberated...

Meanwhile, the dark-skinned girl rises out of the dumpster once more and tells her mother: "There isn't any!"

In spite of all, she, beautiful and smiling, looks like a trademark of hope.

At that very moment, someone is choking on his food, God knows why.

ELEVATORS

When Belgraders wish to soar up to European urban heights, they do it with the most decrepit elevators in the world. Engrossed in thoughts on more important topics, they hardly pay attention to those small and dirty elevator ones, although they are faced with them daily.

It seems that elevators in our new high-rises would get to the top floors even without motors: they would operate on the tepid and stale stench coming from the cellars...

If you are on your way to visit a friend living in a beautifully furnished apartment – a true European oasis of elegance and comfort – and if, by chance, it is located high up in the skyscraper, you will have to get there riding in a movable carved chapel belonging to an incredible mentality.

As soon as he finds himself claustrophobically alone in the movable coffin hung on unsafe cables, above the frightening abyss, our man, willy-nilly, feels the surge of an irrepressible wish to express his dormant, destructive erotic drive and long-suppressed ego. Then, like a prisoner in solitary confinement, he grabs the first sharp object he can find in his pocket and passionately carves his name and the date of this historic ride, to leave a trace of himself for posterity.

If the cabin walls are made of metal, our man gets hold of his keys or a screwdriver, while cabins made of lacquered wood awaken in him a primeval urge to carve images with his pocket knife, presenting excitingly exposed female bodies with all their details, in the style of the most lascivious naive art. Ladies, naturally, resort to different tools, like lipsticks, eye pencils and nail files, while some get ready for the creative ecstasy beforehand and get in with a supply of highlighting pens and color spray cans.

Perhaps it is a matter of our traditional mistrust of all new contraptions coming from foreign lands (elevators, for example), and we therefore take revenge on them while they take us up into the heights of civilization or down into the Balkan underground.

Truth be told, these hieroglyphic-like messages on elevator walls can be useful and edifying. A man who enters a certain building for the first time, for his first long-desired dinner with, say, a certain Vesna, will acquaint himself with the love life of the residents as soon as he gets into the elevator. Holding a bouquet of flowers in his hand, he will soon find out who made love to his beloved in that same elevator, who was the one with whom she cheated on him later, how she denied it (denial carved into the wall with her nail scissors – a double wavering line of her heart) saying that he was a flop, a liar and a faggot.

The walls of our elevators, in addition to telling us who slept with whom and how it was, also disclose the frequently hidden political orientation of its passengers: chauvinist slogans, skulls and crossbones, swastikas, gallows, anarchist insignia and other symbols of all kinds of perversity.

That's why the remaining fuzzy elevator mirrors hate us so much that our reflection in them never looks nice. Although I have to admit that the light in the cabins is poor, as a rule. That is because the residents steal the bulbs, and those that are left, protected by wire cages or crossed metal rods, can hardly give enough light to make themselves visible.

I also have to admit that were it not for the elevator scribblings that I have been studying carefully for years, I would feel desperately stupid in the presence of my accidental fellow-travelers, who blow smoke into my face and don't take off their hats in the presence of ladies. The elevator ride is too short to strike up a friendship, but too long if you ride to the top floor. Although, it can be interesting if the elevator stops at every floor. Then, in an instant you can get an insight into all kinds of tenants of those state-of-the-art Corbusier-style high-rises, given all the important awards for architecture, but not for the contents.

On some floors the step landings are turned into pantries and storage spaces (old refrigerators and cupboards), on others the winter gardens are in full bloom, carpets are taken out to dry, heavy racing motorbikes lean against the walls, on still others cats and dogs reside on old rotting sofas...

In front of many an entrance door, below the brass plate full of academic titles and ranks, there is a row of wooden-soled slippers neatly arranged on a small rug.

There is no doubt that we are the only country on Earth where the mats in front of entrance doors are secured with heavy chains. You can rest assured that if there is no chain and padlock, there is no mat either!

THE MAJESTIC HOTEL

In an old, elegant Belgrade café which has seen better times there are three tables.

Three tables seating the same guests for the last forty years.

Three estranged tables in three different corners of the café.

At the first table sit elderly Belgraders: bowties, black sticks and foreign newspapers bought at the kiosk on Terazije. They sip cappuccinos and take trips down memory lane, talking of balls at the Aero Club, of the Vajfert, Bajloni, Teokarević and Mitić families...

At the second table sit the veterans: retired high-ranking police officials, former inspectors and their victims... The passing of time has brought them reconciliation. They read *Borba,* drink 13 Juli grape brandy and are just about to liberate Livno, Duvno and Glamoč, having already taken Prozor and Kjuč, before ten a.m.

At the third table sit retired actors. They drink white wine from small jugs. An elderly soubrette

У славу мог покојни
пријатеља, Господина
Нитоу Пројковита,
нрорана и с се† ораку
гле миги сусреме
град „Москвом"
ттт куп
1989. јануар

asks an old leading man: "Say, did you and I make love before the war?"

He can't remember.

I sit at all three tables from time to time.

The veterans reproach me: "Why do you sit with those bandits?"

The elderly Belgraders are shocked: "What are you doing in the company of those murderers? If only you knew what they were doing in '49!'"

The occupants of both these tables get angry at me if I sit with the actors, as they are "mere circus performers" and some of them even appeared on stage during the German occupation.

The actors are indifferent: they are self-sufficient people – they still argue about who received the longest applause in nineteenthirtysomething...

There is one thing in common, though, at all three tables: when someone passes away they try not to mention his name and change the subject of their conversation right away.

Three tables, three isolated islands in the sea of Coca-Cola, in the middle of the turbulent high sea of blue jeans. They are surrounded by young, slender bodies, alluring hips, tanned backs, shining teeth, flashing whites of the eyes...

Three tables in the café invaded by boys and girls who communicate in their own secret, mute language of about fifty words. They neither eat nor drink, nor have they any past to speak of.

Perhaps they are waiting for the future that promises nothing? They stand on their feet and keep silent, happy to be together.

Nobody knows why, nobody knows how, nobody knows when, but a day or a night come when the Belgrade youth, as if by some tacit understanding, invades a certain corner, a certain square, a park or a café where until recently only a couple of regulars languished, whiling their time away.

One year it is Lovac, the following year Majestic, then Galerija or Manjež, Stupica or Madera... Now they twist their bodies around the three tables where their occupants still sell shares of Lloyd's, listen to their clapping audience and kill Germans.

The older and the more forgetful they get, the elderly Belgraders see themselves as ever more elegant and rich, the actors ever more famous and the veterans ever more courageous and responsible for winning battles. Had it not been for them, perhaps the Germans would still be sitting in this café.

When they have sat out their morning stint, the elderly Belgraders get up and go home for lunch. They are expected by their nagging wives, angry at them for being late.

From under the veterans' table the cleaning ladies sweep machine gun shells, unexploded bombs, the wounded and the dead...

The actors leave behind dead roses and faded programs.

Nothing remains behind the elderly Belgraders, but their scattered ashes.

Madame Death sits in the cloakroom, smoking and waiting to escort them.

HAPPINESS

We hear from old Belgraders that, before the war, wealthy people in Belgrade used to live rather modestly. Some even wore shabby, worn-out clothes and complained that their bankruptcy was just around the corner! That was probably because they knew the mentality of their fellow Belgraders. Belgraders are very warmhearted people: they love their neighbors best when these fall down to the bottom of misery. As soon as someone rises above them, they want to drag him down with all their might. Every new suit, every new car, expensive furniture or just a man laughing contentedly – lead to hatred. In this city the smartest thing is to be totally inconspicuous. A nobody!

However, nowadays the rich people, who acquired their wealth overnight, try very hard to be noticed. They drive cars which cost a fortune, wear heavy golden chains around their necks and precious wrist-watches on their hands, have fabulously expensive wedding parties and buy the houses of former well-to-do people. Even their tombs! As if they are doing their best to see their names in the crime reports as soon as possible.

But, still, are they happy? I don't think so.

"Money isn't all – there is also some value in golden ingots and real estate!" (maxim of an anonymous philosopher from Ada Ciganlija).

Well, what is happiness, then?

Perhaps it is something very simple: perhaps it is just the amount of time we can devote to ourselves and our dear ones?

Happiness is when we have a sunny day in mid-winter, or happiness is when it rains and we are at home, so we can sleep to our heart's content.

Happiness is also when we see two frail old people, who spent all their life together, crossing the street slowly and fearfully, holding hands, surrounded by unfamiliar faces from another epoch, a company of two, the witnesses of long gone days, events and people, the keepers of secrets...

"If you want to be happy for a day," says an old Georgian proverb, "then get drunk! If you want to be happy for a year, fall in love with a beautiful lady. But, if you want to be happy all your life, then it suffices to drink good wine with your old friends!"

Perhaps happiness is to stop running after happiness in time? Or to live our life fully before doctors forbid us to smoke, drink, eat, swim, sunbathe and make love?

To sum it up, happiness is when I happen to come across a half-full bottle of whiskey, but there is no ice in the fridge and when, at that very moment, a hailstorm comes along.

I take my glass and rush out into the street, waiting for the ice cubes to start falling from heaven.

MAKEDONSKA STREET

We shouldn't be acting high and mighty! True, the buildings in Makedonska Street are much taller than before, but there are fewer and fewer cafés!

On their way to the office, the journalists from *Politika* were exposed to many more temptations than today. They had to resist dropping in for a drink and *mezze* at their favorite haunts: Zora (Dawn), Kolarac, Bulevar, Pašon, Kineski Car (The Chinese Emperor), Persijski Šah (The Shah of Persia), Ginić, Mladi Arapin (The Young Arab), Knez Mihailo, also Musa, Dve Megdandžije (The Two Duelists), Dva Bela Goluba (The Two White Doves), not to mention Oriental bakeries, pastry shops and illegal backyard makeshift inns, with a couple of wonky tables...

It is not easy today either, as in this Fleet Street of Belgrade one has to pass by Scylla and Charybdis and the sirens, that is to say by Šuma-tovac, Grmeč and Lipa, in whose windows evil tomcats and old foxes lie in ambush waiting for journalistic greenhorns to tell them that it is not nice to be ambitious and that, with or without them, the newspapers will appear at the newsstands anyway!

Before it turned into a street, Makedonska was, only some hundred years ago, a regular country road, connecting the town with the nearby district of Palilula, inhabited by the best gardeners, brought in from Pirot and Knjaževac during the rule of Knez Miloš.

In their shady, green gardens they grew eggplants of superior quality, melons and watermelons, onions and garlic, red peppers without par, all kinds of soup greens, but also delightful pears, apples, the Thessalonica grapes "sweeter than honey and smelling of incense", even figs, that were used for making the traditional Belgrade preserve!

Even now all these delicacies grow in Palilula, but in the cans on the shelves of supermarkets constructed on the crumbling foundations of the former Palilula inns with their poetic names, like Mesečina (Moonlight), Pceto Koje Laje (The Barking Cur), Soskina Češma (Soska's Fountain), Sedam Švaba (The Seven Krauts), Srećni dvori Ive Zagorice (the Happy Inn of Ivo Zagorica)...

Here is a passage from the late Nikola Trajković's Book of Memories: "In the late 19th and early 20th century, this street was paved with bumpy cobblestones of very poor quality, leading pedestrians to believe that the street was much longer than it actually was. Sometime before the Balkan wars, it was asphalted and became shorter somehow, and the people wondered what had happened to their street."

Today, while you walk by the taxi stand, goldsmith's shops, boutiques, bookstores and music shops, tread quietly and modestly, as you are treading on history!

Makedonska Street joins Trg Republike (Republic Square), or, more precisely, makes a curve towards Terazije, where I had had the rare privilege to sit quite often in side-walk cafés with Mr. Nikola Trajković, a writer and an excellent translator of French poetry. He used to tell me, while using his straw-hat for a fan, that a century ago Terazije was full of wild dogs, who hid in holes and almost went mad with hunger.

"It is a known fact that packs of dogs used to swarm around the Turkish settlements", Mr. Trajković was telling me. "My father told me that after the Turks had gone, he had been crossing Terazije once and had had a tough time defending himself from the dogs which attacked him furiously, as he had been carrying smoked meat and bacon. That spot was inaccessible even in summertime, in moonlight, because it was far off and dark, as the lamps on Stambol-kapija were turned off at dusk, and stray dogs prowled around, waiting for prey...

It is likely that the fear and hatred from those long gone days stayed with us until the present

210

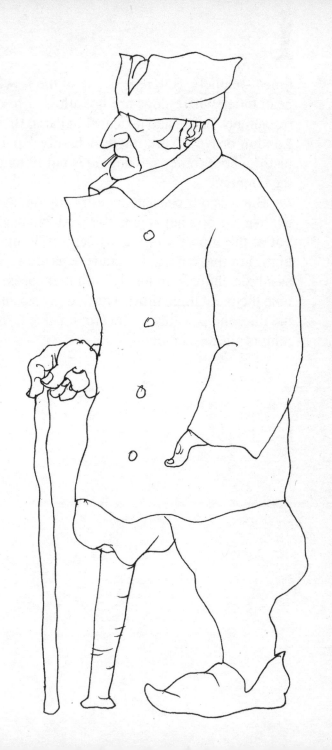

times – namely, Belgrade is one of the few European cities where dogs are not allowed in cafés, restaurants, hotels and taxicabs! In Paris, Brussels, London or New York, there is hardly a pub or a bistro where some lazy doggie is not lying under the counter.

But it is our peasant ancestry saying, through us, that the dog belongs in the yard, chained, and not at the top of a tall apartment building, sky-high! For that reason, Belgrade dogs are as lonely as single children in newly built high-rises. They take them out three times a day, to pee, to sniff, to breathe, and possibly to run around, that is, if running is allowed at all.

THE BOULEVARD

A foreigner, passing though Belgrade, asked me once how to see Belgrade in one hour?

Namely, that's all the time he had at his disposal.

I took him up the Boulevard, on foot...

In Belgrade, we have more boulevard press than real boulevards.

Still, King Alexander Boulevard is the most interesting and the longest of them all.

This broad street, with trees on both sides, is our past, our present and our future!

The first thing to show him, naturally, was its pompous, gloomy-gray, monumental beginning – Trg Marksa i Engelsa (Marx and Engels Square), a unique monument to socialist realism in architecture. Who would ever believe that on this very spot, a century ago, stood a slaughterhouse for sheep?

As everything else on this soil, our boulevards were also born out of ideology. On this Square you see the Trade Unions House, a stone rampart which prevents storms and winds from reaching Downtown. Here also used to stand the nest of collapsed ideology: the editorial offices of the *Borba* and *Komunist* newspapers and of *Socijalizam* magazine, the Komunist bookstore, the Museum of the Labor Movement...

Hardly a hundred or so steps to the north, I showed him the Old Palace and the palace park, as well as the Parliament building, just across the street. The Parliament building used to be enclosed by a most beautiful, ornate fence of forged iron (just as the palace park), which was removed after the Revolution, as a symbol which prevented the people from being in touch with the authorities. Later, someone stole the symbol and used it to fence in his own villa.

Only some two hundred steps from the former Marx and Engels Square, now Nikola Pašić Square, there is a small shop selling church supplies; it smells of incense and sweet Orthodoxy. Here you can buy candlesticks for your patron saint's day, candles, icon lamps, icons, the Holy Bible and prayer books... In St. Mark's Church, across the street, you can pray for the souls of the deceased from both ends of the Boulevard, and also buy tickets in the JAT Airways office to fly to any place on Earth, or send a parcel to someone across the oceans from the Central Post office.

It shouldn't be forgotten that the Boulevard, a hundred or so years ago, was actually a dirt road, commencing from the property of famous Marko Buljubaša, where gun-powder experts lived. Knez

Miloš cautiously moved them away from the town, lest someone be killed should the gun-powder workshop explode.

So, you are now walking a historic trail – I told the foreigner while we strolled – and here is what an old chronicler wrote about it: "In rainy days you could hardly walk here because of the mud, and in summertime because of the dust. Along its entire length, this trail was bordered by deserted tombstones, small second-hand shops, livestock markets, marshes full of reeds and other swamp grasses, as well as by isolated village taverns on bare fields, where the *košava* danced its furious dance..."

A quarter of an hour later we entered the field of science and literature, nibbling peanuts on the way. I pointed out to him the Schools of Law and Engineering, as well as the monuments to our great men, Nikola Tesla and Vuk Karadžić.

At the Metropol hotel we immersed ourselves into a mundane atmosphere. We watched the ladies of the night sitting at the bar and sipping ill-humoredly their cappuccinos, while waiting for Kuwaiti sheiks to return from the mosque, where they had gone to say a couple of prayers.

Still later we walked through the "stomach of Belgrade", the green market called Đeram, and reached the district named "Lyon", after the traditional but unrequited love of Belgraders for France.

The higher up we went along the Boulevard, the smaller the houses appeared to be, the poorer the shops, the cheaper the goods.

215

Step by step, the bookstores, boutiques, cafés, goldsmith's shops, the big windows of furniture and automobile stores, the music and computer shops, were disappearing, and from the twilight of the past there appeared *ćevapčići* eateries, tinsmith's shops with tin tubs, stoves, pipes and weathervanes, Oriental bakeries, modest greengrocers, kiosks with various seeds, chickpeas and peanuts... Fur coats and hats were replaced by calico dresses and robes, plaid flannel shirts and tall shoes with laces. Long cotton underwear, slippers, cheap brooches and fake pearl necklaces – small movable shops on overturned cardboard boxes... At every corner there was a primitive roulette, called *trange-frange*.

The small-town atmosphere was persistently and unstoppably sucking in the Boulevard, which had begun in great style only several kilometers down the road, until it turned it into the Smederevo Road, bordered by huts and shacks, stables and barns, outbuildings and tire-repair shops. It was a gloomy and muggy day and our native mud was getting ready to start its invasion down the Boulevard, all the way to Downtown.

Is there another street like this one anywhere in the world, where you can see all these things, the centuries and the mentality?

"You are a rich country, indeed!" said the foreigner, exhausted by so many wonders.

BRIC-A-BRAC

For decades I collected bric-a-brac which makes me sad. It has grown to be quite an impressive collection. I'll bequeath it to the city of Belgrade. Here are its contents:

Dogs which look like their masters and vice versa.

Elderly Belgraders with black captain's caps from Piraeus, although they never sailed anywhere.

Former smokers sucking on an empty cigarette holder.

Ladies with fresh coiffures, just out of their hairdresser's, on the eve of public holidays.

An elderly married couple dressed in unisex clothes, former boogie-woogie dancers, performing their well-trained routines from the 1950s at the birthday parties of their children, who look at them in astonishment.

A husband and a wife who call each other "Mom" and "Dad".

The phrase: I won't let them make a fool out of me, for my own money. It's not the matter of money, but of principles!

A fireplace with a light bulb wrapped in red tinfoil, to simulate fire.

A house in the Alpine style on the bank of the Danube, in Grocka.

Dachshunds dressed in Scottish tweed waist-coats, so as not to catch a cold.

Burberry scarves over locally-made raincoats.

A fake Rolex from Singapore.

Drina cigarettes in a Marlborough pack.

Reversible raincoats.

Musicians' faces at weddings.

White socks in black shoes and rings with black stones, monogrammed in gold.

Bold men with overly long whiskers.

Feminists without breasts.

A steering wheel covered with fur.

A jolly fellow who knows all the latest jokes. He is said to be "ideal for company" and he feels obliged to justify it, learning new jokes by heart at home.

A slapped-together New Year's Eve orchestra, consisting of an engineer, a tax collector, a dentist and a watchmaker, who used to play at dance halls a long time ago.

A plaque at the railway station hotel: "We ask our esteemed guests to refrain from polishing their shoes with the curtains!"

A hotel room with a view to the wall, instead of to the high sea.

A dressing room after an unsuccessful concert, with a bunch of carnations from the Management.

Our immigrants from the USA (from the state of Ohio) on holiday in Belgrade. In Skadarlija they give a one-dollar note to the singer and then ask their hosts why he felt offended?

A studio borrowed from a bachelor friend, from three to six p.m. The bed sheets have absorbed the sweat of many unknown lovers. In the fridge – half a bottle of sticky orange juice, a piece of cheese turned to stone and a cup of buttermilk, six months old. Also, moldy cashew nuts. An icy desolation and traces of bare feet on the dusty floor. A feeling of another love failure...

A check, in lieu of a wedding gift.

A painter at his own vernissage, not knowing what to do with his hands while a critic praises him excessively, as if he were already dead...

And some other sad things...

A GENETIC LICK

Talking with Westerns about the things that baffle them most in our city, I have come to the conclusion that they are bewildered by the things we are so used to that we do not register them at all!

For example, lukewarm Coca-Cola and cold tea as a rule!

Also, that nowhere in Belgrade do you get tea served with milk. Namely, they do not realize that we drink tea only when sick, and milk only in childhood.

They also find it interesting that cognac is served here as an aperitif and not as a digestif!

Lately, our fellow citizens take it with ice cubes, thinking it's posh, which drives the poor French, who invented cognac in the first place, crazy. A bottle of Napoleon, which we finish off in a jiffy, lasts them several months. Once we see its bottom, in an hour or so, we pass on to something more familiar, a combination of brandy and beer, known as "concrete".

On their first visit to Belgrade, foreigners usually find it astonishing that lettuce is not fresh. If they come again, they'll be surprised that there is any!

Unlike us, Westerners never give money to café musicians. Really, how can one carouse in Vienna? Certainly not by pushing banknotes between the harp strings on which some old lady picks out preludes, or sticking them onto the bow of a cellist performing potpourris from some Jacques Offenbach's operetta.

They are also surprised to see paper napkins in fine restaurants.

If they order wine, it will be served in water glasses (co-called "spritzer glasses"), and in order to have it served properly they'll have to ask for the "table glasses", as if there were others, like, say, "chandelier glasses"! They'll never get used to corrupting their wine with club soda, or to paying their bill as soon as they are served, because the waiter trusts no one.

It is not possible, they say, that sea fish is twice as cheap and twice as readily available inland compared to the coast, where it comes from.

The English absolutely cannot get used to the fact that our waiters sit with their guests, and that drivers sit with their bosses.

The Russians criticize us for not eating while drinking hard liquor.

The Americans cannot understand the phrase: "Leave me a drag!"

221

We are the only city on Earth which brought together two incompatible things: the pagan ground-wheat sweet and European whipped cream!

In our state-of-the-art hotels, the handles on toilet doors are the first to go, there is usually no toilet paper inside, and most hand-dryers are simply out of order. One can also come across holes on toilet doors, which goes to prove our pathological curiosity towards the opposite sex, in the most private moments.

Belgrade is also famous for a special kind of dessert for men: chewing on a movable toothpick, which goes from one corner of the mouth to the other.

Naturally, there is no way that foreigners would understand why we cannot be patient a little bit if we are hungry, but have to eat at someone's grave?

At the Hyatt they certainly overdid it in their attempt to be posh: they bring the bill for dinner on a warm plate!

Igor Stravinsky wrote in his memoirs that at concerts held Belgrade, it is the flowers that get the most applause. Every bouquet receives a new applause! The last one receives a standing ovation!

Following the concert, a breathless girl appears on the stage and tells the popular singer:

"Dear sir, here are your favorite flowers, and here is the change!"

Belgraders adore piano sonatas so much that they cannot resist applauding between movements!

While Westerners always sit in the back of a taxicab, we sit in front with the driver, like buddies, and three minutes into the ride start to badmouth the authorities.

Serbs, for reasons unknown, are more given to kissing the hands of priests than of ladies.

Why do we always lick a cigarette before lighting it? Because our ancestors did not buy their cigarettes, but rolled them with home-grown tobacco.

It is a genetic lick!

EVERYDAY NONSENSE

Future researchers of the mores and mentality of Belgraders will no doubt be interested to find out what was the nonsense that the present-day residents of our capital believed in. In order not to be forgotten, I leave them here, as a legacy, a list of some of the nonsense which makes me laugh – a sure sign that I'm still alive.

Among other things, my fellow Belgraders naively believe that you can stop beer foam from overflowing if you stick your index finger in the glass. Although our cafés are overflowing with characters who stick their dirty fingers into each other's glasses, I have never seen any other effect of this action but wet tablecloths and cuffs full of beer.

Belgraders also invented an incredible thing – that red wine spots on white trousers can be taken out if immediately drenched with white wine. That's why Belgrade is a city of tipsy trousers, as a result of mixing two kinds of wine. If they smear their clothes with grease, they put salt on the stain, even though it is a well-known fact that this kind of smudge can be taken out by scissors alone!

You are right to ask what a glass of water has to do with taking an exam? Nothing. But when a student goes to take an exam, his or her mother or grandmother will not fail to pour a glass of water down the stairs, the result of that being that many have slipped and broken their arms or legs, while those who escaped that misfortune got to the the university dripping wet. The idea is to facilitate the flow of thoughts at the exam – let them flow like water!

A sty – an inflammation on the edge of the eyelid – is brought on exclusively by winking, and those who take a seat at the corner of the table will never marry.

If you happen to have a toothache, elderly Belgraders will tell you to put a grain of sugar on the cigarette embers, to close the nostril on the opposite side of the aching tooth and to inhale this smoky sherbet until you faint.

There are other ways, as well: take some strong plum brandy into the mouth and hold it on the painful tooth for a while, before swallowing it. That's the reason why many of us acquired a tendency to drink from a very tender age.

The best way to cool a watermelon is to wrap it into a wet cloth and leave it in the sun to dry; you'll tan best if you sit in the shade of a fluttering tree top, and if you are hot, the best way to refresh yourself in summertime is to drink hot tea instead of icy water.

Unbelievable!

Many Belgraders boast that they have been using the same razor blade for years, by sharpening it on the inside of a wet glass, while others claim that mineral water will not go flat if you put a teaspoon in the bottleneck. Why a teaspoon and not a zipper or any ordinary stopper – will remain a secret forever.

Also, many people still naively believe that a burning candle on the table will absorb the cigarette smoke and that the broken fan belt in your car can be successfully replaced by a rolled-up nylon stocking, a great excuse to be given to a jealous wife if she happens to stumble on that particular piece of female wardrobe in the car.

Although not fetishists, young Belgraders adore the Mercedes sign. Whenever they have a chance, they break it off the hood of the car and take it away as a talisman, so that most Mercedeses in Belgrade, devoid of their majestic sign, seem to be somehow incomplete, like a frying pan without a handle.

Although they live in an age of synthetic paints, Belgraders remain stubbornly faithful to the most primitive stuff for whitewashing their walls – popularly nicknamed *štricla*, the white traces of which can regularly be seen on their backs or elbows. Namely, they claim that the polycolor or wallpaper prevent their walls "from breathing", causing them to "sweat"! That's probably the result of their fear that the walls might catch cold and fall ill. I wouldn't be in the least surprised if those in favor of the classical, powdery *štricla* should soon take their walls out to Kalemegdan, for a walk and a breath of fresh air.

SPRINGTIME

On March 21st, we get out of a long, winter tunnel, with buckling knees and a yearning in the pit of our stomachs.

Some newly born beauties, the children of suburbia and the New Belgrade residential quarters, throw away their winter coats and emerge from their cocoons, like butterflies from clumsy silkworms. Astounded by their own sudden beauty, they stumble as they pass through the admiring glances bestowed on them.

The macho Belgraders, descendants of warriors and rebels, for centuries embarrassed to carry flowers in the streets, cannot resist a small bouquet of hyacinths, which they buy surreptitiously and hide in a plastic bag holding meat and onions.

Disturbed by the arrival of spring and generally dissatisfied, their angry wives, upon seeing the flowers, forget their famous phrase, prepared well in advance: "I haven't been out of the house for three days! Some life....!"

The spring is upon us when an elderly regular of the Madera café, who became father at an ad-

vanced age, goes to meet his little daughter after school and take her home. He wears thick glasses, and feels somewhat dazed by the March weather. After classes he took his little one's hand and brought her home. When they got there, his wife asked him:

"Where is our pet?"

"What do you mean 'where' – here she is! I brought her home!"

"You wretched creature!" screamed his wife. "This is not our daughter at all!"

The old lady-killer, namely, took home the first child who gave him its hand.

In springtime, the ivy turns those ugly big houses full of communal apartments into green palaces out of Sleeping Beauty.

In springtime, ours is the most beautiful country in the world, which everybody knows and envies us for.

"Oh, Lord", they ask, "why did you shower all this abundance on Serbia? You gave it a nice climate, rich fields, green woods, also swift rivers, high mountains, fertile seasons, you gave it everything..."

"True," replies the Lord, "but that's why I also gave it the Serbs."

THE GERMAN CONSUL'S BARBER

In these tumultuous times, when once omnipotent people fall from power overnight, and everybody is at a loss what to do with them since they are left without jobs and occupations, an old Belgrade hairdresser, Mr. Sava, and his story about crafts, frequently come to my mind.

"You know, it does not hurt to be the master of some craft!" he used to tell me in his backyard, over coffee. "All told, there isn't much use in being in power today. Now you have it, now it's gone..." He mastered his trade with an old German master in the early 20th century, in a small town in Banat, later crossed the Danube and in the Thirties found a job as a young journeyman at the best hairdresser's shop in Terazije Square. One day, a black Mercedes stopped in front of the shop. The chauffer enquired whether anyone among the shop staff spoke German. The owner dispatched Mr. Sava, who spoke excellent Hungarian, Romanian and German, and from that day on he went regularly to a villa in Dedinje, to cut the German consul's hair. Namely, everybody knows that ambassadors and consuls have no time to waste in going to barber shops, as the rest of the world, but that barbers go to their places. That's the way it is. By the way, says Mr. Sava, the consul had a strangely shaped, square head (a true Prussian), but Mr. Sava managed to cut his hair in such a way that the consul was more than satisfied and did not want anyone else to mess with his hair any more.

Back then, Mr. Sava had two new suits made of first-class English cloth; he wore gray spats the color of pigeon feathers, a Borsalino hat and gloves, and he passionately attended afternoon sessions at the Dance Hall in Pašićeva Street. There he met and befriended some young Montenegrin students, notoriously penniless, so he cut their hair for free. He had no idea that they were communists.

And so, cutting hair from various heads – stupid and smart, rich and poor, alive and dead, victorious and defeated – he realized one thing: that everybody is sensitive about one's hairstyle. Even those with only three hairs left want them to be arranged nicely.

On the day Belgrade was bombed, Mr. Sava and his boss were sitting in the empty shop, minding the inventory since the windows had been shattered by the detonations. Two days later, the black Mercedes, all dusty and bullet-riddled, stopped in front of the shop, followed by two German military policemen on motorcycles.

"Wer ist hier Friseur Sava?" yelled the German policeman with a Schmeiser machine gun across his breast. *"Schnell, schnell!"*

It must be on account of those communists that I kept company with, thought Mr. Sava, while tearfully taking leave of his boss, who, in Sava's words, was like a father to him. He took along his leather bag with Solingen tools. Let them bury him with the tools of his trade.

They pushed him, neither dead nor alive, into the Mercedes and took him to another villa in Dedinje, where the German commander of the city of Belgrade was waiting for him. What was going on? The pre-war consul had recommended Mr. Sava to his friend the general, who later passed him on as a legacy to his successor, and so Mr. Sava cut the hair of them all. If he was in a position to save someone from the execution list – he did it. Those he could not save – let their souls rest in peace. In nineteen forty-four, fierce battles were fought all over Belgrade. Mr. Sava and his aged boss were sitting once again in their empty shop with broken windows, when a black Mercedes stopped in front of the shop, accompanied by two armed Partisans on motorcycles.

"Which one of you is Master Sava?" yelled a sturdy partisan with a Russian machine gun across his chest, and Mr. Sava's knees buckled with fear.

Well, now I'm in a real mess, he thought while they shoved him into the car. Why the hell did I accept to cut the German generals' hair! Just in case they spared his life, he took along his old bag with the tools, to have it handy if need be.

They took him to a deserted villa in Dedinje, where a famous Partisan general was waiting. When Mr. Sava finally got in, he recognized, to his great amazement, the Montenegrin student whose hair he had cut for free before the war, in the shop in Terazije, and lent him money, to boot. He had turned completely gray-haired and unkempt, and had given orders that Mr. Sava be found right away in order to cut his hair, as only he knew how! And so, for some time he cut the hair of Partisan generals and made his living out of it, although his old boss intended to make the shop over to him. But he did not consent. He was used to having his entire shop in his bag with brass latches. All that he needed was in that bag. The place where he opens his bag and takes out his tools and accessories – that's where his shop is. He only trusted his skilful hands and his honesty. He helped whomever he could – and if he could not help, he did not do any harm!

I watch Mr. Sava while he brushes carefully his black coat and *geschtraft* trousers, and packs his bag with the Solingen tools.

"Look," he says, "I am eighty four, and naturally my hands tremble, but as soon as I get hold of my clippers, they stop shaking!"

"Where are you off to, Mr. Sava?" I ask him.

"To Dedinje, to give a haircut to the German consul!"

"Who recommended you?" I ask, walking along with him through his garden.

"That general of ours, when he was a military attaché in Bonn..."

Mr. Sava, straight as a flagpole, and carrying his eighty four years with elegance, walks out of the gate, where a big black Mercedes is already waiting. A chauffer in uniform respectfully opens the back door for him and he first puts his old leather bag on the seat and then sits himself. They drive him away while he waves to me from behind the limousine's dark windows.

THE COUNT

On account of his exceptionally noble appearance and behaviour he was nicknamed "The Count", although he spent his entire life working as a night-shift waiter. When he retired, he stuck to his old habit of sleeping during the day and staying up at night.

He would get to our table after midnight, freshly shaved and with his clothes perfectly ironed. The rims of his Borsalino hat spoke of the history of poverty. Yesterday's newspapers, half-smoked cigarettes and dried carnations would disappear into the inside of his big bag, always by his side...

He would tell us that he collected meat leftovers for his cat.

He died the year when they put up the announcement at the entrance to the Madera restaurant saying that DINNER IS OBLIGATORY.

Rumor has it that no cats were found in his solitary room.

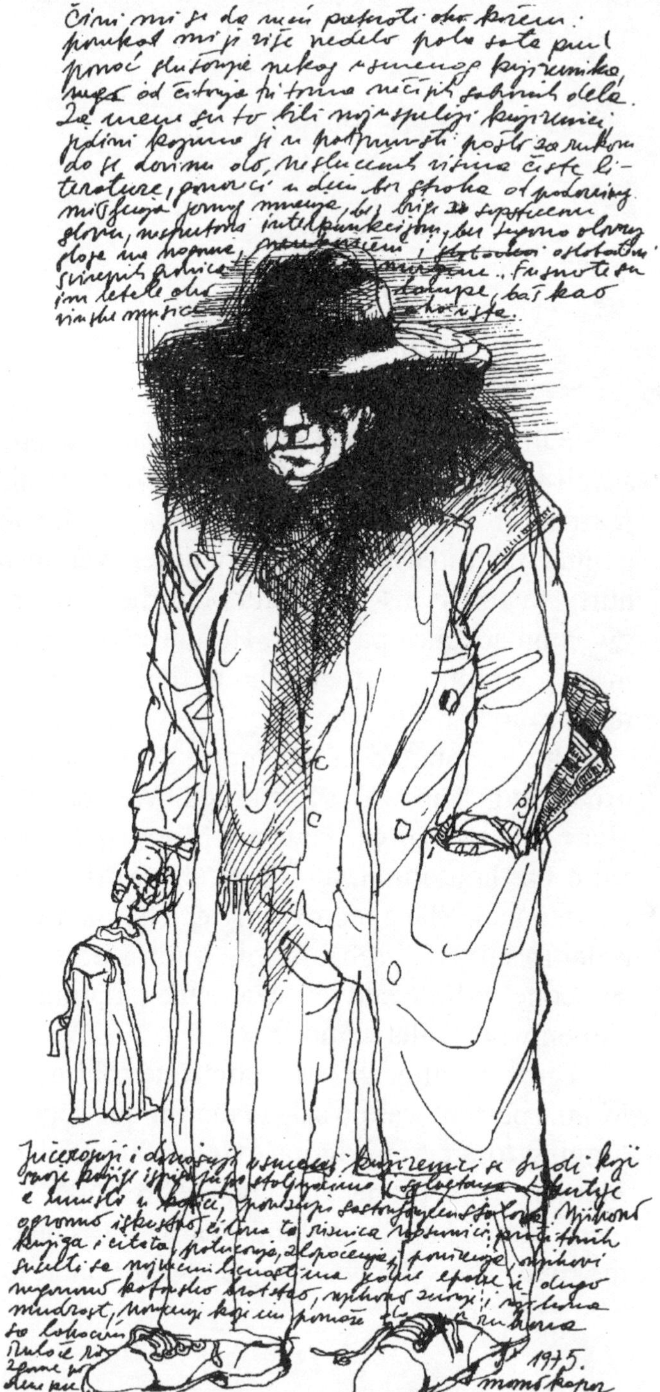
1975.
momo kapor

THE PORTRAIT

In the winter of 1941 my father commissioned a well-known Belgrade painter to make a life-size portrait of my mother. My Mom posed for the painter for three weeks. The painter was in no hurry to finish his work, although he had been given an advance payment. He must have fallen in love with my mother, who at that time was a real beauty.

The war started in the spring. My Dad went off to fight and was soon killed. We remained alone, the two of us. First my Mom sold things from the household, and later she worked as a charwoman. She aged overnight. The painter, in order to survive, probably sold Mom's portrait to someone. Who could tell where the painting was and on what walls it hung?

One day, after the war, someone told us that Mom's portrait was on sale in the antique shop belonging to a certain Ignjačević, nicknamed The Martian, in the former Hartvigova Street. We went there. I remember everything clearly; I was nine at the time. The shop was deep and semi-dark, loaded with junk. A stuffed snake hung above the door, with the inscription underneath saying: "Python snake. Caught in Tašmajdan." Mom's portrait stood close to the entrance door and was nicely illuminated. It was then that I realized how beautiful she had been. The shadow of her straw blue-ribboned hat fell on her enormous dark eyes and on the open book in her lap. She wore a white sleeveless dress. It was obvious that the portrait had been done with great affection. We stood in front of it for a long time.

"How much is it?" asked my mother finally.

"Twenty thousand…" replied the old man.

Back then, it was an enormous amount of money. We lived on two thousand a month. But the painter was one of the best in the pre-war times.

Mom took my hand and we started for the door.

"I am sorry, Madam," said the antiquarian, pointing to the portrait. "Is that you on this painting?"

Mom hesitated for a while. She looked at her ruined hands, brushed an invisible crumb off her faded dress and touched her hair, already turning gray.

"No, it isn't" she said, and we left the shop.

THE MENU

I am not surprised that the Serbs had finally, after so many years, defeated the Turks, nor that the keys of the Kalemegdan fortress were handed over in 1867, nor am I surprised that Ali Riza-pasha, the Turkish commander of Serbian towns, went to the banquet in honor of his defeat, nor that Prince Miloš Obrenović hosted the banquet – they were all well-mannered men of the world, it is all a matter of history and diplomacy; but there is one thing that surprises me – the menu at the banquet held on April 5th, 1867. It truly amazes me!

Huitres
Potage à la Reine
Cassolettes de riz d'Agneau
Turbot à la Chambort
Filets de Boeuf, Jardinière
Saute filets de Beccasse
Epigrames d'Agneau au pois
Aspic d'Homard en belle vue
Asperges Artichauts
Punch imperial

Faisan Perdraux rôtis
Pilaw
Gelee de Marasquin aux fruits
Charlotte à la Russe
Baklava
Fromage glacée
Dessert

(Oysters. Queen's Soup. Cassolettes with rice and lamb meat. Flounder a la Chambort. Beefsteak, garden style. Fried snipe fillets. Lamb medallions with green peas. Lobster in aspic. Asparagus and artichokes. Imperial Punch. Roasted pheasant and partridge. Pilaf. Maraschino jelly with fruit. Charlotte, Russian style. Baklava. Iced cheese. Dessert.)

I am amazed that on that day, April 5th, 1867, fresh oysters had made it to Belgrade. How long had they traveled from Ston or Thessalonica, how were they transported across impassable mountains, over roads rutted by spring waters – where did they find the ice to keep them from spoiling (or were they brought, perchance, in oak barrels filled with sea water)? Across wild rivers, through dark and dangerous woods – oysters in Belgrade, on the fifth day of April, 1867 – that's what amazes me!

THE CAP

"Take your cap off!" the magistrate ordered Handsome George, who stood in the middle of the room with his chums and waited for the interrogation to start.

"Take your cap off!" he repeated, raising his voice.

Handsome George kept silent and looked down. The others looked at him.

"This is the last time I am ordering you to take your cap off!" shouted the magistrate. "You are in an institution, not in the street!"

Handsome George was looking dejectedly at the tip of his worn-out shoes.

"Take your cap off!" yelled the magistrate. "If not, we'll take it off for you!"

"Take it off …" pleaded his chums.

Handsome George looked at the ceiling, as if expecting help from it.

"Take his cap off!" the magistrate ordered the two policemen, who entered the interrogation room at his call. By the way, the cap was a beret, and came down to Handsome George's eyebrows.

The bigger policeman approached the young man and abruptly pulled off the cap. Handsome George put up no resistance. He had been planning to go to a dance that evening.

He had curlers in his hair.

PEANUTS

A dark-haired girl walks into the restaurant Tri Lista Duvana (Three Leaves of Tobacco) at midnight sharp.

She approaches the table in her overly long raincoat, inherited from her mother, and stands quietly, holding her school bag open. There are no notebooks in it, or pencil boxes, or textbooks – only peanuts.

Her mother roasted them in her oven.

Her father made small cone-shaped bags out of the leaves of her last year's calligraphy notebook – fifty cones with straight and slanted lines, and the mark in red ink at the bottom – A-.

The girl stands silently, with her school bag open before guests like a strange, dark shell with some mysterious fruits.

I hear someone's voice:

"Shame on those who let her do this!"

The spendthrifts buy ten cones at once.

Former tenors hit the high C just for her and buy three cones of peanuts.

Two people in love unwrap her paper cone and whisper the rhymes starting with the letter 's': "She sells sea shells at the sea shore…"

A drunkard stares into the dark interior of her open bag and thinks that it is his grave, into which he is being lowered. A hypochondriac asks the girl whether the peanuts were washed, a riddle-lover tries to calculate how many peanut kernels on the average fit into a cone, a businessman gives her one hundred dinars in order to get rid of her, but she returns the money and says that she is not begging, but selling peanuts – and at that moment the maitre d' appears and pushes the girl out into the street, and all the guests keep mum and pretend they are interested in something in their glasses or on their plates.

I sit and ponder on how little stands between us and the moment when our daughters could end up going out to sell peanuts, while we would wait for them to come home before dawn and to fall asleep, sucking on their thumbs.

THE TREEHOUSE

In the 1950s, a Belgrade architect by the name of Peđa the Jesus (nicknamed so on account of his ginger beard) built a house on a tree by the Sava river.

Sometimes we slept in the house, rising with the birds from a nearby nest. As the tree grew, each year the house got a storey higher.

It was at that house that we realized one does not have to live on the ground all the time. But, some people fell out (the tree shook them off), and I can still hear the dull thuds of their encounters with the humdrum.

Occasionally we bump into each other at zebra crossings. We exchange glances through car windows and try to measure the amount of ruin on each other's faces.

KALENIĆ MARKET

You must have noted, surely, that newspapers review even the most tedious theater plays (which, to tell the truth, did have their opening nights, but closed immediately thereafter); the most insignificant volumes of verse, printed in one hundred copies at the most; the prize-winning novels read by approximately fifteen people. There is no newspaper, however, that would publish a review of an open market – that magnificent show which farmers stage daily, like some jolly folk theater, in downtown Belgrade, before a record number of spectators. The reason is probably that Belgrade intellectuals profoundly despise the things that they live on, although in addition to spiritual nourishment, they readily consume the food from the open market, as well. For example, when writing about a theater festival, the critics never fail to compare it to the previous one, although it is a known fact that all festivals are more or less the same.

Kalenić market is always different and unrepeatable, but nowhere can you read a single line about it. If I were to write a review, I would certainly point out that strawberries are much bigger this year than last, but that they are not as sweet, as it rained often in the spring. As for horseradishes, they are redder and crunchier than ever, and scallions' heads are larger than before.

Theater critics seem to write the same review over and over again, changing only the name of the author. The longest part of the review is the introduction, devoted to the author and his play. It is followed by the names of the director and actors, with each protagonist given a couple of words, while the rest of the troupe, like a bereaved family, is lumped together into one single divisible sentence. It all ends in a perennially identical phrase: "stage sets pleasing to the eye, costumes adequate". I have never met a theater critic who would open his review with the description of a costume or the stage lights. Therefore, in this review devoted to Kalenić market, I would like to note that the lights were grayish, reflecting on the counters' awnings, and that the main actors wore, by and large, country-style costumes!

For the sake of those who are not from Belgrade, it should be pointed out that Kalenić market is the biggest and the best supplied market in town, and that it is located in Čubura. Elderly Belgraders call it also Kalenića Gumno. The word Čubura is of Turkish origin and means a wide and shallow well, with water springing from it. Once upon the time, there was such a well right across the street from the legendary café Čubura, at the site of the present-day park. In the late 19th century, this area, overgrown with reeds, was barely populated. Belgraders used to go there for wild duck hunting. An old chronicler noted: "In Čubura people drank and made merry day and night. The singing would start at dawn, with the first cocks, at the same time when revelers, accompanied by Gypsy bands, would call it a night…" It is no wonder, then, that this blessed quarter, always bent on enjoying life and watered by its live well, gave birth to the most luxurious Belgrade market – a true small Babylon, where one can hear all Serbian dialects, interspersed with the Romany, Albanian and Macedonian languages, as well as those of our East European brothers – black marketers and middlemen.

Kalenić market is a sort of village embassy in the capital. It is where, every morning without fail, green credentials are handed over to wan Belgraders, who lost their roots and contact with the soil and its fruits a long time ago. When entering the market from the direction of café Kalenić, one has the impression of having arrived at the bow of Noah's Ark; here you can buy young puppies of the "Čubura barker" breed, songbirds, rabbits, tumblers and aquarium fish…

Regardless of how long I lived abroad, I – a born provincial – cannot for the life of me get used

to the illogical abundance of supermarkets, selling watermelons in January. For us, watermelon was always the sign of the summer at its peak, before fading away. Simply, it does not agree with us in February. Living next to Kalenić market and in it, we grew accustomed to things ripening in nature's cycle.

The appearance of the first cherries on this sumptuous stage was a true festivity. The first cherries were bought in small bunches (to make children happy), while those in pairs were hung on ears, like springtime earrings. I have never seen prettier jewelry! What do I care for the December cherries in New York? They only take away from me the sweet, superstitious waiting for real cherries, because when you eat them for the first time you must wish upon something and your wish will come true, without fail! We climb the cherry tree in some Čubura yard and we pick the only partly ripe cherries, covered in tiny dewdrops. We also use this opportunity to watch the naked thighs of the girls of our age, high up on the trees above our heads, still unaware of their attractiveness...

I must admit that to this very day I have not found out why in fine Western restaurants they serve melon with prosciutto? It is not my cup of tea, particularly melon in March!

We no longer wait for strawberries in May or grapes in August. You can buy them here as well, in the bitter cold, until they die of pneumonia. The modern world has mixed up the rhythm of the seasons. But November roses have no fragrance.

No matter how long it rots in the shop window, the coconut will never learn Serbian.

The only vegetables that resists this terror of the modern world are spring potatoes. You don't see them anywhere out of season. This spring they are the aces of Kalenić market!

Thus, having lost the natural rhythm of the change of seasons, we also lost the capability to enjoy the taste of their fruits.

Kalenić market is, therefore, a sort of a healing spa, where the indifference and snobbism of various rootless cosmopolitans are successfully treated. For that reason they should go there, just like to a therapy, at least twice a week.

FIVE MINUTES OF POWER

We are a people of geniuses indeed!

Stop any Belgrader in the street and ask him whether he would accept the position of Mayor, director of the National Theater or head of the Nuclear Institute; he would take it without hesitation, and even feel slightly offended that you were offering him the top position only now, after so many years which he spent doing nothing.

You could count on the fingers of one hand those who would not welcome a chance to be manager of the national soccer team, ambassador or president of the Serbian Academy of Arts and Science. Even high-school dropouts would consent to be editors to the best Serbian writers and to improve on their style and thoughts. Half of Belgraders are deeply offended that no one suggested them as the right persons to set things right in traffic or urban planning. The houses they live in would be much better had they designed them, instead of architects. That's the reason why nowhere in the world are there so many glass-enclosed terraces, walled-up doors and rooms turned into kitchens.

The well-known Belgrade phrase, "If only I could have five minutes in power…" is the most explicit proof of their inborn longing to have power over others.

Everyone knows what is good for you, better than you do.

Everyone would like to change you and to order you around.

The critics believe that you did not do your best in your collected works.

Your physician demands that you stop smoking.

Your friends tell you that you drink too much.

Your wife meddles in your marriage.

"If only I could have five minutes in power…" confides a waiter, looking crossly at the maitre.

For years I used to come across an elderly man in the supermarket. Good morning! Good morning! He seemed to be a nice, quiet, somewhat withdrawn person

Then, one day I was called up for maneuvers. Bring your uniform. When I put it on, I am the most ridiculous person ever.

At seven a.m. I enter the premises of the community center, smelling foully of some long-forgotten times. Old photographs of masses of volunteers at huge construction projects, faded and colorless. In front of the photos stands – who else but that old coot, completely changed, strict, hot-tempered and cocky – a miniaturized commander.

"Fall in!"

We line up listlessly.

"Count off!

"First! Second! First! Second! First…"

"Comrades, I salute you!"

"Ciao!" we answer languidly.

"Repeat!"

I cannot recognize him.

"What are you waiting for? A lemon?" he roars at us. It turned out that he was a captain, long retired, who could not be promoted further, but still wanted to command.

All of a sudden we are soldiers again, although not as young and lean as we used to be. Our families, our reputations, the years, everything that we have achieved in life, all vanish without a trace in front of this vampire-like commander, who, come tomorrow, will turn again into an insignificant, quiet pensioner with a plastic bag in his hands. In one single move, he wiped us out with the invisible eraser of his minute power. His five minutes of glory have returned!

I am deployed, together with two middle-aged neighbors, to the Zoo!

"Ten-hut! Suck in your guts!"

"I already did!" says one.

"Comrades, in the case of, you understand, bombing or nuclear attack, you are accountable, you understand, for killing wild animals which will, understand, try to escape from their cages

258

and imperil, what, comrades? The lives of our comrades, both male and female, comrades! Because, comrades, a man is our greatest treasure! There are some writers among us, who sneer at my words... We'll take care of them, no problem! To them, you understand, all this looks funny. But we, you understand, we must behave as if the peace is going to last a hundred years and we must be ready as if the war is going to break out tomorrow. For-ward, maaaarch!"

With our unloaded rifles we sit at the tables of the small bar at the Zoo and drink grape brandy. Instead of pink elephants, I see gray ones. They sway their trunks, not understanding what will befall them, you understand, in the case of a nuclear attack.

They watch us in amazement. They probably think that someone is shooting a movie.

"What are you doing here?" asks a lady strolling with her grandson.

"Waiting to kill Cica the elephant..."

What a nice day for huge, gray elephants!

At three p.m. the old coot reappears, accompanied by his retinue.

We jump up and stand at attention.

"Very good, comrade soldiers!"

"We serve the people!" we answer in unison and then have another drink, this time with the commander... His five minutes of power are up...

A BELGRADER IN SWITZERLAND

There is some curse upon us! As soon as we leave Belgrade (where we, usually, object to everything), we immediately start to miss it.

It seems that we miss our misery.

In the paradise of Switzerland we split hairs.

We sulk, backbite and find faults…

We make our hosts' lives miserable, just to show that we are not impressed by their affluence.

We don't let the wide world confuse us.

Look, here they buy meat by the gram, unlike us – we buy it by the half-carcass.

To tell the truth, their tomatoes are nicer and bigger than ours, but they are tasteless. Ours are all gnarled, nothing to boast about, but you eat them just like that, like apples!

They do not peel their cucumbers. Their salads are served unseasoned, and we do not know how to ask for the *karafindl* (oil and vinegar set).

I admit that their peppers are twice as big, and all are sound, but they are not fit for stuffing. They are thick and somehow watery.

Their cheeses are moldy, particularly Roquefort.

Their lilacs have no scent.

And the Serbs living abroad are not like regular Serbs! If the day of Saint George, May 6, falls on a Monday, they postpone the celebration for the following Sunday, May 12, because it is their day off. St. George's Day is St. George's Day! It does not do to wait for the weekend to celebrate it. Isn't the Serbian patron saint's day older than the Swiss weekend?

We stay with our well-to-do relatives, but what good is their wealth to them when they have no time to enjoy it? By the way, the kids do not speak a word of Serbian. Their Swiss mothers took them under their wings.

A *Keva* decided to visit her daughter, married to a Swiss man and living in Lausanne. She wanted to give them a treat, so that, for once, they would eat a decent, home-cooked meal, and made about thirty rolls of *sarma* (just in case, she brought lamb' stomach lining from Belgrade). Out of politeness they took one each, smearing it across their plates. Her daughter kept explaining to the grandchildren how miraculous this national dish was until she was blue in the face. All in vain! Most of the *sarma* remained untouched. *Keva* had to eat them herself for three days in a row; it is a pity to throw them away.

After dinner they drink coffee in the drawing room, as if they were their own guests, and not in the kitchen, where it is most enjoyable.

She felt like looking into the dregs in her coffee cup, so she turned the cup over to drain, but, lo and behold, the cup was clean, without dregs! She could not read what was in store for her, no joy in the house, no expected gain, no dark-haired person in uniform, no love, no blond woman plotting against her; no tears, no trips – there is nothing in the Swiss cup. Only emptiness! Just like their lives!

I often wondered why so many Serbs live in Switzerland?

Now I know. When they left home, they did not buy a return ticket.

But I did.

THE ESCAPE

"And now listen to this!" said, some time before midnight in the café Pod Lipom (Under the Linden Tree), a man who had been sitting in the corner silently, listening to our stories about missing persons:

"My uncle, a kindly soul, one of those people who seem to live so as to be of use to others, could do nothing right according to his wife, my aunt. She kept count of his every outing, every drink and every cigarette. Where have you been? Who with? Why do you slurp when you eat your soup? You are picking your nose again...

"One day their only child, a daughter, got married. The wedding was typical of Belgrade... Joined tables in the Slavija hotel, with two families looking suspiciously at one another and the orchestra listlessly playing old songs. At the top of the table the newly-weds were going through an ordeal, waiting for the time to push off on their honeymoon trip.

"The permanently guilty uncle was silently rolling bread crumbs into balls, while the aunt, like an offended public prosecutor, radiated sour ill-will, so much so that you could pour it into your glass instead of soda water. There are women who do not pay attention to anything, either to cataclysms or to wars, concentrating on one thing only – making their husbands feel as guilty as possible!

"Finally, it was time for my uncle and me to take the newly-weds to the airport. After that we would return to the wedding party, to fetch my aunt.

"When we kissed the newly-weds goodbye and they boarded their plane, my uncle stood looking at the sky for a long time, and when the plane finally disappeared from sight, he asked me to take him home for a minute, to pick up something...

"Once inside, he offered me a drink and told me to wait. I was afraid of my aunt, whom we had left at the wedding party. I could already visualize her hissing at my uncle for being late.

"From the wardrobe he took down a smallish suitcase and put in it some shirts, underwear and a couple of books, and asked me to take him to the railway station. On the way there we did not exchange a single word. I could only imagine what my aunt intended to tell him and what punishment she had in store for him, while waiting for us for hours, at the joined tables amid the people she did not know.

"We said goodbye at the platform and he entered the nearest carriage randomly, not knowing where the train was heading. None of us ever saw him again…"

DULE THE BIGHEAD

Let it be noted: Dule the Bighead from Ada Ciganlija did not live to see the First of May of 1989, the day when the perch jump out of the river, delighted to see another summer and when boys (it is a matter of honor) enter the spring waters of the Sava for the first time,

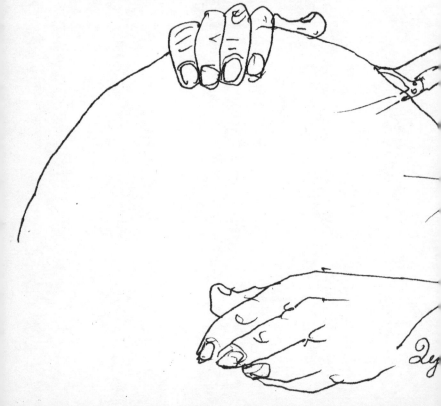

the day when bare-footed, middle-aged housewives, all of a sudden and for no reason whatsoever, feel like running on the damp grass below
the willow trees, and husbands feel like napping,
with newspapers spread over their faces,

the day when all old, leaky boats are being
mended, and the smell of tar and varnish is in the
air,

the day when Ada smells of roast pig on the
spit, and the small red horseradishes and young
scallions crunch under your teeth,

the day when the white sails of the Sava re-
gatta begin to flutter, and the current takes away,
all the way to the Danube, empty beer bottles with
their necks nodding every which way ...

Dule the Bighead died just as he had lived –
quite unexpectedly!

Let is also be noted that Dule the Bighead was
the owner of the strangest tavern in Belgrade,
maybe even in all of Europe; I can vouch for myself that I have never seen anything similar to it,
anywhere on Earth.

First of all, his tavern, located on a half-rotten
and fully run-down wooden raft, displayed no sign
and had no name. We called it simply "At Dule
the Bighead's".

Besides, it was not duly registered as an eatery
and no taxes were paid for it. It would close by itself if tax inspectors happened to come near, and
would open by itself when friends arrived.

Dule the Bighead hardly ever cooked anything on his raft. The guests themselves cooked when they were hungry. There was no set price for food and booze – everyone would place on the cupboard as much as one could afford. The strangest thing of all was that the guests usually prepared meals for Dule as well, as he considered himself to be above it.

He was the happiest and the freest man I have ever met and I envied him deeply for his ability to evade all traps set by life.

If he would fall asleep after lunch (and he slept without fail), his snoring would make small waves on the surface of the river, and the raft would heave, as if alive. Sitting in our boats, we would wait for him to wake up and tell us what he had dreamed of.

A writer from Split, Miljenko Smoje, was once a guest on his raft.

We were expecting excitedly to hear what he would say about the Sava, the love of our life. We even made some preparations beforehand, we painted crows white to make them resemble seagulls, and a man waited upriver with a bag of salt to pour it in, should Smoje decide to take a swim and be puzzled by the fact that the water was not salty.

"You really swim in this?" asked the flabbergasted man from Split, pointing at the turbid water.

The current was carrying away with melancholy the bloated corpse of a cow from Umka, with birds standing on it.

We admitted that we did swim in it and that we were still doing fine. If we happened to spot a bicycle, or a bacterium or an amoeba in the river, we simply swam around them.

Occasionally some curious foreigners would visit the raft belonging to Dule the Bighead. Once I brought a New York TV crew to make a story about him. The Sava troubadour, Old Caruso, joined us soon. Naturally, we had too many drinks, forgot all about filming the story, and launched into singing.

The Americans wanted us to translate the lyrics for them.

Mile walks on the Lajkovac track,
And his mate walks behind his back...

What a crazy people! Who would walk along the railway tracks if there is a road? How, then, to explain the wicked spite to walk on the railway track, across the ties and crunching gravel? Heading straight for the train, which could appear any minute.

Mile walks, his cigarette glows,
His mate he well knows!

Of course he knows him well, if they walk the tracks together! But now come the most difficult lines to be translated, the lines that make your head spin:

> *Dry hay, mowed away, through the village*
> *runs a stream*
> *Fish swim in the stream, not an angler to be*
> *seen ...*

Who mows the dry hay and why isn't there anybody to catch the fish? And what's all this got to do with the railway tracks to Lajkovac?

> *Mile, don't desert your mate so,*
> *There are still many miles to go!*

"As long as I stuck to one liter of wine a day", says a character from along the Lajkovac railroad track, "everything was fine! When I switched to two liters, I occasionally made a mess of myself. But only when I could not live without three liters a day, was I awakened one night by my neighbor, screaming at me: 'Get up from those tracks, *bre,* the fast train to Valjevo is coming...' And that was when I decided to sign up for treatment!"

Who, actually, was Dule the Bighead?

The Colas Breugnon of Ada Ciganlija, Gargantua or Pantagruel, a jester and a host, a friend of cast-outs and the lonely, but also of well-known people, the last king of the Sava, the man out of whose hand the fish ate, the guardian of the river's secrets, a sage, a mythical personage...

I don't know.

But neither do I know where to moor my boat, now that he has turned into a legend.

SUNDAY AFTERNOON

It all started when she, frying onions and wiping away the tears (provoked only by the onions), remarked that her husband had not shaved for two days, to which he answered that – he was giving his beard a rest!

Of course, she says, he does not care what he looks like when he is at home; it is a different matter when he is at work, and everybody knows why! As if she were not aware that weekends for him are like a jail sentence; that he would gladly scamper off to a meeting if he could invent one, but, unfortunately, it is Sunday! He readily agreed that his life was like serving time, but in prison they at least let you walk for an hour and you could read the newspapers in peace, which was not the case in his own home...

Why don't you go out? Please, go! Get out right away; you don't have to come back at all! What kind of life is this? When you are at home, you do three things only: eat, sleep and read newspapers. It's as if we did not exist! As if we were not alive! When did you take the children to the zoo last?

He said that he had asked them only that morning if they wanted to go the zoo, but they were not interested. Besides, the polar bears are still hibernating. Yawning, he declared that he had no guilty conscience! For example, he had gone to the market earlier today. Hadn't he?

Your market! I'm sick and tired of your market! You all but tip the farmers, as if you were in a pub. You pretend to be an expert... Where is this potato from? From Ivanjica, sir. For you, all potatoes are from Ivanjica. Even the ones packed in nylon bags in the supermarket are also from Ivanjica. They are certainly not from Idaho!

He tried to explain that she was great at putting the blame on others. She even cooks in order to make the rest of the family feel guilty. Her meatballs in tomato sauce are actually a hand-grenade, while her noodles look like a hanging noose. Once her Sunday cooking, supposed to make them happy, is over, the whole house is in disarray, brimming with pots and pans, skillets, plates and cutlery. She does it on purpose, to demonstrate that she works herself to the bone, and also so she can wash the dishes and make noise when he wants to take a nap after dinner. It is a different matter when he cooks; everything is always clean! As soon as he is finished with a utensil, he washes it! He has no need to make anyone feel guilty...

Yeah, and when does the gentleman cook at all? Only when we have guests, to show off in front of them and to steal the show. An expert in Chinese food! Shrimps with bamboo shoots in soy sauce. Duck a la Sichuan! Surely he got used to these delicacies as a child, while living in that small town, in the middle of nowhere. And it is even phonier when he tries to play the role of a man of the people, and prepares his famous army-style beans. Good God! Those never-ending stories from the army (starring him); the stories that she is sick and tired of!

He tries to tell her that love is over once the wife stops laughing at the army jokes she had heard two hundred and seventy eight times before. Then love is really over! And as for cooking, it is a known fact that all great cooks are men – not a single woman among them! They simply have no culinary imagination and creativity for it. For women, preparing food is just a chore and an everyday routine...

Yeah, I'd like to see you cooking every day, said she.

Has anyone ever seen a woman chef at a Hilton or a Sheraton, said he. She would surely chase away all the guests in no time, by making them feel guilty for having dined for their own money. She wouldn't be able to resist the urge to make a round of the tables, in order to show her "ruined" hands and the veins on her legs! Who, in his right mind, would ever wish to go to a restaurant where the cook complains of not having left the kitchen for three days in a row!

And who would go to a hotel in which the cook gives his beard a two-day's rest?

He went on reading the newspapers and she asked him what was so important in them, more important than their conversation.

He does not know, he says, but the sentence he has been reading for the last half an hour, is awfully interesting!

They ate in silence. Beef soup, boiled beef. with horseradish sauce and mashed potatoes, all tasting of their morning squabble. The noodles stretched endlessly, like the Sunday afternoon. Wrapping itself in low, gray clouds, Belgrade turned into a provincial town.

Do you want me to drop you off? he asked, for the sake of asking, while she was getting ready to go visit her parents.

You have already dropped me! she said and slammed the door.

TIRED OF HISTORY

In those long-gone years, while we were singing enthusiastically "Now awaken the East and the West / Now awaken the North and the South" – the West had already been awake for quite some time.

Later on the North and the South also awakened and only the East remained dozing in a sweet ideological drowsiness for almost half a century, envious of the affluence of the awakened West.

White wine with club soda in hand, Belgrade spoke ill of socialism for forty-five years, dreaming of capitalism and doing nothing.

When the East finally caved in, the West knocked at our doors. At first we were enthralled by the visit!

Our businessmen, who we felt deeply sorry for when some thirty years ago they had to leave home and go into the wide word, since there were no jobs for them here, started to come back, one after the other.

They came back as true Western millionaires. They surveyed carefully what possible purchases they could make here: we couldn't believe our own eyes! They bought the most beautiful houses in Belgrade, whose owners in the meantime had been reduced to poverty, yearning for the West all along. Then they started to buy everything that was for sale. Some of them even bought the companies they had been fired from a long time ago.

For the West, the East has turned into an El-dorado, where everything can be bought for peanuts! How much is Belgrade?

Naïve as we are, we believed that they returned to help us out, but they came to make a profit out of our misery. Money makes money!

Living amid nonsense for half a century, the East earnestly came to believe that "the man is our greatest treasure".

Yesterday's lords of the surplus of value, the immediate producers who owned the means of production, finally had a close encounter with the West.

Unaccustomed to working endless hours, from morning to midnight, the first ones to faint were the Belgrade children working at McDonald's! They did not employ grown-ups there.

History is repeating itself! The Serbs, who defeated the Germans in the last two wars, now invited German experts to help them overcome the crises.

A smart German earns in our country as much as a hundred lazy Serbs. The sons of those Germans, who picked out every second Serb from the line-up to be shot, today fire every second worker from the factory, as redundant!

Now the East is starting to miss the old East.

How sweet it was to doze off at the workers' meeting! The director-general apologizes to the cleaning lady for having earned two university degrees.

Who dares ask him now why he rides in a Mercedes? First of all, there are no more meetings, and then the owner does not drive a Mercedes, but a Jaguar.

Those who dared ask were fired on the spot. Overwhelmed, they still stand in the street, in front of their company. Only now it is not called a "suspension of work" - but strike!

I remember the year when passes were introduced for entering the premises of Belgrade TV, and when the doorman boasted to everyone and his brother that he did not allow even the director-general to get in!

"Yes, I do know you..." he told the director, "but no one can get in without a pass! Those are the orders!"

The new owners do not even say hello to the doorman. When he sees them approaching from a distance of twenty meters, he jumps to his feet as if scalded. But they just pass by, pretending not to see him.

The East is parting from itself with great pain...

Where are those great days of endless workers' councils meetings? Where is voluntary blood donation for the heroic people of Vietnam? Where are the meal coupons? Sick leaves and paid absence from work? Who dares, if working for a private company, drink six cups of coffee in the morning in order to get going, read the newspapers from the editorial to the ad page, and analyze the previous night's TV program, to boot!

Where are those good old times when "technocrats" were being arrested all over the place?

Whatever happened to those companies that were labeled as "alienated centers of power"?

Where are the office parties with roasted pig, the trade-union-organized trips for March 8th, the early morning gatherings for May Day, the mutual assistance fund?

Who ever got properly drunk with the Westerners, who do sums on their calculators all the time and constantly rush someplace? And the old director-general – you could drink with him to your heart's content and get the keys to a new apartment, as well. Those were the days!

What we had to live through and to suffer, how many years went down the drain, all to make the rich even richer and the poor even poorer!

I pass by a group of workers striking on the street and I know: soon, emaciated types with small beards and thick glasses will appear and offer fliers to the workers. There will be secret readings of the novel *How the Steel was Tempered*, Maxim Gorky will be in vogue again and his novel *Mother* will be passed from hand to hand. Then two jailbirds doing time in prison will translate Capital once more and everything will start all over again.

I am tired of history, which repeats itself like a worn-out record...

BELGRADE ECCENTRICS

The first Belgrade eccentrics was mentioned in writing by old chroniclers in 1813. He was called Crazy Nastas. He embellished himself with tinkling bells and was followed by a pack of hungry dogs. In the completely deserted town of Belgrade, he was the only one to meet the Turks when they regained power. No one knows how and why Crazy Nastas was turned into Crazy Nasta – an expression still used by Belgraders for persons off their rocker, also called muggins.

The last city eccentric, whom everyone in Belgrade knew and liked, was the famous Pera Balon, who passed through the 1950s and 60s like an apostle, whose apocalyptic messages no one could decipher. He was an old coot with strong gray beard, clothed in an enormous overcoat, with a rope for a belt, with a heap of medals and decorations on his chest. He always lugged a number of bundles with him, a wicker wine demijohn, filled with water from the Hajdučka Česma spring in Topčider, a stick and a ball. By tapping the ball against the ground he would mark the rhythm and the diction of his sermons, announcing in this way

momo kapa
sojenica na Adi
Ciganliji, 1988

his arrival at the cafés. He was a fan of the Crvena Zvezda (Red Star) football team and he had a precisely set route through the city. Both the waiters and the guests gave him food and cigarettes, even though he never asked for anything. A strange phrase remained after him, full of ambiguous and mysterious meanings, which he would repeat to no end: "As a man says, it is known…"

After he passed away, there were no prominent town fools worth mentioning. Small-bore freaks have become fixtures on radio talk shows with ludic tendencies. Bigger nuts are paid for their craziness, which is too full of phoniness and egotism to be interesting or sincere. They are already in show business.

The true town fruitcakes have practically vanished, while craziness turned into a mass phenomenon. A newspaper reporter noted that "there are too many people in the streets who talk to themselves…"

In the present-day Belgrade slang, these persons are said to have lost their marbles, or to have "burst".

"You've burst, man!"

Truly, if schizophrenia is the splitting of personality, its duality, then we all are, more or less, ready for the psychiatric ward.

One half of our being is bent to peace, while the other longs for fights and revenge for previous injustices!

We long for the love of our friends who opted for the opposite, enemy side, hating them all along because they betrayed us.

We sleep in Belgrade and dream of the coast...

We swear that we will never ever go to the places where they offended us brutally, hoping all the time that we'll make it there some day, nevertheless.

The fight is going on in us between the outlaws and the diplomats!

The spendthrifts are fighting with beggars, economists with squanderers...

Inside our beings a battle is going on of revanchism against forgiveness, of an eye against an eye, of a tooth against a tooth, of Orthodoxy against sin.

A part of us is a historian issuing warnings, while the other part is a futurist, pulling us towards the future.

A conflict is going on within us between the patriarchal Serbs and blasé cosmopolitans, who are totally indifferent to where they live.

The monarchists and the republicans, those on the left and those on the right, the red and the black, are at each others' throats!

If this is not madness, what is?

It remains to be seen whether and how we'll find a way out and who is going to win.

"As a man says, it is known..."

A MADHOUSE

The best proof that Belgrade is the most agreeable place to live in is that apartments in it are much more expensive than in New York City, although the earnings are incomparably lower here than over there.

Newspapers are full of ads, mostly for swapping houses in the interior for Belgrade. You can count on the fingers of one hand those who want to move out of Belgrade. Are they out of their minds?

Even a son of a war hero, living in the interior, would gladly swap the street bearing his father's name for a small two-bedroom apartment in Belgrade!

It is not my intention to praise Belgrade excessively, far from it, but, all things considered, the safest place to be in is Belgrade.

In this city no one was killed on the grounds of being of a different religion. If you happen to be shot by a Magnum in some café, it is only because they did not like the color of your tie. You are the sole culprit.

In Belgrade, no stranger had his car tires punctured.

Belgraders only puncture the tires of other Belgraders, for parking in front of their garages. This is something they can't resist!

In Belgrade, no one was fired for not being a Serb.

It is the only place in the world where newcomers fire born-and-bred Belgraders.

Namely, there are so many country people in Belgrade that the urbanites represent a national minority.

Judging by the accents, the only people in the National Assembly who are from Belgrade are the drivers, since someone must know the streets that lead out of town, to the highway.

There is no place in the world like Belgrade, where each day is a historical one.

Belgrade has three hundred and sixty five historical days in a year. As this is very strenuous for its inhabitants, each day spent in it should be counted double in terms of length of service!

Just take the historical unrest on the streets! Belgrade breaks its own windows – it does need others to do it for it. (Glasscutters are much obliged.)

Taking all this into account, Belgrade seems to be a masochist city.

Were it different, would it still award extraordinary pensions to those who conspired against it all their lives?

It is interesting that more and more former politicians are becoming writers and vice versa.

It's hard to tell which has more to lose, literature or politics?

Former politicians' bodyguards now guard former writers. They used to protect the former from the latter, and the latter from third parties ... a crazy city!

The best proof of the downfall of Belgrade is that it is being praised and defended by myself, an out-of-towner!

ILL-GOTTEN GOODS NEVER PROSPER!

There was a man in Belgrade, named Mane Cvetković, a tinsmith, who lived to be 120. He lived in the borough of Voždovac, in a small run-down cottage. Hundreds of roofs in Belgrade sported tin weathervanes, hand-made and set on chimneys by Uncle Mane. With the *košava* blowing, those weathervanes would turn and their tin wings and metallic feathers would perform a clinking, clattering music.

Those who knew him tell me that he went to City Hall on the day he reached a full hundred years of service, to ask for a pension, which he had earned by honest work, but there they told him that he would have to provide two witnesses to vouch for him.

"It could be only Prince Miloš and Toma Vučić-Perišić", said Uncle Mane. "They were the first ones to get my weathervanes on their roofs!"

When asked for the amount of his pension, he answered, "it is not important how big your pension is, but how long you'll enjoy it".

Uncle Mane was in the funeral cortege when one of the richest people in Belgrade died, a well-known man from Herzegovina, Luka Ćelović. All of a sudden, a man appeared before the cortege, spread his arms and ordered the cortege to stop!

"What do you want, man?" asked the bishop, heading the cortege.

"I want to see what is Luka Ćelović taking to his grave," answered the man.

Luka Ćelović did not take anything. He came to Belgrade as a poor boy from Trebinje, with a one-dinar coin in his pocket. He was leaving this world without so much as a one-dinar coin, but he left everything he had earned to Belgrade University.

Day in, day out he used to go to his own hotel, the Bristol, taking with him his own sugar, as coffee would then cost a couple of cents less. His endowment to Belgrade University was seized in its entirety by the new state in 1944, but that is another story.

Strolling in shady or snow-covered streets of Senjak and Dedinje, I often think about the late Mane Cvetković and the man who stopped Luka Ćelović's funeral cortege. I look at the pompous villas of the nouveaux riches, their sumptuous gates and fences, and I ask myself whether they would feel sorry on their dying day to leave all their worldly goods behind? Luka Ćelović can rest in peace, because thanks to his endowment his name has remained forever engraved into the collective memory of Belgrade. But, these new ones! I haven't seen a single one of them endow a building, be it much smaller than those given to the Homeland by Kolarac, Spasić, Captain Miša or Igumanov, who were paupers compared to the wealth of these new classes.

Wealth acquired overnight, that an English family would require at least five generations to amass, is spent just as fast, leaving no other trace but suspicions as to its provenance.

Rade, the son of Nikola Pašić, the famous prime minister of Serbia, will be remembered only by that he sold the bust from his father's tomb, made by Meštrović, and that his own mother reported him to the authorities.

The history of the most beautiful buildings in town, its villas and palaces, is also the history of its downfall and decay. There is hardly a single villa that did not change owners at least several times. The original owner's house, built for his family, to live in it happily and to cultivate a garden, was first taken by the Germans, and the owner and his family were dispatched to live somewhere in town as subtenants. The liberation in 1944 liberated him from all worries inherent to ownership of property, as the liberators moved into his house, leaving him, if he was lucky, the choice of living either in the garage or in the gardener's hut. Once the liberators grew older and fell from power, they sold the villa at the request of their children and their families, until finally the nouveaux riches would come into possession of it. But regardless of all efforts to renovate these old neglected mansions, regardless of how many times their façades were repainted, the curse of other people's nurseries will follow them to their dying day, as announced by the old saying: Ill-gotten goods never prosper!

THE BLOCKADE

Amidst the blockade, Belgrade was full of refugees.

An elderly couple lost all their possessions, their house in the hills was razed, everything they had acquired in half a century went up in flames, and so – deliberating what to do, where to go – they decided to go to Belgrade and stay with their son and daughter-in-law. Their whole life changed overnight.

The apartment was not big, but it was nicely furnished – the paintings, books, wallpaper, and lampshades soon became impregnated by the strong smell of the old man's tobacco.

At night the young ones would open the convertible sofa in the living room to sleep there. Lovemaking – no way! The walls are thin and to get to the bathroom you have to pass through the living room. And there, in the bathroom, the old man's ancient shaving brush is fighting all night long with the Gillette shaving foam.

The mother, in mourning clothes, knits gloves for an unknown soldier and cries silently.

The father, a giant of a man, sits with his leather cap on his head and watches TV, without seeing anything. He just sighs deeply from time to time. In the high-rise where he feels as if living in a cage, he calls out "good morning" to everyone, which gets on his daughter's-in-law nerves in particular. When eating soup, he slurps. He also scatters cigarette ashes all over the place.

How is it possible, under these circumstances, to invite over their Belgrade friends, who gossip about them anyway? They are already six dinners and two cocktail parties in arrears. The worst of all is that nobody knows how long this is going to last. Nevertheless, they are his parents and they are in dire straits. They deprived themselves of many things in order to put him through school. He still remembers those yellowish postal checks, which would reach him regularly on the first day of each month. When he became a journalist, his father, in just one sentence (completely untranslatable into any existing language), gave him the shortest and the strictest quintessence of morals in the history of journalism:

"Woe is to you if you lie!"

Once they tried to throw a party, but the mother refused to put on her daughters-in-law's violet dress with pearls for the occasion. The conversation about the latest premiere died down the moment his father sighed deeply, got up and went to the kitchenette. At half past ten he joined the party again, looked at each and every one of their elegant guests and asked:

"Children, don't you have homes of your own?"

They departed hastily, in a tense silence.

She couldn't take it any longer. She ran up the stairs to the roof terrace. She was crying. He came after her and gave her a hug. Her face was damp. They started kissing, leaning on the chimney.

"It's been a long time since you kissed me like this", she whispered.

They kissed for a long time under the cold stars over Belgrade.

Later on, they went down to the apartment and opened the sofa.

ŽUĆKO[8]

He was sitting in an open cardboard box, while rain slicked down his short yellowish-red coat, blinking his dark, intelligent eyes and watching with curiosity the gloomy day and the feet of passers-by. I bent and patted him, and he politely licked my palm.

"What's your name?"

"Žućko!" answered the man who was selling him.

Žućko…

Every Sunday the poor people in Belgrade take out to Kalenić market everything that they can do without, and that's how Žućko found himself in the company of rabbits, new-born puppies, canaries and parrots, tiny fish and ducklings resembling a puff of yellow down… He snorted angrily at his two beautiful neighbors in the basket – two Siamese pussycats, and openly demonstrated his scorn for the cackling chickens. But he was also utterly confused by the hectic crowd at

---

[8] Žućko – from "žut", yellow: a typical name for a yellow-haired dog, especially a mongrel.

the market, by the noise, shouting and strange smells of autumn fruits and fresh meat; everything was so different from his peaceful yard in Čubura.

He still hears his mother Lisa whimpering when they took him away from her: "Take care, Žućko, God only knows if we shall meet again in this dog's life!" They took him away at dawn, before his little master got up, since he would undoubtedly stop them, and now he sits in the rain among these unfamiliar people and waits for someone to come along and buy him.

In this country and in this town everything is both expensive and cheap, including a dog's life. I asked and learned that Žućko cost thirty German marks. We do not express the worth of our lives, or dogs' lives, in dinars – they buy us for marks and dollars!

It is true, though, that Žućko cannot boast of being of a fine breed. He belongs to a widespread Belgrade family of mongrels without pedigree, but he counts among his remote ancestors a purebred dog from Šar Planina and a good-looking bitch of Scottish decent.

His father is the famous Steppenwolf – today the leader of a pack of wild dogs in Ada Ciganlija, forgotten and abandoned by their fickle summer owners. Žućko and his lost brothers are the fruit of a short-lived love affair with gentle Lisa, whose puppies were sold as soon as they were born.

Žućko is now four months old, but when he grows up he will surely reveal the best traits of his mixed blood: endurance, a strange elegance and, before all, sweetness and blind loyalty – the most important traits of Belgrade dogs' character.

He senses that something unusual is going on; he was never touched, felt and patted by so many unfamiliar human paws, and he was rather frightened by those white ones with long, painted claws.

"Wow, look how sweet it is! Let's buy it."

"That's all you need! Where do you intend to keep it?"

"Well, in the apartment, like everybody else!"

"Yeah, and I'll be the one to take him out to the park three times a day, right?"

"What breed is it?" asks a passer-by? "A mongrel? A street cur?"

"A Čubura barker", replies his owner.

"Dad, please, let's buy him!" a child whimpers.

"I can hardly feed you, let alone him!"

"Twenty marks", the owner lowers the price.

It is the twenty-fifth week of the blockade. At first, doggies like this one cost one hundred marks. Regardless of how smart he is, Žućko cannot understand what he had done wrong to be here, in the rain, and not in his home yard, where everything is safe and familiar.

Like Belgraders, their pets are also not very demanding. Žućko is certainly not the hound of the Baskervilles, nor the famous Jerry of the Islands, nor the small Pomeranian from Chekhov's The Lady with the Dog, nor White Fang, pulling Jack London through the snow, nor Kachalov's Dog from Yesenin, nor the nostalgic Johnny fed on caviar and herring, nor Disney's Scamp... Žućko lives on leftovers, but there are no leftovers any more!

I stand in the rain, which drenches the autumn marigolds and the bags of potatos, waiting to see who is going to buy Žućko. I wouldn't like it to be someone who does not understand all this. Although, such people do not frequent Kalenić market on Sundays.

It is noon, the market is gradually withering away, and old ladies rummage through the remnants of half-rotten vegetables on wet counters.

"Žućko, let's go home", I hear his owner's voice as he lifts him together with the cardboard box. Žućko licks his hands and waves his tail merrily.

Thank God, all is well! We have not been sold this Sunday, I say to myself and go to celebrate at the market bar.

THE CELL PHONE

In hard and crazy times (are there different ones?), I used to come across people who walked the streets and talked to themselves. Poor souls. Did they not have anyone to hear them out, so they found the one person in the world who would listen to them, or were they starring in some drama of their own, uttering long monologues; who can say? The harder the times, the more of them in the streets.

These days I see them again all over Belgrade. There, a man walks in Knez Mihailova Street and talks to himself!

They usually put their hand on their right ear while talking. The passers-by wonder and make the sign of the cross. They are somewhat similar to that legendary eccentric, the late Pera Balon.

All right, we sort of got used to them in the streets, but here we are at a party – everybody's standing, drinking and talking but one person, apparently quite normal and elegant, who stands in the corner and talks to himself, with his hand on his right ear. I am intrigued to know what is going on, and, being shortsighted, I come nearer, only to see that he has a phone in his hand (who could see it?). I thought he was shaving with an electric razor, but no, it is a phone! I have never seen a smaller one in my whole life. And there is another character, with two phones in his hands.

So, you are invited to a dinner party by some wise and powerful people; you expect to hear all kinds of important things and drink good wine, but the moment you start on your entrée, three mobile phones begin to shriek and squeal. There is no way to have a conversation. If a table is longer, the one sitting at the top calls the host on his mobile phone to ask for more Scotch.

A true wonder!

I know a man who deals in these telephones, and he offers to get one for me. He says I'll pay him when I pay him. Thank you, I tell him, but even my old bakelite black phone, weighing a ton, is off most of the time.

SCHIZOPHRENIA

I lounge on a worm-eaten raft on Ada Ciganlija and ponder whether to take a swim in the Sava.

A man from Herzegovina and a Belgrader are fighting in me...

The Belgrader finds the water cold, the man from Herzegovina finds it murky and dirty, and I am hot!

The Belgrader, born cautious, whispers to me that we, all three of us, will catch cold.

The man from Herzegovina remembers with sadness the turquoise waters of the river Trebišnjica, so clear that you can drink it, and the green waters of the river Neretva, into which he used to jump from the Old Bridge in Mostar. He swears he would not swim in the Sava, not for love or money! (As if something were being offered to him, to start with!)

Many rivers flow through my memories: the pretty, feminine Sava, the treacherous Danube, Mark Twain's Mississippi rolling sluggishly (forget it, waves it aside the man from Herzegovina, a born Russophile), the sly whore Seine capable of cajoling your last penny, the murky Thames wrapped in its gray robe, the Miljacka murmuring below the bridges with changed names, the holy river Krka, golden and shining, I tread through the Kupa, the Cetina and the Zrmanja – Hey, Morava, my village on your banks...

And while the two of them are carrying on their dispute, I jump into the Sava, what do I care!

The Belgrader swims crawl from the start, and the man from Herzegovina swims butterfly, but I swim on my back!

You cannot imagine how all this looks to observers from the bank.

The man from Herzegovina has been living in me even before my birth, the Belgader since I was nine, when in 1946 we moved to this town.

One speaks in the ekavian dialect, the other in the ijekavian one.

I have a particularly tough time at the concerts at the Kolarac Concert Hall. The Belgrader, allegedly, adores Mahler's boring symphonies, while the man from Herzegovina goes to sleep right away and, pardon my French, breathes heavily, while the people around him try to wake him up and hush him.

He would prefer to listen to the *gusle*[9].

---

[9] *Gusle* – a one-stringed folk fiddle used to accompany recitals of epic poetry.

On the other hand, the Belgrader yawns while listening to a *gusle* player singing about heroes of old and looks in amazement at men with moustaches weep.

I admit they make my life miserable all the time. I don't know how to escape from these two.

For example, a couple of days ago I was on my way to be interviewed by an important British TV station. The man from Herzegovina insisted that I put on fatigues. The Belgrader opted for a dark suit and a tie. So I put on my faded jeans and dirty sneakers. They did not speak to me for two whole hours!

One is adamant that we should sign everything they demand of us (so we can disregard it later), and the other is dead against it!

The reporter of Frontline New Television, Mr. Adam Kaliher, was at a loss. These two shout, slam their fists on the table – they don't let me get a word in edgewise!

All right, I appease them somehow and explain to Mr. Kaliher that in every Serb there live many different Serbs.

The other day they quarreled again, while I was asleep. What was it about?

It seems that the man from Herzegovina dreamt, as usual, that he was at the front line with his people, and the Belgrader called him a warmonger and closed his part of the left auricle for him. I almost suffocated in that ugly dream.

When I woke up, I fried two eggs sunny side up and washed young horseradishes, but it was a no-go! The man from Herzegovina wouldn't eat and only looked at us with his mouth shut. He was on hunger strike. The Belgrader's food stuck in his mouth. He threw his fork onto the plate...

A well-known psychiatrist used to come to Ada Ciganlija, to cure his depression. He would sit on the bank all day long and stare at the river. I tell him about my problem and he says that I probably have a mild case of schizophrenia. Which is to say, a split personality.

"But, it is the three of us, not two!" I explained to him. "Is it possible for a personality to split into three?" And there could soon be even more of us! A few are already making occasional appearances: refugees from Sarajevo, Europeans, pacifists and warmongers, the Orthodox and the Slavophiles, diplomats and people with suicidal tendencies...

The psychiatrist told me that my case was quite unusual and that he had not come across anything like it in his practice:

"Put down on paper everything you feel,..." he told me. And that's what I'm doing. That's how I make my living.

"You could make your living by doing something more serious", grumbled the man from Herzegovina in me.

At that very instant a Belgrade belle passed by us.

307

Both the man from Herzegovina and the Belgrader turned to look at her.

I pretend I am not interested.

But they are unable to talk about anything but politics. Time and again they disagree on the issue of patriots and traitors. What am I to do?

I order a shot of grape brandy for the man from Herzegovina and a cold beer for the Belgrader. I take sedatives to help me bear them and go back to sleep.

Only, I shudder at the thought of having to wake up eventually…

GIRL SMOKERS

I notice that the number of girl smokers is constantly on the rise. You might say it's a nasty habit, and I couldn't agree more, but don't expect me to be disgusted! I even dare say – I like the way they do it, while swaying their bodies and holding prettily the burning cigarettes in their elongated fingers. I don't know why, but while I look at them, some of them remind me vividly of the portraits of Georges Sand, who, a long time ago, shocked her contemporaries with her long cigarette-holders and cropped hair. And these are the fruits of her wonderful, nutty rebellion, born so many decades later!

The only explanation, I think, is that we have finally become part of the world. We stopped being a small-town place in the Balkans. And those burning cigarettes in the hands of young women in the streets are one of many small proofs that essential changes have taken place, with us probably not even being aware of them.

I feel the pulsing of the big city, I feel the people in their kitchens, in their rooms, in attics, in cars, in underground passages, I feel the rhythm and hope, I see how the city heaves and grows, feeding on energy, space and youth... And in that great, feline leap forward, Belgrade skips centuries.

What a change! Only half a century ago the rules of bon-ton prescribed that young Belgrade women walk and behave humbly, look straight ahead, neither to the left nor to the right, with their eyes modestly cast down to the ground. According to the notes of old Belgraders, these virtuous brides walked with tiny, oriental steps and carried baking dishes full of pies to their mothers' and sisters' in law. Between the two wars they were also capable of pushing baby carriages devotedly, with the restrained pride of one who had carried the line forward. Their postwar successors marched proudly, with their heads held high, carrying flags and shovels.

The girls from the beginning of this incidental little note reflect in their gait something of each of these past epochs. They are taller than their mothers by a head, more liberated than their married elder sisters, more beautiful than any other Belgrade girls that have ever lived in this windy city. And, anyway, they have come the longest way: they smoke in the street and nobody finds it strange! And why would it be?

Or, perhaps, you'd prefer a Belgrade girl with a baking pan on her head, in lieu of a hat?

SUPER!

Many Belgrade girls wander all over the world...

Their moms, dads and grannies stayed behind. Just like their childhood rooms. The posters of Michael Jackson and Madonna on the walls, the old sneakers, broken tennis rackets, winter clothes, school notebooks, dolls, plaids and the sentences written in felt pen on the closet door:

"Sex isn't everything. There is something in holding hands, as well!"

Their neighborhood chums also stayed behind. They meet the girls' mothers every morning and ask the same question:

"How is Sneška? Does she call?"

Have you ever seen tears dropping on greens in a string bag?

The children of Belgrade sell trinkets on Charles Bridge in the golden city of Prague (and it seems it was only yesterday that we felt sorry for the poor Czechs); the finest Belgrade girls work as cloakroom attendants in New York, or as waitresses in Paris, or baby-sitters in London suburbs; occasionally, as poorly paid models in icy

Stockholm. Some of them work at night and study by day. They live by moonlighting.

Many ballet, English and piano lessons were wasted on them.

Munching a tasteless tuna fish sandwich, they dream of spring potatoes, which are about to appear at Kalenić market, and the first cherries, shiny with dewdrops…

They lost weight and turned adults prematurely, but they don't mention it when they call home, they say everything's super.

Granny has a weak heart. Dad is going to get drunk with despair. Mom dusts her room regularly, airs it and puts fresh flowers into the vase, as if she is going to breeze in suddenly, throw her bag on the sofa and yell from the door: "What's for grub?"

"Wash your hands first!"

"Oh, *Keva*, you're no fun!"

But she will not be present for Sunday dinner, which is inconsolably getting cold, and will not bring her best friend for whom a place was not set ("Look, I have nothing against your Ceca, but you have to tell us in advance if you are bringing someone to dinner. That's civilized behaviour!"). No one eats Sunday soup with boiled beef and homemade noodles, no one fights for the breaded chicken leg… To put it in simple terms, everyone misses that countless times repeated phrase, which gave flavour to their meals:

"Get your hair out of the soup!"

They are silent, but above the dishes an unutterable question hangs in the air:

"Dear God, does that child have anything to eat over there?"

Their closets with left-behind clothes are full of ghosts and pangs of conscience. There is the old raincoat, over which a bitter quarrel broke out some five years ago, and they were not on speaking terms with one another for two days. On the hanger, together with the raincoat, hangs also a famous sentence: "You already have two!" or: "What do you think, that money grows on trees!"

Also, there are many sleepless nights, the seasons of measles, mumps and whooping cough, the first prize for the essay "My Mother" and a bouquet of dried flowers fetched from the open-air school on Mt. Divčibare. Also, some undeserved slaps in the face, which resonate in the echo of the empty room, and the crying over the too long satin dress for the graduation party and its zipper which broke at the very last moment. The end of the world!

The panic when she did not return home before eleven p.m. as she was told to but at eleven fifteen, a cigarette accidentally found (Ah, she smokes!") and her father's reply: "So what, I also started smoking at sixteen!" "Yeah, you are just the person to set a good example!"

And now their princess, the pet and the apple of their eye, the smartest kid in school, waits on some stupid foreigners who, if justice prevailed in the world, would not be fit to clean her shoes, and the meal is getting colder and colder, Granny is looking for her pills, Dad is already on his third beer and goes to lie down for a while on the cot in her room.

Of course, she will come back one day, when all this passes…

Granny is right when she says that "no morning sun shines the whole day". The same applies to our adversaries!

Still, the girls will come back one day, exhausted from grappling with the battles for survival, somewhat tired, somewhat despondent, their eyes still having that hidden spark that the West did not manage to extinguish, the naiveté and hope; strangely stingy (although they used to be regular little spendthrifts), sure of themselves, full of distrust of people, with a slight foreign accent.

"Let's call the child, to see how she's doing", says Granny.

"But you called her only the other day", her father pretends to grumble. "Do you have any idea what our phone bill was last month?"

"And how much goes on your beer?" her Mom jumps at him. And, naturally, they call her, forgetting all about the time difference and not minding that on the other side of the Ocean it is still dawn. First they hear the murmur of the universe and the roar of the big lead-colored sea.

"Listen, they are bugging us again", says Dad.

The faraway ringing of the phone, quite unlike our ringing; it is strange and refined, somehow.

"What time is it over there?" Granny remembers that there must be some mix-up about time.

"Six o'clock."

"In the afternoon?" asks Granny.

"No, in the morning."

"And is it Sunday over there as well?"

"No, it's Thursday," says Dad, to confuse matters further.

The phone is still ringing and the tension in the kitchen is growing. Maybe she moved, or maybe there is someone with her, or maybe she sleeps at his place, or has something happened?

Finally, someone lifts the receiver – click. A voice, still warm from sleep, says:

"Heeeelllooo?"

"Sweetheart, how are you?"

"Super!"

WHAT ARE YOU DOING?

The other day, while walking in the street, I met a man whom I barely knew. The only thing I know about him is that he is retired and that in the past he held a certain high position where he did not overexert himself. Now he moves with dignity, his arms on his back, as if performing some ritual of inspection of the city and life in general. He asks what I've been doing lately.

What can I tell him?

"Nothing…"

"Are you writing?" he asks reproachfully, as if I hadn't done my homework.

"Yes, I am," I say apologetically.

"What are you writing?"

"Well, I write for the Sunday newspapers…"

"I know that," he cuts in. "I mean, do you write anything serious?"

"This is as serious as I can manage"! I excuse myself involuntarily, while this character, whom I hardly know, looks down on me as if I were a failed talent.

Still, he succeeds in imposing a feeling of guilt on me!

I go back home, lie down on my sofa, stare at the ceiling and ask myself – really, maybe I should be writing something more serious?

In the meantime, the character has erased me from his memory. He meets someone else and with his arms on his back asks him:

"What have you been doing lately?"

PASTRIES

This is not a big topic, but it is sweet – pastries!

Thanks to political commentators and chroniclers, future readers will undoubtedly know how we used to devour one another, but not what we had for dessert!

For that reason I see the pastry shops' windows as battlefields of historical struggles lost and won.

Baklava next to a Parisian tartlet – you can see that only in Belgrade! What a clash between the East and the West, what a Waterloo!

By invading us, the invaders also invaded our cuisine and our stomachs.

There are stories that in the past, when we were the Old Slavs, we used to eat honey and drink mead. Ice cream was nowhere in sight! There was too much ice in the river basins of the Oder, Vistula and Dnieper, where we originated.

During the five centuries of Turkish rule, we got used to oriental sweets. When we finally threw the Turks out, we kept their *baklava, tulumbe, kadaif, tufahije* and *ćeten-alva,* just like the Viennese bakers who still make their rolls in the shape of the Turkish crescent.

After having expelled them, we turned to Europe, naturally. Elderly Belgraders still remember many nice pastry shops between the two world wars that would not shame either Paris or Vienna. Belgrade housewives used to make quince 'cheese', almond puffs, ladies' fingers, walnut rolls, vanilla cookies, "princess-doughnuts"...

The new age brought along a collective style of ready-made sweets, manufactured impersonally, with no feelings for those intended to eat them, in gloomy state-owned pastry shops, where cheese pies and pastries with cracklings rotted under swarms of flies, next to chestnut purée and flat meringue puffs. The inscriptions on the wall read: "Do not spit on the floor!" and "With healthy food to a brighter future!"

One by one, the old Belgrade pastry shops with the typical Belgrade spirit and pedigree, frequented by old ladies who ate mignonette cakes with birdlike, pecking gestures, slowly folded.

Finally only three or four remained (in Sremska, Zmaj Jovina, Makedonska and Mišarska streets), resisting stubbornly the influence of the Orient, swarming in on us once more from all directions.

Tufahije are rolling down Banovo Brdo.

Sudžuk already got as far as New Belgrade.

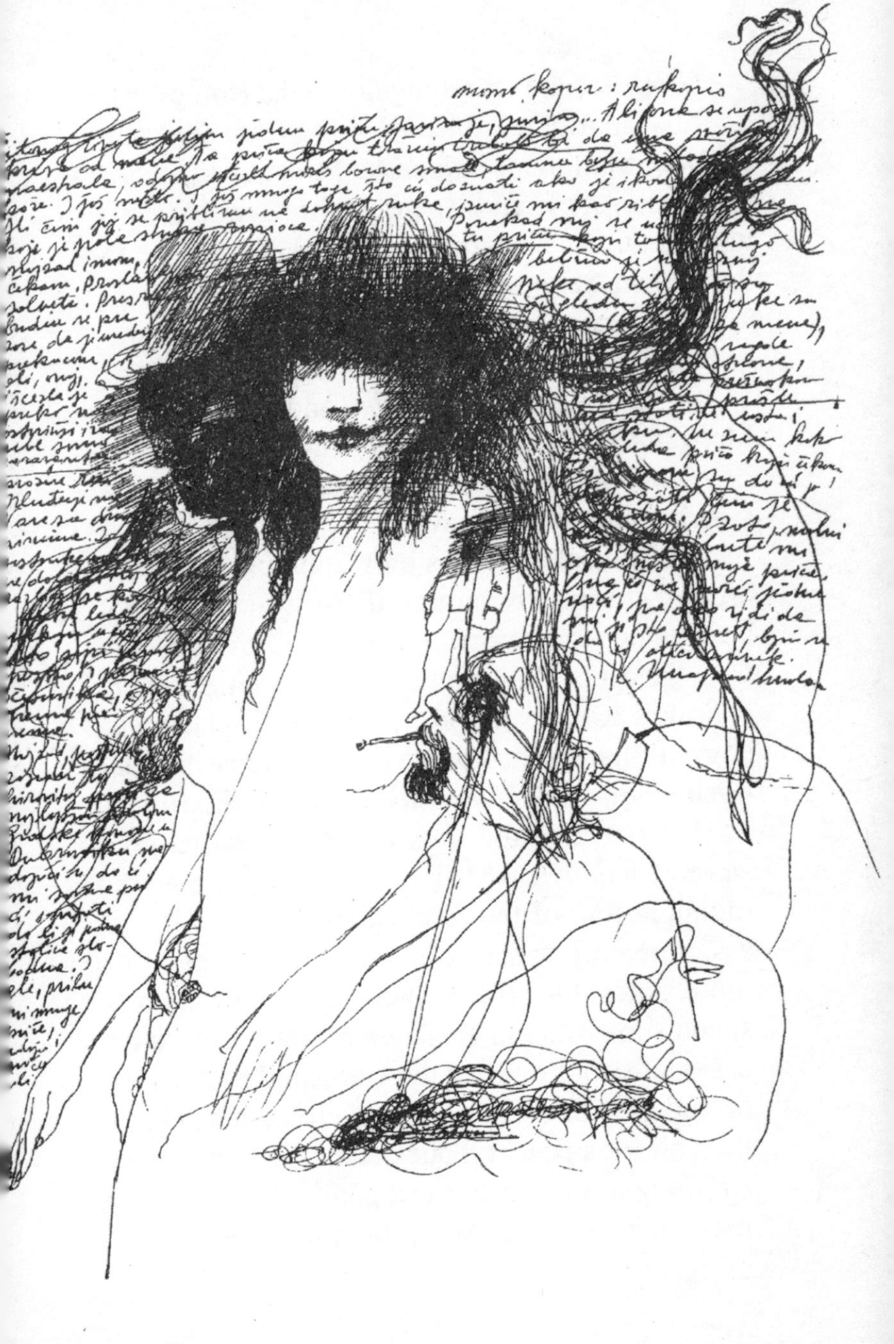

Urmašice are marching down the Boulevard.

Like an irrepressible tide rising from the Main Railway Station up Balkanska Street, *salep*, *boza* and lemonade from dispensers threaten to drown what little has remained of the sweet Europe in downtown Belgrade.

Ćeten-alva scared the "London almond bars" so badly that they melted away out of fear!

Sachertorte divorced *kadaif* and returned to its Mom in Vienna.

Tulumbe are scattering the frantic Mozart-kugeln every which way.

We can eat pancakes only at home. When we order them in a restaurant, if the waiter does not beat us up – we most certainly will get our due from the cook! Unlike other European cities, where pancakes are sold at every corner, we find them so unusual that we had to invent an impossibly derived word – *palačinkarnica* (pancake shop)!

I have nothing against *tahan-halva* and *sudžuk*; *baklava* is still a treat, the same as the midnight tour of the candied-fruit seller with his assortment of sweets to make our bitter nightlife more digestible. But a man, besides wishing to spend some time in an Oriental town, craves occasionally to drop in at the Gerbeaud pastry shop in Budapest or to have a bite of croissants in Paris. I am all for a peaceful coexistence between *Turkish delight* and Sachertorte, and I would like to make it public by beating on a *drum layer cake* with forks, as I have always had certain misgivings about all reforms, including the *reform layer cake*!

For all these reasons I lend moral support to the three remaining true Belgrade pastry shops, which have kept their souls. In the post-war times they were the first to make those big round cakes for patron saints' days, which we would buy furtively and carry home under our winter coats, as if they were heroin. Maybe they were, as we have been told repeatedly that religion is the "opium of the masses".

In the meantime, the new generations indifferently chew their gums and lick their ice creams, not noticing that anything is amiss.

Enjoy!

VANILLA COOKIES

I don't know the exact day of her first appearance at Kalenić market, perhaps it was a year ago, but I noticed her right away. Somehow she did not belong to the market crowd, noisy and frantic, sure of itself and the goods that were on offer...

Dressed in black, tiny as a bird, she stood there, lost among the counters and the big loud women selling eggs, home-made noodles, pastry for cheese pies, honey and yogurt. In front of her, on a metal counter, there were two trays with a neatly arranged assortment of cookies, as if prepared to be served on a patron saint's day.

Round vanilla cookies and wafers – the most common sweets of the poor in Belgrade.

It was an unheard-of wonder at Kalenić market! Everybody knows that from time immemorial pastries in Belgrade were sold in pastry shops only, but who knows what troubles made this tiny woman take her cookies out to the market, among the slaughtered chickens, *kajmak* from Čačak, pasta squares to be mixed with sautéed cabbage, and the smoked sheep meat from Zlatibor. Poverty made many Belgraders take out and sell everything they had in their households, so that the so-called green market was diminished by half and turned into a true flea market. Whoever had anything to sell – has sold it, but this old lady, probably a retired clerk, had nothing to sell. It occurred to her that she was well known in her street for her vanilla cookies (her whole yard smelled of vanilla powder sugar), and so she made two baking dishes of cookies and sold them quickly. Anyone who passed by her counter would be stopped in their tracks by that beautiful sweet smell and would not be able resist buying her cookies. The first time she went to the market she was, naturally, quite embarrassed. She was used to enquiring about prices at the market, and now she was standing on the other side of the counter and citing the price, with her eyes almost closed out of fear that the price was too steep, but it was so ridiculously low that the women who were selling home-made noodles nearby made her raise it. She, who could not make ends meet for one week on her pension and whose children had scattered all over the world, leaving behind two granddaughters from two failed marriages, found salvation in vanilla cookies. For, who makes them any longer, anyway? Young people buy sweets by the kilo in supermarkets and fashionable bakeries. Therefore, for those ladies who have forgotten all about vanilla cookies, I enclose this touching, old recipe:

Vanilla cookies. For vanilla cookies, prepare the following: two hundred and fifty grams of butter or two hundred grams of lard, half a kilo of flour, an egg yolk and one whole egg, four spoonfuls of sugar and the juice of one lemon. Beat the butter or lard until light and foamy, add the egg yolk, whole egg, sugar and lemon juice. Add the flour, put everything on a dough board, mix the dough and use a rolling pin to make a crust half a centimeter thick. Use a mold to make cookies out of the crust, dip each cookie into the foam of two beaten egg whites, strew with finely cut walnuts, arrange them in a greased baking dish, put it in the oven and bake, taking care that the cookies stay light in color. Spread jam over the baked cookies, join two and two together, sprinkle with powder sugar and scent with vanilla, and serve."

The vanilla cookies at Kalenić market are not just any old cookies for me – they are the image of Belgrade, pressed by wretchedness and misery, selling its last personal secrets!

I buy ten cookies, and the old lady gives me an extra one, which I put into my mouth on the spot. Look, it melts on my tongue right away – a real delight for the palate – and after many years I feel again the flavor of the long-gone backyards of Neimar in Cerska and Šumatovačka streets – the fragrance of recently baked vanilla cookies on an oval, yellow ceramic tray, a little chipped…

Your vanilla cookies, my dear lady, are absolutely priceless!

OBITUARY

Lately I meet an ever-growing number of Belgraders who boast about not reading newspapers any longer, not listening to the radio nor watching TV.

They say it's much better for them; they sleep better (and even dream in color), they don't get upset and their appetite is back.

Anyway, newspapers are becoming more expensive and on TV you only see horrors and hideousness.

What you don't see and don't read about – does not exist!

I am amused by this movingly naïve escape into a temporary happiness and serenity, so typical of Belgraders.

Good for them!

They'll never know who visited our country, who left it and what they declared.

Nor who spoke to whom, who received whom to their mutual satisfaction...

Those who abstain from reading newspapers and watching TV will not know what kind of weather they'll have the following day.

Partly cloudy, with winds blowing at a speed of about two meters, or sunny with possible local storms in the afternoon.

Those not watching TV don't know how much they are missing – they'll never know how Spanish media report on the situation in Vojvodina, what are the reactions in Greece, what are the decisions of European leaders, where the Queen of Great Britain intends to travel and what her foreign secretary had to say to that.

I wonder how they can live without knowing the results of the presidential elections in Cambodia or the outcome of the political upheaval in Japan? They don't give a second thought to the news that last week the election results in Nigeria were annulled. They did not even notice that the Big Rock asteroid failed to hitt the Earth by a mere ninety thousand miles.

They know nothing about wars and battles, about sporadic shootings, fierce reactions, counter-attacks, nor about the night that was relatively quiet…

When all is said and done, whether they read the papers or not – it makes no difference.

Neither those who avoid reading newspapers, nor we who read them, will be able to read the most important piece of news in our lives – our own obituary in *Politika*.

FISH CHOWDER

There is an island called Ada Ciganlija, on the Sava river.

A raft built on empty barrels is anchored next to Ada.

This raft houses the café called Embargo. It belongs to three mates: Boban, Drlja and Ciga, and because of them the café is also known as "At the Three Sanctions".

The river is as clean as can be.

That's because none of the factories upstream are operating.

In this way, willy-nilly, Belgrade became the first ecological city in the world.

They have few visitors – those who stumble on them by chance.

Boba, Drlja and Ciga make the best fish chowder on the river.

The only problem is that they get drunk by the time the chowder is ready.

And the chowder simmers on a low flame. It contains four kinds of fish: perch, bream, carp and catfish. A small jug is used to take water from the river, as specified in the recipe. Boban and Ciga lie on the grass, drink Banat Riesling and reminisce about the good old times. Fish jump from the river, nervous that they are not being caught. They are almost ready to jump into the kettle by themselves.

Way back, I knew a man who was fascinated by fish chowder. He was a painter called Jarak, from Čačak. During World War II he was a prisoner in a German camp and he was so hungry there that later, when he got out, he felt he never had enough food

to stuff himself.

He would come to the Šumatovac café around eleven a.m., with a recently finished painting; he painted flowers only. His flowers emanated some unusual, quiet joy. His bouquets consoled many a disappointed Belgrade lady. Jarak would prop his canvas against the chair and order a double portion of goulash. He was a stout man of low stature, with thick gray hair which shone like a lamp. At the beginning of his meal, the painting would cost as much as a double portion of goulash and a beer. But, the more he ordered, the higher the price went. It is a miracle how all that food – goulash, Wiener schnitzels and meat patties, fit into such a small man like Jarak. While eating pancakes for two, someone would come along and buy his painting and Jarak would go home to take a nap.

Fish chowder was what he most often dreamt of. He had an ingenious idea – to drill a hole in

Пензионисани рибар Деза Лукаш, који је
послење горине свог дугог живота провео
и крлми Мијал_ка, на Сави, на
Маришу, испод спорт Обреновачкт
_уна.

the Earth so that the water from the Pacific would get to the other side of the planet, where else but to Čačak, which for Jarak was the true center of the world.

He used to say enthusiastically:

"And then, you see, buddy, as the sea water is salty and full of fish, it would pass through the center of the Earth which is, clearly, red hot, and the fish would cook itself in it, and all ready and piping it would fall out from the other hole in Čačak, where we would, you see, put an enormous caldron and stuff ourselves to our heart's content!"

But, let's go back to the Embargo raft, where two out of the three "sanctions", Boban and Ciga, were preparing their Sava fish chowder, dreaming about rich guests who would happen to come by and get them out of a jam which had been following them for weeks on end.

At that instant the third partner, Drlja, appears from somewhere, bringing with him a roasted pig's head. It is not clear whether he was given it or stole it, but he certainly did not buy it! And as for stealing – he is not opposed to it!

Once, for example, he had to get up early, but he had no watch, so he nicked an alarm clock from a supermarket in Čukarica. He put it under his greasy straw hat, but when it was his turn to pay the cashier, the alarm clock began to ring full blast! Everyone turned to him, but Drlja kept his cool:

"Excuse me, Miss, which of my ears is ringing?"

And so Boban, Drlja and Ciga applied themselves to the pig's head while waiting for the fish chowder to be ready, but it turned out that one ear was undercooked. Boban threw it into the kettle and forgot all about it.

But, as fate would have it, that same night some really rich guests happened on them. They wanted to see the twilight on the Sava and to meet some original Ada dwellers. Naturally, they ordered fish chowder, for starters.

All of a sudden, a lady guest screamed and fainted – there was a pig's ear in her bowl!

They asked for an explanation from Ciga.

"Are you a waiter?" they asked, looking at the white tablecloth which he used for apron.

"No, I'm a ship's carpenter."

"Then get me the waiter", said the man in the white suit.

They dispatched Drlja to see him.

"Is this fish chowder?" asked another gentleman, in black suit and white socks, with a Rolex watch on his wrist.

"Yes, it is!" affirmed Drlja.

"Well, what is this, then?" asked the gentleman, pointing to the pig's ear.

"That's from the catfish!"

"Get me the owner!"

After a while, there appeared drowsy Boban, whom they managed to wake up at long last.

"What is this?"

"It's an ear", said Boban calmly.

"What is it doing in the fish chowder?"

"Well, I'll tell you in confidence – this is the way that the cops eavesdrop on guests!" replied Boban, ate the pig's ear, which was finally cooked to perfection, and went back to sleep.

JUVENILE INSANITY

I am going to describe for you a very strange encounter that of a friend of mine, a poet, had when he woke up one morning, sobered up, in a psychiatric ward. He used to go there from time to time, when he felt like seeing normal people and having agreeable chats. There he would get a free haircut, a shave and a good breakfast and no one was laughing at him when he said that he was "Oscar Wilde and that he had just had a child". Anyway, that morning, the poet saw an eighty-year-old woman, with her gray hair plaited into braids, skipping rope by his bed.

"What's your illness, Madam?" he asked her.

"Juvenile insanity", she twittered.

To tell the truth, it seems that the middle-aged Belgade has been afflicted by juvenile insanity. Grandpas run like mad in parks and along jogging tracks, regardless of the fact that the American who invented jogging dropped dead of a heart attack while running. You know what drunkards like to say – how could dropsy kill him when he drank by the gallon!

One spring day the late Zuko Džumhur was sitting with a friend of his at a table in a café on the Herceg-Novi promenade, when a man of their age ran by them, in a tracksuit, sweating profusely.

"Look at that fool", Zuko Džumhur said to his friend. "Allah gave us a determined number of steps that we are going to make in our lifetime, and he, like a madman, is in a hurry to spend them as quickly as he can!"

We are getting old, yes, we are, my dear reader, and there is nothing one can do about it. We do not run across the street any longer, we do not play chicken with the oncoming traffic – we look left and right and then, in the middle of the street, we suddenly feel so lonely and helpless, so unprotected and frail. Some people take aging in stride, others find it hard, while there are those who do not yield to old age.

Strolling along the jogging track in Košutn-jak, I came across a tree trunk.

"Walk over me!" it said.

I walked over it and found myself in front of a fence.

"Jump over me", said the fence.

I did, but then a ditch blocked my way.

"Go around me," said the ditch, and I went around it and got to a wooden board nailed to a tree, saying:

NOW INHALE DEEPLY THREE TIMES AND EXHALE SLOWLY!

I breathed in deeply three times and then slowly breathed the air out, until there was none left. I stuck my tongue out and just in case I said "Aaaaaa..." although there were no such instructions. Then I lit a cigarette.

"You are smoking on a jogging track!" a peer of mine, who was in good condition, was amazed. My peer, who was in good condition, had a tracksuit on and we met at the very spot where we were supposed to inhale three times deeply and exhale slowly. Were it not for that peer of mine, who was in good condition, I would have thought that I had lost my way in Alice's Wonderland and that any moment now I would come across the White Rabbit, which is notoriously late. But it was not a fairy tale. It was only a jogging track for people who were in good condition.

"So, you are smoking on the jogging track, ha?" he asked me disgustedly, while I sat on the tree trunk, swinging my legs and smoking. He had caught me *in flagrante delicto*, and I tried to change the subject.

"Tell me, please, what is better for our health – to run or to make love?"

"It has been proved scientifically", said he, "that it is much healthier to make love, as our whole body participates in the act."

"Why do you run, then?" I asked him.

"You see, it takes two to make love, and it is not always easy to arrange, while for running you

337

only need sneakers!" he replied and ran away across the meadow.

A Croatian poet, whose name I will not mention because it might seem that we used to be on friendly terms before the war (a possible source of trouble for me in my country), wrote an immortal poem on this topic:

Get old properly,
Get old with expedition.
I really hate those people
Who are in good condition!
Those who've given up
Smoking, girls and booze
And done all they could
Their former selves to lose…

But modern cities are made for young people only. I circle around the tables on the sidewalk in vain – they are all taken by hordes of kids. There is not a single dancing hall left where I could ask a lady of my age, with tiny wrinkles around her eyes, to dance with me the English waltz from the movie *Love in the Afternoon*. And I'm not in the mood to go down to some basements and shake like a palsied monkey. What I mean is that I like to touch and be touched while dancing. I like to whisper endearing words into someone's ear. I like to love and be loved!

338

The tyranny of youth squeezes me around my waist, chest, hips, legs and heart. I find it ridiculous to carry, at my age, a small ladies' bag for petty items or to fasten what looks like ammunition clip holders onto my belt. My ID card, in the back pocket of my slacks, is all shabby. The police cannot identify me as the photo is rather worn. I ruin my most expensive trouser belts by using a screwdriver to drill holes in them that are not supposed to be there, but which I need.

I don't have who to share meals with – everybody's on a diet!

Old coots run like mad on jogging tracks and sweat in saunas. Recently they discovered tennis. Some of them, when young, used to make their living by collecting tennis balls for fine people, vowing to plough over all tennis courts once they come to power. Now some other tykes collect the balls, while the former collectors yell to each other "game" and "break"! They are disgustingly tanned. They are insufferably young. It's enough to drive one mad.

The cities are replete with young old men and fake young men, with grannies who look like their granddaughters' elder sisters.

My peers play football or basketball every Saturday. More often than not someone's leg is broken, or someone's spine gives away, or someone's head is gone. And the worst of all is that, no sooner having lost two hundred grams during the match, they go to the café by the football ground, drink a crate of beer, wolf down a whole tray of pork and veal in aspic, followed by calf's head in tripe, and gain two kilos each on the spot.

But, what counts is that, at least, they are not at home!

REVERSE

Recently there appeared on Ada Ciganlija a new face, with a brand new boat and an even newer engine. A Doctor! While we lie around on the anchored raft, two old Ada dwellers, Isa and Mile the Chicken, just for the kick of it, dive in, turn the propeller back to front, get out and continue to doze in the weak sun.

Finally, here he comes to the anchorage. He gets into his boat, polishes it, plugs the reservoir cable in and turns the engine on. But the boat starts to move backwards, stern first. It almost collides with the other boats. The Doctor, totally bewildered, opens the throttle, but the boat keeps moving backwards!

"What's the matter with this boat, people, in the name of God?" he asks Isa and Mile the Chicken.

"It's the gasoline, as far as I can tell", says Mile the Chicken.

"What do you mean – the gasoline?"

"Where did you fill 'er up?" Isa asks him.

"In Čukarica", says the Doctor.

Смиьанилев силов

"I thought as much..." says Mile the Chicken philosophically.

"What's wrong with the gasoline from Čukarica?"

"That gas station sells gasoline from Albania, for reverse gear only", say Mile the Chicken. "That's the catch!"

"In Banovo Brdo they sell gasoline from Greece, for sailing bow-first", adds Isa with the air of someone in the know.

The Doctor packs up, gets into his car and drives to Banovo Brdo.

Mile the Chicken and Isa dive in again, put the propeller in its regular position. The Doctor comes back, pours the new gasoline in and starts the engine. The boat moves properly.

"What am I to do with this 'reverse' gasoline?" asks the Doctor. "Maybe you could use it?"

"Much obliged", Isa gives his thanks to the Doctor. "We live in reverse anyway!"

HOMECOMING

Each December the West lets our people go home to see their families. The West, naturally, does it for its own Christmas and not for ours, but our people rob the West of a couple of days, just to satisfy their yearning for the *badnjak* (Yule log), as they are fed up with fir trees only.

Here they are, then, after a long time, in their hometown, but Belgrade has turned into a rather run-down place, just like the first love who for a long time lacked make-up and new clothes and decided to give up the fight and indulge in eating pastries with cracklings washed down with yogurt. Truth be told, she still resembles her old self, wonderful and unique, but it seems that some of her magic and mysterious splendor, which made her absolutely irreplaceable, is gone. When covered with snow, the old love looks as if it were dressed in a precious white polar fox fur coat, but as soon as the snow melts, its inconsolable decay rises to the surface; the plaster falls off the façades, the antique ornaments crumble away, and the mud from Mali Mokri Lug and Batajnica crawls in and infiltrates itself slyly into the once untouchable downtown Belgrade. Belgrade is supposed to be festively decorated with lampions and shining garlands, but every now and then the bulbs give up the ghost, grieving for the better days gone by.

They longed so much to see it while out there in the wide world, and now, when they made it here, full of nostalgia and sweet expectations, they almost regret having come at all – the city was much nicer in their dreams. Who, for example, could imagine the odor of sauerkraut from the cellar, rising up the stairs, together with the smell of many a roux, and impregnating all the apartments in the building with the smell of the Balkans and Eastern Europe, still not able to break off with the old times. And who can tell them why, in their own dining room, in the chandelier with supposedly twelve bulbs, only one is left to shed its meager light?

And that's how our man from the West, after a long time sleeps in his former room, and his *Keva* makes his cot longer by putting a stool at its end, for he has outgrown his berth by now. And so he lies in his unheated room and looks at old posters on the walls: James Dean, Jimi Hendrix, Janis Joplin, a psychedelic skyline of Manhattan, old sneakers hanging from a nail and a stringless guitar, a framed diploma and a letter from a friend who invited him to go to the West and start a new life there – the things which made him leave home and go to the place from which he returned a winner, after many long years. It was the post-cards that prompted us to leave, by awakening our desire to see the wide world. He is under the impression that in the meantime everything has grown smaller somehow. Is it possible that I studied in this small kitchen for my final exam, our man asks himself? It was the only room that was heated in wintertime, and in his child's eyes the cupboard on which a balance with weights and a brass mortar and pestle stood – as indeed they still stand today – was bigger than Notre-Dame Cathedral.

The bedroom was not heated in winter, naturally, so he and his brother drew matchsticks to see who would be the first one to crawl into the icy bed, with the bed linen almost crackling from cold, to make the berth warm for the other one. His granny was privileged: they placed tiles in the oven of their old stove, wrapped them in a towel and, once warm, put them under the eiderdown before she went to bed. In the yard Papa chopped wood for the fire, cursing his fate and his maker. They bathed on Saturday afternoons only, in a bronze bathtub, having started the fire an hour earlier under the red tin caldron (the maternal grandfather of today's boiler) with a manometer for gauging the steam pressure, which rumbled and puffed like a locomotive on a narrow gauge railway tracks.

Who took daily showers daily in those times? Only whores and American spies! Serbs are known to believe that your skin gets thinner if you bathe too often. We bathed only when we got really dirty, but even then we did not stink— on the contrary, we smelled of the *Schicht* soap, and our hair smelled of vinegar. It's been a long time since our man in the wide world smelled in his nostrils the exciting fragrance of vinegar in the hair of Belgrade girls. There, where he resides now, he takes showers both in the morning and in the evening, after work, but he still cannot oust the smell of futility from his skin.

Keva is eating her heart out: she wanted to paint the apartment before her son's arrival, but the painter did not finish the dining room. Besides, he is drunk all the time. Not to mention the ladders and buckets all over the apartment. A disaster!

As for food, it's a real orgy of long-forgotten flavors. First of all, the *sarma* with spare ribs, cooked in a big pan with white dots and cracked blackened rims, just like the dentures of the surviving neighbors and best friends who came to lunch. His *Keva*, namely, mistrusts the Zepter utensils that he gave her as a present on some earlier occasion; she still cooks in the old pan from her childhood, and the Zepter set stands in the cupboard and serves to boast in front of her guests about her son's generosity. She says she is so used to her old pan that she knows the exact quantity of ingredients needed for any dish. The pork and veal aspic are golden and shaky, the melted cheese drips from the corn bread, apple fritters await their turn ... after each *sarma* roll our man from the wide world calculates how long he will have to jog when he goes back there; every crackling raises his blood pressure and blood sugar by a notch, sends him into throes of guilt while visualizing his next meeting with the expensive physician who takes care of his health, but, in spite of all, his *Keva's* sautéed sauerkraut and liverwurst win the battle which he had lost in advance. "You only live once!" he thinks. "I don't give a fig for what Elsa will say over her oatmeal bowl when I get back. But, I swear, starting tomorrow, not a bite more than prescribed by the astronauts' diet."

And the following morning the painter appears, with his two assistants, to finish the dining room and take away his tools. At ten, as expected, he sends his apprentice to the bakery and the butcher shop to buy breakfast for them. Our man from the wide world happens on them by accident and, lo and behold: he sees the most beautiful still life, spread on newspapers – half a kilo of headcheese, tiny hot peppers from the jar and freshly baked bread with a pink and crunchy crust. He said to them, "Enjoy your meal", and they unanimously answered "Thank you, please help yourself". That was all he was waiting for.

And here is the sight which would make the blood freeze in the veins of his employees out there in the world: the powerful man sits on a covered bucket full of peach paint and tears at the loaf of white bread with three house-painters, stuffing himself full of headcheese and beer, which he drinks straight from the bottle.

THE FOOL

"You fool!" this beautiful girl screamed at me through the open window of her fast and expensive car, which she was driving at breakneck speed. She barely missed me on the zebra crossing.

Well, if you ask if I had a few – yes, I had, and I don't deny it. I was standing in the middle of the zebra crossing and her posh car almost grazed me. It happened at the intersection of Skadarska and Twenty-ninth of November streets.

"You, fool!" – the words were hurled at me from the immediate vicinity, in a young voice full of some strange Belgrade charm, a combination of mischief and female neuroticism, which I absolutely adore in Belgrade women.

And so I was standing there, at the top of Skadarlija, just across from Dva Bela Goluba (The Two White Doves), looking down the street which resembled the ninth circle of hell, what with music and clouds of barbecue grill smoke pouring out of it. If you are a person who stands on his dignity you must wash your hair after strolling through this street, lest it should smell of *ćevap-*

čići, pljeskavice and *gyros*. And while standing there, in the middle of the night, I realized what a fool I had been.

It all started over forty years ago (a whole span of a human life), when in the small kitchen of the shabby cottage next to the restaurant Tri Šešira (The Three Hats) restaurant I sat at the table together with Zuko Džumhur, architect Uglješa "Yogi" Bogunović and some other people, and when, in that small, illicit eating place Yogi had a brainstrom – to raise Skadarlija from the dead. Its lanterns were all broken, the cobblestoned streets potholed and patched up all over again, and the light in the three remaining eateries was dim, with the bulbs all coated with dead flies. I must say that the food there was good and cheap, though: bean soup, tripe, pigs' trotters in sauce, and naturally, *spritzer.* After its romantic past, Skadarlija, to which some of the most beautiful pages of Serbian literature had been devoted, seemed to have snuffed out its stars in the period of "socialism with a human face".

And so, we started from scratch. First Yogi turned Skadarlija into the first pedestrian zone in Belgrade, then Zuko Džumhur made most attractive chandeliers from brandy shot glasses or jiggers for Tri Šešira, which sparkled like the most precious Murano crystal. Following that, Zuko and Yogi hauled from someplace in Vojvodina three beautiful 19th-century ceramic tile stoves and

351

out of the three they made one, in the tavern Zlatni Bokal (The Golden Mug), where it is still in use. The sculptress Milica Ribnikar built a beautiful fountain at the top of Skadarlija, and the painter Mario Maskareli adorned the restaurant Ima Dana (There Are Days) with portraits of celebrities. Finally, Yogi and myself created from our imagination the restaurant Dva Bela Goluba, where my old pastels can still be seen on the walls.

Very soon after that, things took off like a charm. Young people from Belgrade "dormitories", prompted by nostalgia, swarmed on Skadarlija. The real estate in this street, where we replaced even the cobblestones, turned out to be the most expensive in Belgrade, beating even New York City.

The house in which Đura Jakšić had spent the last years of his life was razed to the ground and rebuilt again. The house, with its earthen floor and two damp little rooms, was so pitiful that Đura Jakšić, ashamed of its wretchedness, did not let anyone in. Now the poet and the painter finally got a spacious house befitting him, with an office and a restaurant in the basement, and a garden to be opened in front of it soon. The sculptor Jovan Soldatović placed in front of the house one of the most beautiful sculptures in town, depicting the poet with his hat pushed back on his head and slightly tipsy, sitting there and trying to make up his mind whether to go in at all. One of my old

friends, Žika *Pljeskavica*[10], the owner of the café, a legendary opponent of McDonald's hamburgers, set a table in front of the monument to Đura, and the waiters occasionally put on it a jug of wine and a siphon of soda water. Could there be a more fitting ambiance for the poet!

Many of my friends with whom I, as a young writer, restored Skadarlija to its old splendor, are already dead, but their spirits sometimes, in some mild autumn night, still wander through this legendary street, finding their way laboriously among the tables which have made the cobblestones almost invisible.

In Skadarlija restaurants, dinner is obligatory, instead of love. The residents of the few remaining apartment buildings sleep with ear plugs in their ears and already shake slightly with some unknown disease. The cats hide in dumpsters and stray dogs avoid this neighborhood.

Well, there I was, standing at the top of Skadarlija, while the lovely and vibrant young voice still echoed in my ears: "You fool!"

The girl did not crush me with her car, but with her voice.

If she is ever to read this little story, she'll know that she was right.

I really was an honest-to-God fool forty years ago when I was raising Skadarlija from the dead.

---

[10] *Pljeskavica* – a hamburger-like spiced grilled meat patty, a much-beloved national specialty.

354

SKADARLIJA

Going down the cobblestoned Skadarlija Street to Bajloni's open market, I pass by the bronze statue of Đura Jakšić, sculpted and mounted in front of the house at No. 34 by the brilliant sculptor Jovan Soldatović. With the cape over his shoulders and his hat pushed back on his head, my neighbor Đura sits outside the house in which he died in 1878. He looks as if he came back at dawn, rather tipsy, and decided to sit down on the steps, after having whiled away the night, and have a breather before going to sleep.

In the morning Skadarlija looks freshly shaved and washed up, like a drunkard who wants to conceal the telltale signs of a night on the town. It resembles a country street, which unexpectedly found itself in the metropolis. Old ladies sit on benches, the waiters read newspapers, and table-cloths are freshly starched. The first autumn leaves look for vanished poets, to fall on them and become part of a poem.

"Good morning, neighbor!" I say to Đura Jakšić, just in case. Occasionally, in a neighborly way, I borrow some blue color from his *Girl in Blue*.

"Any luck with the paintings?" I ask, to pass the time.

"None…" answers the bronze painter.

The same situation as on the day he returned from the Drina battlefield, where he had been a war reporter. It was in 1876, during the war between Serbia and Turkey, when he kept company with an Italian volunteer, a Garibaldian on the Drina front, Antonio Paganini.

"Ashamed of the miserable area where he lodged, the poet did not disclose his address to anyone, including his relatives or best friends," wrote down Arsa Pajević.

Nowadays children sit in Đura's bronze lap.

A little bit higher up from Đura's house, at Zetska Street No. 2, there is a plaque with a succinct inscription: "This house rejoiced in the presence of Branislav Nušić". Milan Predić wrote down:

"Many mornings I used to see Nušić crossing the huge backyard, wan from the lack of sleep and yellowish from the cigarette smoke and café air. These nightly sprees, even without heavy drinking, were ruining his strength…"

Other contemporaries also remembered Nušić's nightly binges in Skadarlija, affirming that he never overindulged in drinking, but mostly smoked cigarettes, drank countless cups of coffee and entertained his company with his stories.

Another dweller of Skadarlija, Jovan Dučić, temporarily ousted from diplomatic service for the

lack of a university degree, worked for a year as a journalist for the daily *Politika*. On October 5th, 1908, following the news of the Austrian annexation of Bosnia, he wrote an announcement, saying: *Belgraders, The Fatherland Is In Danger!* In the wake of the proclamation, one half of the inhabitants of Belgrade, which at that time numbered barely fifty thousand people, went out to what is now Republic Square. On October 7th, Branislav Nušić, pen name Ben Akiba, also a journalist at *Politika*, led the Belgraders to demonstrate outside the Ministry of Foreign Affairs. Along the way, the demonstrators placed him on a white horse, preceded by a certain Milisav, a giant man with the Serbian tricolor flag in his hands. Pushed by the demonstrators, on the back of the horse which reared and neighed, Nušić found himself in the Ministry hall, where the doorman Jovan, on seeing him, exclaimed frantically:

"No, for the love of God, Mr. Nušić! Don't enter the Ministry on horse!"

Hardly keeping himself upright on the back of the frenzied horse, Nušić replied:

"This would not be the first horse, Mr. Jovo, to enter the Ministry."

Writers and journalists, actors and bohemians, joined the ranks of volunteers for the Drina front, among them Vladislav Ribnikar, the founder of *Politika*, the legendary Diša Stevanović, who carried the whole editorial desk on his shoulders, the unavoidable Jovan Dučić…

In the fall of 1994 someone delivered to my address in Skadarlijska Street a white horse of Scottish breed. It was a bottle of whiskey called *The White Horse.* When we finished "the horse" we moved to Dva Jelena (The Two Deer). Dusk was falling and the Skadarlija night, full of cacophony, was about to start.

"What kind of people are you?" an accidental tourist, a foreigner, asked me.

"Crazy," I replied, recalling the splendid title of the late Jovan Rašković's book.

There is no shorter street in Europe with more music. A *tamburitza* orchestra, full of optimism, starts to play *Hey, a rotten plank / So the boat sank.* Outside Đura's house, an ensemble of music veterans plays, free of charge, for the strollers in Skadarlija *Oh, my darling, I love you, dee-doo lee-doo doo...*

A well-known Belgrade poet, Petar Pajić, born in Valjevo, climbs the stage and recites in his stentorian voice one of his poems:

The Serbs sit in an inn,
Some drunk, some done in!
By the road the Serbs lie low,
From their heads the trees grow...

At that moment, in Dva Jelena a Russian brass orchestra thunders the notes of *The March on the Drina!* Where did they spring form? Half of them are Cossacks and the rest stayed here after the tour of the Aleksandrov Russian army orchestra and vanished from sight. The conductor failed to get hold of them and take them back to Russia.

Reacting to this, our musicians start to howl *Ryabinushka*, and then, joined by the Russians, launch into *Đurđevdan!* A former tenor appears from somewhere and spills out his belcanto *I'll Return to Sorento*. Petar Pajić continues to thunder from the stage:

> *And from every Serb's head,*
> *Three murky rivers led...*
> *Karađorđe, the Serb's pride,*
> *Killed by one of his own side.*
> *And the place of that fight*
> *By the Serbs is called Delight.*[11]

Listening to *O, Sole Mio,* a local drunkard came up with a philosophical thought: "A tenor is not an occupation – it is a state of mind!"

When the general crescendo reached its culmination, a brass band from Dragačevo showed up, with their nicked and chipped trumpets. *Hey, the green walnuts fell on the ground / Hey, baby, how does a little ... sound?* Three Russians found

---

[11] Karađorđe, the leader of the First Serbian Uprising, was killed on the orders of Prince Miloš in the village of Radovanje, whose name can mean "delight" or "joy".

themselves under the table, and three Belgrade ladies on the table! They are called "the table ladies", since they can't resist dancing on the table. From the tavern Šešir Moj (My Hat) comes the sound of a *tamburitza* played by the Gypsies from the plains: *Hey, the Stukas fly, the airplanes fly...* Everyone plays his own music, trying with all his might to outdo the others.

Skadarlija is gradually turning into something like New Orleans's Bourbon Street.

THE GUARDIANS
OF SKADARLIJA GATE

If you want to enter Skadarlija by car, you have to pass though a huge wrought-iron gate, at the very spot where Gospodar Jevremova Street ends and Skadarska Street commences. The gate is guarded by day by one Uncle Lale, a retired journalist, and by night by one Mića, a passionate chess player and avid reader. Uncle Lale's job is less interesting, as he is there during the day when lots of lorries loaded with crates of various drinks, supply vans and small refrigerator trucks delivering fish and meat for restaurants, enter Skadarlija, particularly in the morning hours... From time to time there appears in this steep, cobblestoned street, an armored van, bringing fresh money to the National Bank. But, all told, Uncle Lale can drink his beer at ease, sitting at the table in the company of the poet Đura Jakšić in bronze, outside the house where he lived and died.

If he were a writer, Mića could have written many stories or novels about those entering Skadarlija at dusk and leaving at dawn. Couples come at about eight p.m. –a man dressed to kill with a lady on his arm who went to a lot of trouble to look her best for the evening outing. The uneven cobblestones are the sworn enemy of her high heels, which frequently go askew and break in the contact with the Turkish times. Full of expectations and all smiles, these happy couples scatter into nearby restaurants, where some true miracles may await them. One may propose, another may break off a seemingly solid relationship of many years at the most unexpected moment. Mića is in a position to see some women run off with tears in their eyes and make-up running down their cheeks, but also others who leave hand-in-hand, after having entered through his gate with someone else. He will also welcome freshly shaved musicians and their instruments, and usher them out in the early hours of dawn with the stubble on their cheeks again and their ties askew and hanging loosely from their no-longer-white collars. He unlocks and locks the rusty padlock on Skadarlija gate, and from time to time he is temporarily out of job, as his place is occasionally taken by a squadron of inconspicuously clothed men in gray, with a slight bulge under their armpits. For example, both Mića and I saw with our own eyes Lord Owen eating *ćevapčići* with onions and drinking white wine in the company of Cyrus Vance. He must have found Belgrade, as regards its male population, the most elegant place in Europe, as all tables at Tri Šešira

(The Three Hats) were occupied by men in impeccable suits who only drank fruit juices and kept their eyes on the VIPs. Only the orchestra was the same as always, and it successfully played a song which explained to the visitors the politics of the host country in the best possible way: *Come on, Jana, come on, sweetheart, let's sell the house / Let's sell it now, in order to dance as we know how!"*

But, one cannot say that the life in Skadarlija runs smoothly all the time. My problem, for example, is to get down to Bajloni market unnoticed, and, what's worse, to climb back, passing the rows of tables on the sidewalk, where, from the early hours of the morning (some did not go home at all) sit the people I know, inviting me to join them for a drink. You don't spur a willing horse! But nevertheless I'm a strong character and I always get back home with my shopping bag full, like every good housekeeper. The only problem is that more often than not the vegetables and meat get there in time for dinner, not for lunch! During these morning open-air sessions I am often invited to visit someone or to hear stories that I jot down later on and make my living out of them.

Among many others, I received an invitation from a wine drinker to visit him at his summer home somewhere on the Danube. He promised to make a real feast – goose cooked the Romanian way.

"How do you prepare goose the Romanian way?" I asked him.

"First you steal it and then you roast it like a chicken!"

Another one, who lives in Skadarska Street, did not go home for days on end because his apartment was being painted. He is not inclined to novelties or to the latest vogue that all rooms have to be painted white. He prefers, he says, the old-fashioned *štricla,* with the patterned roller and the straight line separating the ceiling from the walls. He dropped by his apartment yesterday, to check on the works, but the painter was dead drunk and asleep at the top of the ladder, while the separating line went zigzag, all awry and uneven. When he objected to the state of affairs, the painter shook off his sleepiness and appeased him by saying that the line would "straighten out and tighten up once it was dry!"

I am not a celebrity, but nevertheless I am well guarded in this city. Uncle Lale looks after me by day and good Mića by night. As in these hard times I'm often short of money to give them a tip, like I should, I dedicate to them this small medallion about the guardians of Skadarlija gate.

TOULOUSE-LAUTREC
IN SKADARLILJA

As I get older, I leave Skadarlija less and less frequently… If so many Belgraders come to the cobblestoned Skadarska Street every night, why should I go out to where they come from willingly? This is probably the best place to be – otherwise they would not be rushing here.

I am accustomed to sitting at the corner of Zetska and Skadarska streets, in what used to be an old and shabby optician's shop, and is now an art gallery known as *Monmartre*. The gallery, as if fallen from the sky, is the property of a Mr. Pierre Božović, who spent a good part of his interesting life in France. Nostalgia for those days prompted him to name the gallery after the famous Parisian quarter – the gathering place of painters and other artists. Strangely, Skadarlija, as it used to be, was never known for its painters, but rather for actors and poets. Namely, painters prefer to live high up, in attics and lofts, where the light is at its best and the rent at its lowest. High-rises were rare in Skadarlija, it was an area of small houses and lean-tos, where a man who had had one too many was never in danger of tumbling down the stairs.

Your chronicler had the rare privilege of having his painting celebrating Toulouse-Lautrec become something of a hallmark of the gallery. Namely, I once painted a portrait of Toulouse-Lautrec on an old dishcloth, bought some twenty or so years ago at the Clignancourt flea market in Paris and featuring Toulouse-Lautrec's Aristide Briand, a well-known Parisian turn-of-the-century chansonnier. It seems that Toulouse-Lautrec feels quite at home in Skadarlija. At night, when Pierre and his guests leave, he leaves his framed dishcloth and crosses the street to the Spasojević bakery for a kidney goulash and a loaf of bread. After that he goes to the restaurant Dva Jelena (The Two Deer), sits way in the back and sips his grape brandy until morning, when he can be seen wobbling up the street and tiptoeing through the keyhole into Pierre's gallery and back into his frame.

From time to time Pierre has to leave the gallery for an hour or so on some errand, and he leaves me in charge of *Monmartre*, to mind it and talk with visitors and buyers. For this service I am paid in whisky. I drink it straight, no ice, just like the Scots, who invented it, do. If whisky went well with ice – they say – we would bottle it that way!

Once Skadarlija becomes deserted, I talk to the paintings on the walls. I used to know the painters, even kept company with several. Some of them were not on speaking terms with each other, but time reconciled them. Here they are now, in Skadarlija, waiting patiently to see what is going to happen with their names and works. They have all the time in the world. And their paintings travel through that time, changing owners and room walls.

A STROLL IN KALEMEGDAN

There is a very nice path for strolling in Kalemegdan, in the shadow of the old fortress, suitable for lovers and those who have been defeated and now avoid people's gazes. If the weather is nice, you can meet on the path two old gaffers, one a retired general from Montenegro, and the other, his compatriot who opted for the Cominform. On the island called Goli Otok, the general was the interrogator of the old supporter of the Cominform, his former war comrade.

Both of them are tall, bony and hot-tempered people. When they take a nap after lunch, their families go on tiptoe. Originating from Crmnica, they are both obstinate. Even though both of them know that they will meet every day on the same path and that they have to pass each other, almost touching shoulders, they do not give up or change the place and the time of their morning stroll. It seems to be a tacit matter of honor.

When discussing the subject of the Cominform, the general would often say:

"Had we not jailed them in 1948, they would have jailed us!"

The old Cominform supporter keeps asserting that as early as 1948 Joseph Vissarionovich had been absolutely right. He had realized the dangers of revisionism by then. A visionary! And what happened? Now you have it! They sold out their empire to the American capitalists and servants of imperialism!

When they pass by each other, they cast their eyes down, dark, silent, frowning... When they meet for the fifth time, they look at each other for a second, and the old sparkle of hatred appears in their old, extinguished eyes:

"The same to you, fellow", says the general through his clenched teeth.

INFLATION

An old lady, who lives in Kosovska Street, takes her daily walks in Tašmajdan Park. To get to the park she has to cross the noisy Takovska Street, in front of the Main Post Office. At the corner of Kosovska and Takovska streets there is a traffic light, with the longest-lasting red light in town. Some Belgrade boys know it very well, and at this very corner they jump on the hoods of the waiting cars to wash their windshields. Between the red and the green light they manage to wash some three to four windshields. It is not a very neat job, and drivers often get angry with them, but the boys do not mind. They pass their dirty cloth and a squeegee over the glass a couple of times and ask to be paid. Drivers give them money, just to get rid of them. But, still, these kids do not rob or steal; from early childhood they try to earn a couple of bucks!

The old lady I mentioned before, a retired physician, who has been crossing Takovska Street at the same corner for years, knows almost all of them. Her favorite is a boy who, you could say, has grown up before her eyes. Today he is a good-looking, slim youngster, with dark curly hair, quick and diligent, the leader of his small group.

As the time goes by, the nice old lady is getting smaller and smaller and the boy taller and stronger. He jumps on the waiting cars from a running start and throws himself on the windshield, as if taming a bull and not a machine.

The blockade is on. Poverty. Inflation. The old lady persists in going to Tašmajdan Park, albeit not as elegant as she used to be. One day, on the spur of the moment, the boy puts aside his cloth and sponge, signals her to stop and pushes a thick bundle of paper notes into her hands.

The old lady is befuddled. Not ever in her life has anybody pushed money on her. She tries to give it back to the boy, but he is already washing another car, wiping the windshield with quick and resolute gestures.

"Please…" mutters the old lady, trying to pass the money back to him, but her soft voice is not heard in the noise of rumbling cars. "Please…"

"Take it!" the boy shouts. "I don't need it! There is plenty more where this came from!

Dazed, she crosses the street, firmly holding a bundle of notes in her hand and not knowing what to do with it. Then she enters the small Russian church, where the choir's song is mixed with the fragrance of incense. She puts the crumpled notes on the stand and takes two thin candles. She lights them separately for the dead and for the living, and prays for the boy, his parents and for all of us in our wretched circumstances.

Then she goes home and writes me a letter about what has happened, and I am retelling it to you rather clumsily.

I wish the boy from the intersection of Kosovska and Takovska streets would happen to come across these lines and find out how his money was spent.

AT THE OPEN MARKET

If you don't go to open markets, you'll never get to know the Serbian people. It is true that they like to short-weigh their goods, that they like to steal, and also to haggle, but once it is over and they have scored in this little game, just at the moment when a customer opens his bag to receive onions or potatoes in it, at that very moment, when the fraud is over and the slyness and short-weighing done with, the peasant will steal a glance at you, remember his God and with a broad gesture of his hand, as if giving you a blessing, will add a potato or an onion, to atone before people and Heaven.

"Here goes," he'll say, "this will not ruin either you or me!"

In the West no one will short-weigh you, not even by a gram (their scales are electronic, though), but at the same time will not add a single lentil pea more than you have paid for. Let them short-weigh me even by half a kilo; that one extra potato is more precious to me than the whole potato production in Idaho!

And another thing, our people are endowed with an innate megalomania… They never put on the scales the quantity you ask for, always more. If you want to buy a kilo of apples, there is always a kilo and a half on the scales, and the peasant woman does not fail to ask: "Why not take two kilos?"

You reply that you want one kilo only, but she has already weighed two and garnished them with a piece of advice:

"Take two, *bre*! It's better to have them in excess than to pine for them!"

ON OLD TIMES

Engrossed in tumultuous historical upheavals, we tend to miss the change of seasons. We have lost the naiveté and innocence of the times gone with the wind. When we put down the newspapers for a moment and look around, there – it is spring-time and we have grown old; young beauties pass by, pretending not to see us. I hear one of them telling her friend that she knows a man who is aw-fully old – he must be forty at least! On their slim shoulders they carry small backpacks, as if ready to push off any moment to some Promised Land and new adventures. Our backpacks were bulky and heavy, either the ones for hiking, or the other ones, from the time of the German occupation, containing the bare essentials for survival in exile or for the black market. We regularly read the obituaries and comment on the passing of some-one we used to know: What a pity, he was only 75! And it seems that only yesterday we were twenty and waiting for the elderly people of 35 to go away and make room for us...

As for the seasons, we were waiting for their changes as we used to wait for the few movie houses to change their repertoire.

Another thing has completely turned around in the way of our family life, without anyone having paid much attention to it: our children go out at night at the hour we had to be back home, for fear of our fathers. That is to say that young Belgraders, as a rule, go out at midnight, and return at dawn. Had they, at least, gone on a binge, we would say that they were carrying on the glorious tradition of their fathers. But what did they do? Drank Coca-Cola! Why do they have to go out so late? Because the discotheques which they frequent open their doors at midnight. If, for example, they got there at nine – they'd make a laughing-stock of themselves. In order to protect them from possible traumas, we let them go out late at night, albeit unwillingly, as all other parents do.

I recall, with a mild melancholy, the bickering between a friend of mine, a Dalmatian, and his father, when on one occasion the latter started to scream at his son for having returned home late.

"But, Dad, don't shout at me, I'm in puberty!"

"Be wherever you want", replied the father, "but be at home at ten!"

Namely, when we were young, neither puberty nor the menopause had yet been invented. To make matters worse, neither had staying in bed until two p.m.

I'm not a cantankerous old man, but what are these boys going to achieve in their lives if they have breakfast at half past two in the afternoon?

Whether it has anything to do with age or with the fact that I also saw many a dawn, but I feel like hitting the sack as early as midnight. And if I happen (and I do) to stay out late and get home around three in the morning, it takes me three days before I feel my usual self again

But I must say that the daylight saving time makes things easier for me, since I live by standard time. If I sleep until eleven, I tell myself that it is ten o'clock! If I stay out until one a.m. it's only midnight.

My dog Archibald wakes me up at eight thirty sharp, standard time. He licks my drowsy lids, which means that I am to put on two different shoes and take him out to the park to pee at the base of an important historical monument. I was harboring the illusion that he, as a worldly dog, with a pedigree surpassing mine in quality, would grasp the need to keep abreast of the rest of the world by moving the clock one hour ahead, thus giving me a chance to sleep until half past nine, like other honest artists in town, not expected anywhere by anyone. Rubbish! He keeps waking me up at half past eight, standard time. Then I think to myself: surely Archie knows the time better than all those international accords.

ST. JOHN'S DAY GARLAND

Regardless of how poor they are, regardless of their problems in making ends meet and attempts to strike a bargain with farmers on the price of every tomato or eggplant, elderly Belgrade ladies never haggle when buying a St. John's Day garland at the market. They take it home and hang it above the door, taking the risk of falling from the rackety step stool and breaking a hip or a leg. They used to do it before World War II, also during the German occupation, and took the risk of being labeled church-lovers after the liberation, but in spite of everything the garland was always there, suspended above the entrance door. Old Belgrade in its quiet and steady way defended itself from evil with the help of this touching garland of entwined wild flowers. I have seen many countries and cities in my time, entered many homes, but nowhere in the world have I seen that people keep garlands above their entrance doors. It is interesting to point out that you see the garlands much more often in the houses of the poor, while there are almost none in the new,

380

luxurious apartment buildings with wide glass entrance doors and marble halls. They are rarely encountered in New Belgrade but you see them much more often in the municipalities of Stari Grad and Vračar. Back in the time when religion was considered to be the "opium of the people", the district, neighborhood and house spies and informers had no problem in establishing, by the garlands, the addresses of devout persons. Naturally, they did not know that the weaving of garlands was a true pagan custom and that it had as much to do with Christianity as ground sweet wheat has to do with whipped cream.

"In folk beliefs," claim ethnologists, "the flowers woven in the form of a circle have an exceptionally strong magic power, protecting from evil eyes, demons and jinxes. If woven for a holiday, the garland represents the Sun itself, which will help make the growing season fertile. St. John's Day garlands are kept throughout the year, as they are believed to have therapeutic powers."

At this day and hour we cannot count on any kind of help, except perhaps on the help of this fine garland of entwined flowers, with its gentle scent of some bygone, happy fields.

NEW TENANTS

I have changed quite a number of apartments in Belgrade since I came to live in it!

There is no other place where new tenants are as disliked as here. As soon as a man moves into some run-down apartment, he starts to alter and renovate it. He tears down a couple of dividing walls, moves the kitchen to the former pantry, the workers relocate his water pipes and telephone connection, then he drills the walls for a three-phase electrical supply which wasn't there before, and the whole building hates his guts!

Those from the first floor protest because the rubble is taken out down the stairs, those above the new tenant are annoyed by the noise, and those on the left and on the right object to having to walk over the spilled sand and cement. The chairman of the residents' council calls in the inspectors from City Hall, who find only the indifferent painters having breakfast on spread newspapers instead of a tablecloth and drinking tepid beer from the bottle.

The painters have developed a philosophical attitude towards this kind of old hatred. They shrug and explain that they know nothing; they do what they are told to.

The origin of this hatred is very simple. Who is this new tenant, anyway, to move the walls, drill holes and alter the color of the doors, when the previous tenants, who lived here for many years, did not change anything and were none the worse for it; look, he is sanding the parquet floor now – the house is shaking as if in an attack of epilepsy; then he'll certainly coat it with varnish, and we'll all die of noxious vapors! And the former tenants, they used to put some parquet grease on their floors once a year, and they did not bother anyone. And how, in the name of God, could he afford this apartment in the first place? It's certainly monkey business. When they happen to ride the elevator together with the new tenant, they don't utter a word, but there is a look of unconcealed hatred in their eyes.

In New Hampshire, when the Smith family moves into an old clapboard house, and when they begin to mend the porch and paint the shutters, their neighbors, the Johnson family, put on their overalls and go to give a helping hand; Henry's wife fetches her apple pie, and while the work is in progress the Smith children have their meals at the McKinley's. Everyone is happy to see the old house rising from the dead.

Belgraders lack the knowledge of living in the present, today and right now. They wait all the time for some big historical decisions to be made and to start living afterwards. The good Lord gave them this day as a present, and it is up to them either to live it to the full or to waste it. And so they sit, mulling over important political issues and chewing the cud on whether we are all alone in the world and no one loves us (including ourselves), waiting for the big Russian bear to wake up and take us under its protection. Will China strike back at the USA economically? Will Western Europe free itself from the American influence or not? And the lock on the entrance gate has been broken for more than a year now. Someone stole the bulb from the elevator. The cellar cannot be locked as someone pushed chewing gum into the lock. Most apartments were painted fifteen years ago and the kitchen tiles sport greasy mold as a reminder of many thousands of roux.

Apartments do not get gray overnight, but gradually, surreptitiously, day in day out, just like the people living in them. Only when you paint the walls can you see that the window frames and doors have also turned yellowish.

Belgraders do not deal with small things. History comes first, and only then the fixing of the bathroom tap, dripping for a year. At present they are waiting for new elections. If their favorites win, the walls will turn white all by themselves, the bulb in the elevator will find its way back, and the key of the common laundry room will reappear. No one will throw garbage into the light shaft, or steal other people's mail from the mailbox. A better and a healthier life requires new doormats first.

In the meantime, the new tenant has moved into his refurbished apartment and put the plaque with his name on the door, while the traces of paint have already faded away from the stairs and the yard.

But, look, someone's bought the apartment on the fourth floor, he is already tearing down the walls, relocating the doors, enclosing his terrace with glass panes. A man cannot doze after lunch for the noise. Furthermore, this one has a dog, to boot. The former new tenant, already domesticated and drinking coffee with his neighbors, does not miss a chance to grumble about the new one. He threatens to bring in the inspectors. He is well connected at City Hall, he says!

SWEET GOSSIP

It happens to all of us occasionally to get carried away by an avalanche of thoughts and words at some social function and, enjoying the sound of our own voice, to utter many things which normally we would never dream of saying.

Borne on the wings of excitement, of sharp phrases, of judgments and criticism of the person on the carpet, you simply cannot hold your tongue and shut up, even though your opinions and remarks will sooner or later, through the strangest grapevine, reach the person talked about, and cause irreconcilable hatred and rage.

When I find myself in this kind of situation, Zuko Džumhur's mother comes to my mind – a fragile bey's wife, tiny and moving like a bird, who enjoyed visiting with her female friends, given to gossiping about the neighborhood, the city and the state. Whenever she was about to say something, she would address her tongue silently: "If you keep quiet, you'll get a treat when we get home!"

And, true to her word, if her tongue complied and kept silent before the sweet challenge of gossip, the old Muslim lady would make *urmašice* (a Bosnian sweet) and, nibbling on them, would say:

"Here, eat, this treat is for you for having been silent…"

I promised my tongue (a biting one, at that) that I'd give it a treat if it refrained from talking about politics today.

If I had eggs, I'd treat it to ham and eggs, but I have no ham!

THE RECIPE

Ever since the citizens of Belgrade went broke, the number of fishermen at its river banks is constantly on the rise. Even those who never

dreamt of fishing, now dabble in it! They sit quietly, looking at the river and expecting to catch the goldfish which will fulfill their three wishes. The first wish is for this misery to go away, and for them to finally stop fishing and eating fish every single day, as they are already sick and tired of it. Serbs, namely, eat fish only when they have to – for fasting patron saint days, such as St. Nicholas.

Nowadays there is almost no raft restaurant at Ada Ciganlija without a caldron of simmering fish chowder. Everyone has his own way of preparing it and believes that his chowder is the tastiest by far. Ada is crawling with reporters for women's magazines who diligently write down recipes for fish chowder, fish stew and "drunken carp"... At some of these floating restaurants you cannot tell who is tipsier – the carp or the cook!

Recently a TV team boarded the raft of Isa the Unlucky, who, supposedly, makes the best fish chowder on the Sava river. Live on the air, they asked him for his recipe:

"First I fill the caldron with the river water", Isa begins his story, "then I add three kinds of fish, bream, perch and carp, and also fish roe (if there is any); then I add a few carrots, bay leaves and a jigger of ground paprika. In another pan I fry onions. When they are tender, I mash them and put them into the caldron, together with pepper and other spices, to be sure. The chowder is ready when the foam from the top dissipates. Then I take the caldron off the fire, pour its contents into the Sava and put a suckling pig on the spit!"

ON BELGRADE

In the Puerta del Sol square in Madrid, there is a bronze marking pressed into the ground, reading – *Kilometro Zero*. Kilometer Zero! A mysterious inscription surrounds the marking:

ORIGEN DE LAS CARRETERAS RADIALES

Wherever they are, all Spaniards measure the distance from this simple but decisively important point, representing the center of the Spanish world.

I stand at the *Kilometro Zero* and, naturally, I think of Belgrade (what else could I do), wondering where that imagined point would be if it were pressed into the Belgrade ground? For me, it is a small slice of the sidewalk at the beginning of Knez Mihailova Street, in front of the café Ruski Car (The Russian Emperor), where I spent many years of my life, leaning against a certain tree, to prevent it from falling on the passers-by.

The marking I am talking about would be a very useful thing in Belgrade. Dispersed all over the world, we could use it to measure how far we have wandered off from our substance.

That is, a man must have at least one important point in life, in order not to go astray and lose himself among other peoples, other nations... The marking by the Ruski Car would be that blessed unit of measurement for us all.

In the aftermath of my ramblings all over the world, I seem to have grasped something crucial. It is a very simple truth: the closer you live to the imagined point – the happier you are than those Belgraders who live elsewhere and are as rich and flourishing as they please.

In my opinion, the happiest of them all are probably those who live in the building above, for they can see the marking through their window every single morning!

Regardless of all the advantages of Belgrade over other places, there is always some grouch from the interior, who amidst the Terazije noon throng says with disgust:

"Well, I'd never live in Belgrade, not for a million dinars a day!"

To start with, no one forces him to live here, and besides, no one is offering him a million!

I treated my old typewriter to a new black ribbon and pulled out the typed text.

After having read it, I came to like Belgrade so much that I myself would be glad to live in it.

Providing I get a million a day!

On second thought, this city is not, after all, the best place for people with serious professions, for politicians, economists, lawyers, planners, scientists and the like, but it is absolutely ideal for writers!

The Belgrade writers do not have to resort to their imagination at all.

It suffices to start a day listening to a local radio station or reading the newspapers: wonders galore! Compared to average Belgraders, the French Surrealists are pure amateurs, devoid of fantasy! Anyway, with the exception of Paris, wasn't Belgrade the only place where Surrealism took root? The poor Americans and Frenchmen, the wretched Englishmen and Swedes... They go to so much trouble in order to invent something out of the ordinary and illogical, while every literary rookie in Belgrade is given it on a plate every morning!

Is there any other place in the world where at the very onset of a new day the radio broadcasters inform you how long you'll be without electricity or water?

And out of those miserable few minutes of the blackout in New York, piles of books were written, several movies made, and whole libraries of scholarly studies published by sociologists and psychologists.

Is there any other place in the world, situated on the banks of two mighty rivers, with frequent water supply cuts? What a citizen of Belgrade can take in stride would easily kill any average European, not to mention the sensitive Americans!

Which one of them, for example, would be able to survive a winter without heating and electricity? To crawl with a hand torch or a dripping candle through downtown, snowed in and dark as a well?

But we can always sleep longer than they can switch off the electricity!

And which one of these pampered foreigners would get out of the polluted Sava river alive and kicking, while we swim in it regularly, none the worse for wear. They'd be felled by plague and cholera – while we, thank God, thrive! That's because we, from early childhood, keep adapting to the cruelties of life, and thus become immune. Every child in Belgrade swallows in childhood, together with unwashed fruit, at least three and a half kilos of various bacteria, bacilli and amoebas. Later on, diseases avoid us like the plague, as if we were contagious!

There is a theory going around in Belgrade that the Westerners, by taking showers daily, have made their skin so thin that the bacilli easily pass through it, like mice through Swiss cheese. We, however, are nothing like that! Although we have been using hot water boilers for a long time, we take baths mainly on Saturdays, just like our ancestors did.

Belgrade drunkards are, actually, the toughest human beings ever. It's a zilch for Frenchmen and Italians to drink their reputable wines, it's no problem for Russians to get drunk on vodka and Scots to booze it up on whisky – I'd like to see them the following morning, after having consumed two liters of Banat Riesling, the favorite wine of Belgrade *spritzer* drinkers!

I don't think there is any other place in the world where so many drunkards vow each morning that they'll abstain from drinking wine forever, as in Belgrade. Here they have an endearing name for Banat Riesling – they call it "the wine with the speech impediment", since the following day they – stumble over words.

Summertime in Belgrade – it mercifully covers with a lush green robe of fluttering tree crowns the inconsolably ruined façades shedding their flowery ornaments in the Vienna Secession style. Why did we neglect them so mercilessly? Is it, perhaps, a proof of subconscious escape into a nurtured amnesia, to help us forget the time when the idyllic, two-storied Belgrade truly cherished itself and its snug urban homes? Or is it the complex of father and grandfather, whom we never equaled? Or the Orwellian wiping out of the past?

Carried away by our success, skipping centuries, we managed to raise modern buildings almost overnight, but not to keep the locks on toilet doors in our hotels. The indestructible, centuries-old odor of roux and grilled meat creeps mercilessly even into the most beautiful architectural masterpieces, which were meant to help us conquer time and mentality. A point of interest: there are considerably more people in Belgrade allergic to blooming linden trees than to a calf's head in tripe.

The surest sign that a town is in decline is a great number of Italians in it. Strangely, when we had it good and did not lack anything, our neighbors came to Belgrade only rarely. Conceited as we are, in those good times we went as far as feeling ashamed to go shopping in Italy. Belgrade ladies did their shopping in London, Paris, New

York… It was a sweet revenge for the years when the Italians kidnapped our most beautiful boys and girls, the most talented athletes and painters, the most succulent baby beef. Then we became too expensive for our neighbors from across the sea. They simply disappeared! But history repeats itself. Once more they take away our prettiest girls and kill the most precious fowl in our native woods and hills. Our shoe shiners polish the shoes of the Italian ones.

What is an economic crisis?

Economic crisis is when our relatives and friends living in the West come to Belgrade and look at us amazement: over there they read and hear all kinds of things about us, but we are still doing well. Only the soles of our *Bally* shoes, remnants of more prosperous times, have grown somewhat thinner, the elbows of our cashmere sweaters are protruding, but we sew leather patches over them (claiming it is in vogue), we take out from our closets out-of-date jackets with wide lapels, and, to sum it up, we do not smell of cosmetics but of ourselves and of the first drink we had in the morning.

And when they ask us how we are doing, we lie to them that it has never been better, as history has taught us to be proud, but we think to ourselves: you'll have your black day again, like in the year nineteen hundred and something, when your bankers were jumping from skyscrapers' windows. We suffer and do not complain and when they ask if we need anything, we tell them: Not a thing! We do not need anything. We have plenty of everything!

If that is not a crisis, then I don't know what is.

"We moved the kitchen into the pantry (what do we need such a big kitchen for?), and in this way we got a living room, and we partitioned our bedroom with a closet, so that now we have two separate rooms – one for us and one for the child who will soon need a space of his own. The bathroom is big enough to accommodate my husband's small photo laboratory (it's his hobby!). Luckily the entrance hall is more spacious than usual, big enough for a deep freeze, with a leg of pork and some frozen sour cherries in it. Actually, I would never exchange our one-room apartment for a two-room one, like the one our neighbors across the hall have: theirs has more square meters, but the floor layout is awful!"

In Belgrade, everything comes late.

The seasons are late, buses are late, and so are trains, airplanes, even lovers for their dates…

The only things that come early are the electricity, water, telephone, TV, rent, garbage disposal and loan installment bills. Also, the bills from Diner's Club, which we naively believed would never come, as we used the credit card in some faraway places.

Will the New Year also be late?

If its arrival depended on our innate talent for organization and punctuality, it would probably arrive some time in the spring.

If we agree that in Belgrade, as nice and cultured a city as it is, the Menu is still the most frequently read printed text since the early days of literacy to this day, than it is rather amazing that not once, anywhere, in any newspaper have I read even the shortest review of this, undoubtedly the most successful best-seller of all times. I come across reviews of the most boring books, eulogies to a poor collection of poems, studies on novels printed in as few as five hundred copies (and which, by the way, ten years later are still not out of print!), awards given to essays no one ever attempted to read, and the Menu – the most popular text of the hungry army of millions of readers, is ignored. After all, the selfsame writers, as well as the critics, following the book launch attended only by their close relatives, grab the Menu, which they shun elitistically in their writing, and study it carefully.

It is true that authors of menus are partly to blame, since they remain anonymous most of the time. The only signature on the menu is that of the manager, whose function would correspond to the function of an editor-in-chief, and you can count on the fingers of one hand the restaurants in Belgrade which employ an editor or a proofreader, the result being that even in the finest restaurants you can find menus with stylistic flaws.

Bakd beans whiff spare ribs, Chat O'Brian for two, Tornado Rossini, *hemendeks* with ham and eggs, park chops, gillette mignon, champignons made from mushrooms on a rice risotto...

There is hardly any newspaper or weekly in the world, which stands on its dignity, without a regular column devoted to the culinary arts and restaurants. Specially trained reviewers make the rounds of restaurants, test, appraise and examine menus, kitchens and wine lists. In that regard we are still at the level of oral literature; our knowledge of the matter can fit into one single sentence. "I hear you can eat well there!"

And, yet, is there a more rewarding subject than the Menu! So many possibilities for an introduction even at the very top of it (hot and cold starters), so many twists and turns in the spaghetti! What a catharsis at the end of the meal, when we have to make a difficult choice between the walnut pie and pancakes with jam!

You read in history books that Belgrade has been razed to the ground about forty times. There are no records, naturally, of the times it has been razed by architects, with the aim of disposing of all things that could remind them of the way it used to be.

As a result, magnificent new modern settlements began to sprout along the road which takes distinguished foreign guests from the airport to downtown Belgrade. These new apartment blocks were devoid of chimneys, shops, cafés, urinals and storage rooms.

The cobblestoned streets in Skadarlija were coated in asphalt, but some thirty years ago, for reasons of tourism and nostalgia, the city fathers decided to replace asphalt with cobblestones once again!

The Old Dorćol was torn down, the idea being to make a New Dorćol, which would conjure up the unique atmosphere of the Old Dorćol.

After a series of megalomaniac architects, builders of Potemkin villages, there appeared a new generation of architects – the nostalgic ones, who apply an antique coating all over the town.

Genetically accustomed to having their city razed to the ground at regular intervals, Belgraders themselves wish that their own houses be torn down, so that they can get hold of an apartment in some newly built residential development.

Every morning the local radio stations have to give answer to a horde of impatient listeners enquiring about the date when their houses are going to be torn down.

Can you imagine the reaction of a Londoner, for example, if he heard the following statement on the radio?

"We regret to inform you, but at present there are no plans for your house in Carnaby Street to be torn down in the near future!"

Instructions for use:

In summertime, Belgrade should be sipped though a straw.

In July, it turns into a therapeutic provincial spa for neurotics and barren women.

To start with, you have to relax sitting at some shady table with a view to a bottle of white wine, a siphon of soda water and exciting sidewalks, trod upon by a flood of agitated beauty in search of itself.

The city discovers once more its long-lost measure of humanness and turns into a small town.

Afraid of spending the night alone, those who are not at the coast telephone each other with a hint of panic: "What are you doing tonight?"

On the other hand, those who spend their holidays at the coast envy their courageous neighbors, capable of saying no to the specter of vacationing which is haunting Europe. They leave their homes helplessly to be at the mercy of the terror of this compulsory ritual, which in its senseless enforcement is not unlike the New Year's Eve party.

Clandestine lovers finally have a choice of some ten empty apartments where to water the ficuses and feed the parrots.

An absent-minded friend of mine drowned an undisclosed number of parrots, because he used to water them, instead of the flowers. The rhododendrons also died, but of excess of bird feed.

Swimming in the tepid Sava water, hypochondriacs take great care to avoid all bacteria and beer bottles, which, with their necks nodding, float nostalgically to join the Danube and the Black Sea.

Belgraders, actually brave people, for centuries have been scared of two things only: ice in their drinks and the draft! That's a reason why ice in Belgrade has been kept out of consumers' sight for decades now. You can get it only if you are related to the waiter and even then on the sly. I presume that's because Belgraders usually keep meat in the deep-freeze part of their refrigerators.

I divide my friends and acquaintance, whom I visit occasionally, into two groups: those who have whisky and no ice, and vice-versa. I was never wrong.

Our people still believe that ice gives you a sore throat and inflamed tonsils. If that were true,

at least three quarters of the population of the USA would be hospitalized at this hour. Thanks to this old fear, in Belgrade we serve hot entrées cold, and Coca-Cola lukewarm …

The other traditional bogeyman is the draft.

What is draft? It is a common air circulation between rooms! Belgraders, who stroll unperturbed in the strongest *košava*, are appalled at the sight of open doors and windows, even in August. If you try to open a window in the taxicab when it is 35 degrees in shade, the driver will throw you out right away, or, at best, if you are stronger than him, will implore you: "Please, close the window, for God's sake, the draft is killing me!"

This is the way that we in Belgrade discovered a very rare phenomenon – the wind that kills.

The plea is followed by the notorious explanation: "You'd see if you were in my seat. The draft is dislodging my kidneys!"

That's probably the reason why there are only two or three cabriolets in Belgrade.

But their drivers won't last long, either.

Once upon a time, the story goes, a certain man decided to sell his house for three thousand dinars. "But the house is not worth more than a thousand", said the buyer. The owner answered that it was true as far as the house itself was concerned, but that the neighbor on the right was good for a thousand, and the one on the left as much! In New York, for example, there are no nameplates on apartment doors, only numbers and letters: D-16, C-24, F-18… I never met any of my neighbors there. Besides, how can you tell your kid: "Go quickly to apartment C-25 and borrow a cup of cooking oil!" But, for the sake of truth, I must admit that those people are never in want of oil.

As for us, we grew up borrowing vinegar, yeast, eggs, a little sugar, bread or tools from our neighbors. In every kitchen and at every moment there used to be at least two plates, a pan or a grater, belonging to our neighbor, which we had not yet returned. Our doorbell rings: "My Mom sends apple fritters!" Good neighborly customs require that you never return empty utensils and we therefore hastily fill the plate which held the apple fritters with our own "lazy pie".

If we are lucky to have neighbors, they are much closer to us than even our closest relatives. We chose our neighbors ourselves – as opposed to relatives!

Our neighbors knew everything about our household – we did not hide anything from them. In summertime, we left our apartment keys with them, to water the flowers and feed the birds.

In the gentle September sun, Belgrade languidly washes itself, like a big drowsy tomcat…

It grabs the Sava water with its left paw – and washes New Belgrade.

Then it grabs some Danube water with its right paw and washes off the gray patina from the old buildings framing the street leading from Kalemegdan to Slavija.

It shakes off the scaffoldings to demonstrate to its dwellers that they are not without roots, that they are the offspring of those Belgraders who were capable of raising the stately neoclassicist mansions whose beauty is comparable to those in Vienna and Paris.

Then it sweeps away the layers of memory and discovers that, for half a century, ashes and soot have systematically covered Belgrade, to prevent it, Cinderella-like, from joining the grand ball of the other European cities – to make it lose its memory and forget what it used to be like…

Even the new copper dome on St. Sava Cathedral has turned green under the envious glances of those who do not like us!

Luckily, the church was separated from the state in time, for otherwise it would certainly have gone under, just like so many other things under state jurisdiction.

This fall, Belgrade is so attractive that I myself would not mind living in it.

In early September our compatriots living in Europe return from the coast. They'll stay in Belgrade a couple of days, in passing. Their foreign wives look as fresh as horseradishes in August…However much they tried to get a tan, the southern sun did not restore their youth, and that's why they are constantly angry. The bronze tan did not cover their wrinkled skin, resembling the creased surface of a sand desert. Withered, as thin as rails, sporting their jangling jewelry, they sit as living rebukes among us, immersed in our memories…

Is there anything worse than a male company sitting at a table together with a foreign lady, who does not speak a word of Serbian? What a horror!

"What are you laughing at now?" ask Elisabeth. "Speak English, George!"

Translated jokes die a sorrowful death by the saltshaker. Mujo, Haso, Fata. …an Englishman, a Russian and a Serb! When she hears what we were uproariously laughing at, she'll surely think we are some sorts of imbeciles! Which we are.

"And do you know the one when comrade Tito issued the order that *Prozor*[12] must fall! It did fall! They took it later to a glasscutter to be fixed. When we were studying the enemy offensives at school, a professor asked me whether I had an inkling of where *Ključ*[13] was? "I certainly do! It is under the doormat…"

"Speak English, George!"

---

[12] A town in Bosnia. Also the Serbian word for "window".

[13] Also a town in Bosnia, as well as the Serbian word for "key".

The problems with translation start as early as the starters:

"And what is this," asks Elisabeth. "Cheese?"

"No, not cheese. It's *kajmak*!"

"How do you say *kajmak* in English?

We don't. How can we explain?

"See, Madam, it's not cheese, although it is similar to it; it's neither sour cream, nor butter, neither mozzarella nor half-and-half... it is something that only we, the Serbs, possess. Kaj-mak!"

We eat prosciutto with our fingers, naturally. Elisabeth – with a knife and a fork. She enquires as to the chance of getting a slice of melon? What melon? How can you eat prosciutto with melon? Nonsense!

Only half an hour ago we tried to convince her that forks had been invented at the courts of the Serbian Medieval rulers in, at the time when her ancestors, the Anglo-Saxons, were tearing off pieces of meat with their hands, like savages, and now it is us who eat prosciutto with our fingers. If you eat it with a knife and a fork, it stops being prosciutto. There are things that have to be eaten with one's fingers. Roast lamb, for example...

Also, it is interesting to note that Elisabeth is the only one who uses a napkin. We do not touch ours. I remember that in my childhood, at home, we all wiped our fingers with the same piece of cloth. "Hey, pass me the cloth!" The faded linen cloth of my youth, washed countless times... Napkins were set by the plates only when we had guests, for them to see that we, too, had napkins. Even then, if by chance one of us would reach for a napkin, grandma would give us a dirty look and we would resort to the cloth again. Who is going to wash and starch all those napkins! That's why my generation and napkins were never on familiar terms...

As the name indicates, the Serbian salad is made of thinly sliced onions, tomatoes, peppers, cucumbers and chili peppers. Its borders are not well defined: as soon as you sprinkle it with grated cheese, it turns into *Šopska* (Bulgarian) salad.

However, the Serbian salad does not officially exist. I have searched through many cookbooks, written by domestic and foreign authors, and found no trace of it anywhere.

The most reliable cookbook, the Great Folk Cookbook, cites one hundred and twenty different salads and gives the recipes for the French, Italian, Greek, Russian and English salads, but there is no mention of the Serbian salad!

Until recently we were cited in international menus (albeit at the bottom) exclusively by way of fruit salad – *Salade de fruit Macédoine*, which, the story goes, got its name after the Greek region of Macedonia, so chopped up and partitioned in the early 19th century that it became a symbol of things being as mixed up as they could be. The

Serbian salad is, unfortunately, even more of a jumble. It contains both tears (provoked by the onions) and spiciness (from the chili peppers); it is minced and muddled just like the present-day political life in Serbia.

Will they make a salad out of us, or shall we simply gobble it up and solve the problem –it is up to us!

Once in a while and all of a sudden we wish for a quiet, somewhat boring Sunday morning in a small place in the remotest provinces; a table with a red and white checkered cloth, the Sunday newspapers and that obligatory ritual coffee drinking called "the works" – coffee with a piece of Turkish delight on a toothpick and a misted glass of cold water.

Prior to the war there hardly existed a small town in Serbia without a café by the glamorous name of Evropa (Europe) on Main Street. Small marble tables, newspapers spread on wicker frames and groups of old men, meeting every Sunday for more than half a century around the same table… There was an established order in this: the shopkeepers and journeymen at the Bristol, the craftsmen at the Srbija (Serbia), while the teachers, the pharmacist, the physician, the local newspapermen, the local poet and visitors from out of town met at the café Evropa, where coffee was more expensive by a couple of *paras*[14].

---

[14] *Para* – 1/100th part of a dinar.

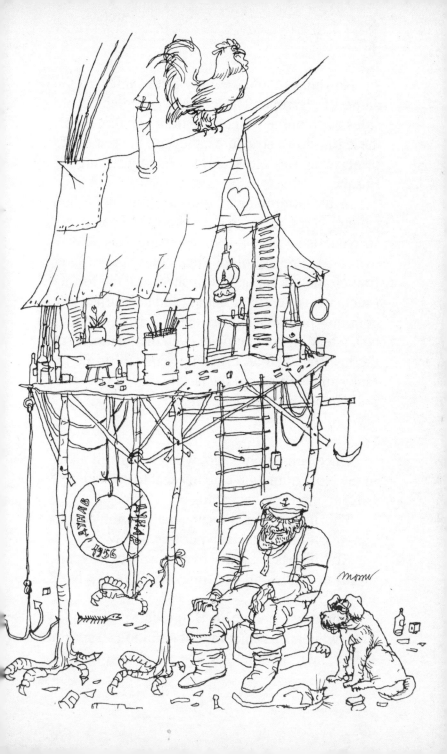

Nowadays there are only a few cafés by the name of Evropa. These shabby, neglected old cafés, with linseed-oil on the floor and dim bulbs, these run-down structures, they are the last traces of our centuries-old secret love and yearning for Europe.

In the aftermath of the war, the institution called Evropa seems to have been deliberately destroyed. Its Secession-style wallpaper was painted over in a greasy, olive-gray color, the wicker frames and the cappella vanished, and the former sanctuaries of coffee-drinking and talk turned into common public-sector cafeterias, as if someone was intending to annihilate even the memories of the last traces of an urban nucleus still in its infancy and to break off the last threads of our symbolic bond with Europe.

Once, a long time ago, when I was still a kid, in the No.2 tram I gave up my seat to an "elderly" lady, about thirty years old.

This morning, in the same tram, a pretty eighteen-year-old girl gave up her seat to me!

My life has passed between these two events, going in circles all the time, just like the No.2 tram ....

There are people in Belgrade, of advanced age, who still remember the famous sausage maker, Mr. Rosulek, a Czech, who owned a butcher shop and where, before the war, one could buy the so-called "*sitnice u fišeku*" – trifles in a wrapper – a cone-shaped paper bag containing mixed end cuts of headcheese, pressed ham, liverwurst, blood sausages and salami, as well as the remnants of sausages, bologna and saveloy - all those tasty things that today we have to pay for dearly.

Mr. Rosulek, Mr. Smejkal and Mr. Novotny themselves sat at the cash registers in their butcher shops, clean like pharmacies, drinking red wine and eating headcheese as a *mezze*, cherishing the tradition of their Czech ancestors who had brought the delicate craft of sausage-making from Central Europe to Serbia. Only one of this wonderful Czech trio, pan Rosulek, was saved from oblivion, thanks to his "*sitnice*", which the poor in Belgrade used to buy as a treat for their children's supper, having previously bought a quarter loaf of bread for half a dinar.

Great writers, naturally, devote themselves to great issues (like half a pig, whole hams or legs), while I myself adore pan Rosulek's "*sitnice*" and I sell them to you for peanuts, or, in other words, for what it's worth!

"When I get up in the morning", I overhear a man telling his friend, "I cannot decide whether to shave or go lie in my grave!"

They stand by a stall at Palilula open market and drink grape brandy from the small vials called "*unučići*" ("grandchildren"). A heavy, damp snow is falling…

"What is it that ties me to my nation – just the force of gravitation!" hums another, hopping from cold.

Yet another asks me to pay for a round of drinks.

"Why don't you write, *bre*?

"What about?"

Well, about this…" says he, pointing with a broad gesture to the market, with its counters full of frozen carrots.

In this neurotic city, these people seem to be perfectly happy. They have lost all they could lose, and now they are out of harm's way. They are not competing, they are not fighting. They keep to one another, in their heavy, worn-out winter coats, like in movable homes. A small club of morning birds…

I stand with them, forgetting where I had set off to.

"Write, *bre*, do you hear!"

How can I explain to him that this is the time for reading and not for writing?

It is a known fact that Belgraders are distrustful by nature of the Sava and the Danube. They carefully separated themselves from their rivers with railway tracks, warehouses, fairgrounds, walls, the ugly Karađorđeva Street with its roaring heavy trucks… They even beached the whole fleet of hydrofoils (which used to run all the way to Đerdap), because it is safer to be on dry land! To tell the truth, Belgraders have been wishing for years for someone to remove the obstacles between the city and its rivers, but it seems that the City of Belgrade has other fish to fry!

Finally, this spring the rivers had enough of these complaints, they rose as never before and reached up towards their old dream – the city that had been evading them for centuries. "If the mountain won't come to Mohammed, Mohammed will go to the mountain!" But, the Headquarters for the Defense from the Sava and the Danube rose to the occasion, and the rivers withdrew into their basins resignedly, leaving behind hordes of invincible mosquitoes.

Just like the second generation of mosquitoes, turned insecticide-resistant, the second generation of Belgraders also turned resistant to all regimes and authorities, which succeeded one another, as well as to everyday increases in prices that would easily kill every average European.

Belgraders, thank goodness – are still alive and kicking!

There are fewer and fewer trees in this city, and more and more plausible explanations why they are being felled. If we carry on like this, the time will soon come for us to take our children to the Botanical Garden, to see and hear the white locust humming its melody behind the bars…

It's not easy to be a tree in Belgrade.

The Međed pastry shop, a dream of all Belgrade boys, was located in Knez Mihailova Street. In order to prove his loyalty to the new authorities, Međed hung above the glass cabinet full of *halva, baklava* and *kadaif* enormous photos of all the members of the Politburo.

One day, a friend of mine who stuttered slightly (albeit only when speaking), went into the pastry shop and asked the owner:

"S-s-s-sorry, Mr. M-m-međ-đ-đed, why not make th-these ph-ph-photos a b-bit sssmaller and the *t-t-tulumbas* a b-b-bit b-b-big-ger?"

I stand at an intersection and watch the drivers: each and every one has a tense and threatening face. If the guy in front of them fails to start his car in a split second, they immediately begin honking their horns and roaring hysterically: "Who gave you a driver's license, you hick! Everybody and his brother is allowed to drive today!"

Clenched teeth, bulging neck veins, strong hands, a wild glare in the eyes – they are all mortal enemies to one another, ready to fight to the death at the drop of a hat on account of a scratched fender or an insignificant unacknowledged right of way…

I have been to many countries and cities, but only in Belgrade have I seen people playing a game called "throwing a matchbox into a glass".

That is, by the way, the only sport that I have indulged in passionately all my life.

The local drunkards gather in front of the Kalenić café. First they have a shot or two of some hard drink ("one nail drives out another"), then proceed to *spritzer* and then ask the waiter to clean the table of everything and take off the tablecloth. It is a certain sign that the Čubura championship in throwing a matchbox into a glass is about to begin.

It's café basketball!

The matchbox is launched from the rim of the table and the glass is set in the middle, at an equal distance from each player.

The late Libero Markoni was able to score with his eyes closed. He was the absolute world champion in this sport, which can be played by tipsy players only. That is when a true Zen-like concentration is achieved and when a player identifies himself with the flying matchbox and its aim, the clinking glass bottom.

If the matchbox lands on the bottom –fifty points. A hundred points if your matchbox stays on the glass's rim. The loser pays for another round of drinks…

In these hairy and unstable times, when in the thunderstorm of history new leaders, unknown yesterday, but dazed today by their sudden and temporary glory (having no inkling of their future downfall) appear in the limelight, act for a while and vanish once more into the anonymous darkness of the theater, defeated and ridiculed, a certain housewife brags to her neighbors over a cup of coffee: "Lucky me," she says, "my husband is a nobody!"

In present-day Belgrade the only thing that people talk about is politics! And if they happen to ask you what's your opinion of it, your answer does not interest them in the least; they only wait for a cue to launch into their own monologue, to present their opinion, their theory on how to overcome the crisis. And all arguments fall on deaf ears! In that respect, Belgrade is a city of the deaf.

Belgrade is also a city where its inhabitants have a great number of things in common. For example, they all read the same newspaper, patronize the same open market and watch the same TV channel. It is most likely the only place in the world where the previous night's TV program is widely talked about the following morning.

"Did you see THAT THING last night?" says a man on entering his office, and he is positive that all of his colleagues did see THAT THING the previous night!

He does not say what, he does not say when, and the fact is that all those present know without fail what he has in mind!

Can you imagine a New York white-collar worker coming into his office in some Wall Street bank and asking his colleagues whether they saw THAT THING the previous night, in the metropolis of at least forty TV channels? What THAT THING? What last night? Where? What channel? What time? In Italian? In Spanish? In Chinese?

But we know at once and comment on it:

"What a scandal! Who let him speak on TV! A disgrace! Super! They should broadcast more programs of this kind! He had him for breakfast! He probably does not dare show his face today…"

See why I don't live in New York? There is no one there who would be able to give me the answer to a simple question: "Did you see THAT THING last night?"

When in the West, we pay no attention to the way people heat their homes. No stoves to be seen, no radiators – their heating comes in through the floor or from the ceiling.

On the other hand, if you want to avoid freezing in Belgrade in winter, you must have at least

421

five to six kinds of heating contraptions. What an abundance of imagination! If the electricity is out, Belgraders turn on their oil stoves. If there is no oil, they resort to gas heaters. If gas is in short supply, they have storage heaters. Luckily, we kept our old ceramic-tile stoves, while some coal and wood, left behind from better times, can be found in our cellars... In the kitchen we have the cooking stove, called the "fiacre" (*keva* did not want to part with for all the tea in China), while in the attic we still keep, just in case, our ancient pot-belly stove, from the times of the German occupation, which burns sawdust, all kinds of junk, as well as old newspapers! We gather wooden crates in the markets, because we don't intend to freeze or be at the mercy of only one kind of heating. And many houses in Belgrade resemble rich museums of the history of heating through centuries! Regardless of whether we make fun of them or not, these Belgraders will keep warm in the winter, come what may, and as for us – we'll see!

Belgraders are tougher and more resourceful than the inhabitants of many other world capitals, pampered by affluence and relaxed by security. Belgraders do not trust anyone and are able to outwit any system, any ideology – and to pull through any hardship!

"Excuse me, sir," a certain lady asked my old friend, the painter Cibe Jeremić, who at that moment was painting the confluence of the Sava and the Danube from Kalemegdan fortress, "is that War Island over there?"

"No! It's prewar!" replied the painter crossly.

For Sunday dinner, consisting of boiled beef and hash potatoes, Belgrade housewives used to prepare tomato sauce as well, until ketchup appeared in these parts.

Ketchup arrived here more or less simultaneously with democracy. Come to think of it, ketchup and democracy have something in common.

You take a bottle of ketchup and shake it as long as you please, but you manage to squeeze out just a drop or two. Edgy and hungry, you slap the bottom of the bottle and ketchup suddenly gushes out, ruining both the dish and your clothes.

One should be cautious when dealing both with democracy and with ketchup.

Ever since the café where they used to meet every day at noon for the last forty years came to be too expensive for their ever-diminishing pensions, they meet rarely, only in passing... Previously people of high standing, they now feel embarrassed for having come a long way down in the world. Their wives make every effort to bring back the elegance to their old, worn-out and shiny suits. The waiters who knew them as gracious guests who tipped well, have all died. The big companies sitting at joined tables, vying to pay for a round of drinks, have broken up.

They meet occasionally in Kalemegdan Park, shamed by life, with their eyes cast down, walking listlessly and aimlessly. In passing, they glance at each other furtively:

"Hello!"

"Yes!"

"Well?"

"Well…"

"So-so. And you?"

"The same."

"See you!"

" See you!"

And all is said.

A policeman in mufti was dispatched to find out whether drugs were being consumed at a certain Belgrade café. He went there, leaned on the bar, drank five glasses of apple juice and almost turned deaf from the overly loud music. When he returned to the precinct, he filed the following report:

"No way! These kids don't even have money for cigarettes. They roll one cigarette and then they pass it around to each other, just for a puff or two!"

"I am forced to be what I am!" says a cab driver, obviously offended by life, while taking me to Ada Ciganlija.

"We are all forced to be what we are…" I try to console him, musing on the number of great philosophers hidden in our seemingly ordinary contemporaries.

"I'm forced to be what I am."

This sentence, so true, could perhaps be used as the basis for some new French philosopher's system; essays and studies would be written about it, it would be translated, analyzed and quoted, just like the sentence "I think, therefore I am", while my cab driver, instead of being praised, is fined by the police at Ada Ciganlija for having entered a oneway street from the wrong direction.

You try being a philosopher in Serbia, then!

THEN AND NOW

Rumor has it that a certain Belgrader spent a whole day taking his foreign guest around town, to show him all its wonders.

When, exhausted, they finally sat in front of a café to have a beer, the host sighed deeply and said:

"What a pity you were not here thirty years ago…"

"You mean when Belgrade was the true Belgrade?" asked the visitor.

"No – when I was the true me!"

CIAO!

I haven't met anyone who could tell me what year Belgrade was occupied by "ciao!" – that short Italian greeting, readily adopted by both the old and the young, including the youngest Belgraders.

Perhaps "ciao" arrived together with the song "O, bella, ciao, ciao…" Who can tell?

But, why not Zdravstvuyte! Ahooy! Why not Hello! Or Salut!

Why "ciao", of all greetings?

We have not even noticed how this ciao, this pitiful greeting word, four letters (down), has edged out all other phrases of salutation; for example, the touching, prewar:

Kiss the hands! (shortened to: Hands!) A hand kiss for your esteemed mother!

Good morning! Good afternoon! Good evening! Goodbye!

And that threatening greeting, reproachful, progressive and strict (but just):

Hello, comrade! Hello, *comradess*!

How did this "ciao", this little chiu-chi-ciao, creep into our cerebellum, into our ear concha, into the Eustachian tube!

It will definitely drive me crazy!

Well, ciao!

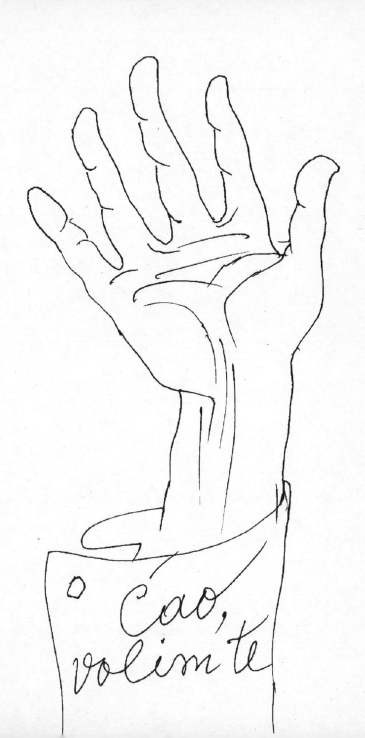

CONTENTS

MOMO KAPOR
THE MAGIC OF BELGRADE

Published by
KNJIGA-KOMERC
Belgrade, Vojvode Petka 5

Publisher
BOBAN STOJILJKOVIĆ

Illustrated by
MOMO KAPOR

Editor
BOBAN STOJILJKOVIĆ

Translated by
LJILJANA BAJIĆ

Designer
PERA STANISAVLJEV BURA

Photography
BRANKO JOVANOVIĆ

Print run
2000 copies

Printed by
KNJIGA-KOMERC

Distribution
KNJIGA-KOMERC
Telephone numbers: +381-11/344-13-84, 344-18-47

ISBN 978-86-7712-240-9

CIP – Каталогизација у публикацији
Народна библиотека Србије, Београд

821.163.41–32

KAPOR, Momo, 1937
    The Magic of Belgrade / Momo Kapor ; ilustrated by
the Author ; [translated by Ljiljana Bajić ; photography
Branko Jovanović]. – Belgrade : Knjiga-komerc, 2008
(Belgrade : Knjiga-komerc). – 435 str. : ilustr. ; 21 cm

Izv. stv. nasl.: Magija Beograda. – Tiraž 2.000.

ISBN 978-86-7712-240-9

COBISS.SR-ID 152094732